OUR MOTHER:

THE HOLY SPIRIT

MARIANNE WIDMALM

PUBLISHERS LLC

SUTTON, ALASKA

Relevant Publishers LLC
P.O. Box 505
Sutton, AK 99674

Visit our website at www.relevantpublishers.com

Printed in the United States of America

Widmalm, Marianne
Our Mother: The Holy Spirit / Marianne Widmalm – 1st ed.
Includes references.

ISBN: 978-0-9909984-7-1 SB Print
ISBN: 978-0-9909984-8-8 eBook
LCCN: 2018963631

DEDICATION

This book is dedicated to:

My father, Sven-Erik, and my mother, Ulla,
in gratitude for everything.

My son, Johannes, and daughter, Rebekah,
because you are the best gift God ever gave me.

My horse, Brian, who carried me for two decades,
in more ways than one, and at a crucial time in my life,
which eventually led to this book.

TABLE OF CONTENTS

TABLE OF CONTENTS
continued

TABLE OF CONTENTS
continued

PREFACE

My Own Story

I was born and raised in Sweden during the exact time when the country transitioned from being a Christian country to a secular one. The Lutheran Church was state sponsored until year 2000 when there was an official split. Atheism began to deeply permeate the culture that had been steeped in Christianity for a millennia. The first schools in Sweden started thanks to the spread of Christianity beginning in Christian convents. Cathedral schools were built along with them, with the earliest one being situated in Lund 1085. Despite this long Christian history, the country turning secular/atheist, in the latter part of the last century, did so at an exponential speed.

When I grew up we sang Psalms on Monday mornings the first few years in school and at age twelve, in the early 1970's, we still said prayer before lunch break. But, that all stopped, and they changed the school curriculum from where we used to be taught Christianity, to Christianity being just one of many topics in a class about religion. Most of all, culture was changing, and although people were still keeping old Christian traditions, like celebrating Easter or being baptized and confirmed, anything to do with actually believing in God was mocked.

I was baptized at home by a priest, but never taken to church by my parents. Aside from an occasional evening prayer, when I was very young, approximately four to six years old, religion was wholly absent in my home. However, I did attend Sunday school at age five or six because my best friend's father was a Pastor. I first learned about the Bible there. Though Christianity was not part of any conversation or everyday life at home, I had a personal experience with God at age seven. From that point on I knew He existed and believed. However, I was still a product of the culture I grew up in. As an adult there have been things I had to unlearn from it. One thing I knew as I was beginning to reach adulthood was that when I had my own kids, I would have God be an open part in our lives. Never would I relegate Him to the background, ignore Him or pretend He did not exist. God would be the center of our lives. I would talk openly about Him and teach my children that if you put Him first, everything will be okay. Without God, the rest does not matter much.

In my mid-twenties I changed from having studied art history in Sweden and theatre in the U.S. to politics. It was during this I also took a class about the Bible. The Bible was still a secret interest of mine, and little did I know where it would eventually lead me. But just when I decided to take a class about the Bible something else happened on a personal level. Like many, my dream was to marry Mr. Right, have children with him, and be together forever. But, this dream is not what happened. Instead I got pregnant outside of marriage while studying in the U.S. It was not one of those planned joyful events, nor an accidental happy surprise. It was more of a shock. The situation was far from ideal, and I was devastated. Yet, due to my lifelong belief that life is sacred, I did not want an abortion but held on to do what I believed was right to give birth to my children. The father was not present until half a year later, and when he finally was involved, the situation got much worse. My faith deepened though while going through this difficult time. In spite of the lack of a husband and father to my children I grew much closer to God. I cannot imagine what I would have done without Him.

It was contemplating the thoughts of Mary, the mother of Jesus, that gave me the strength I needed. Parallels between our lives such as Mary not being married when she surprisingly found herself pregnant gave me comfort and helped me more than anything else to not feel so alone. What was special about my consolation from Mary was that this was a situation that could only be shared by another *female*. Mary was as spiritually esteemed as any woman can be; yet she was also just a simple girl. I felt as if I could both relate and look up to her. Knowing it all worked out for her, and that she was blessed despite her circumstances, gave me hope. Originally I had a hard time thinking anything positive about my own pregnancy. We are given nine months to get ready for childbirth by God for a reason, and my sorrow was exchanged for joy. I turned out to be carrying twins. Having my son and daughter was the best thing that ever happened to me in my life. For these reasons, I feel a special affinity and love for Mary. She became real to me and a spiritual mother figure, which was what I needed and had missed more throughout my life than I had ever even realized until then. I am forever grateful for what the Holy Spirit did through Mary's story for me at such a crucial time in my life.

My own story is an example of how people need role spiritual role models to look to for guidance, especially with the most serious issues we face in life. We need someone to relate to and believe in who by example shows us the way. Most of all, we need someone who believes in us. We all have an earthly mother and father. We may or may not know them, but we know that is how we came to be on the physical plane. When it comes to our spiritual ancestry though, many of us believe we came from one Creator, mostly seen as a single male god. It leaves many, in particular women, left with a spot that needs to be filled. Since the main source for this belief comes from the Bible, it was all the more surprising when it was there I found the missing piece.

Shortly after the birth of my children I started going to a church on a regular basis for the first time in my life. It was a Catholic church located downtown Detroit and a few years after that I converted to Catholicism. Once my children started school, I went back to the University and finished a B.A. in international politics and religion. By that time my passion for studying the Bible had greatly taken over my interest in politics. I continued with a Masters in Near Eastern Studies with a concentration in Ancient Israel and the Hebrew Bible at the University of Michigan. During the last year of my Master's degree I was writing a paper on Psalm 29 right before our Christmas break and had a new interpretation of a crucial Hebrew word in it. I wrote about how this one word in Psalm 29 revealed both the feminine and masculine aspects of God. I was very excited to get feedback on it after the break, but never did. Later I proceeded to pursue my interpretation discovery by writing an article about it after graduating.

This eventually led me to Professor Noel Freedman. This brilliant gentleman took me under his wings and published my article, *"God's Wife,"* in his own journal called "the Biblical Historian: Journal of the Biblical Colloquium West," at the University of San Diego, 2005. After publishing my thesis about the Creation story in Genesis I had so much more to say and started writing a very long, dense, book called **God is not Alone: Our Mother – the Holy Spirit** published in the spring of 2015 by Avalonia, UK. This book: **Our Mother – the Holy Spirit** is a revised and updated version of one, major, extracted part of that book. The rest of the original book will follow in likewise fashions later.

I think it is time for the world to know and understand what the Bible truly tells us about the Divine, and its feminine aspect. Too long, this truth has been buried by ignorance, ignored or denied. Women are represented in the divine realm, and our presence matters. Mary mattered for me when I was pregnant. When I was filled with the Holy Spirit at age seven, I did not know that this was my heavenly Mother. Now I do, and I want you to know too.

Marianne Widmalm

CHAPTER 1

THE BIBLE

And he gave to Moses, when he had made an end of speaking
with him upon Mount Sinai, the two tables of the testimony,
tables of stone, written with the finger of God.

Exodus 31:18

BACKGROUND

This first chapter is a brief introduction to the Bible
and a glimpse of its complexity. This background
knowledge is essential to make the premise of this book
easier to understand. You do not have to be an expert on the
Bible to learn and be inspired from it. In this sense, it is
accessible to all. However, there is quite a bit of knowledge
that lies hidden without in-depth studies. For example,
sometimes the easier parts of the Bible get more attention
while the problematic texts are ignored or even used by
some to disregard the entire book. Over simplifying or
dismissing the texts are two sides of the same coin. Neither
gives it justice. How to read the Bible is a subject all of its
own. Even the seemingly "simple" parts at times can be
misunderstood. The scholarly aspect of Bible study is
therefore of great importance, and, moreover, that this
information gets passed on. By the same token, it is vital to
know that scholars themselves, just like theologians, do not
always agree. In short, an academic's interpretation, no

matter how prominent, may not be the final or accurate word.

Researching the Bible involves many areas such as looking at how it has been read traditionally, the different literary genres, the multitude of authorships, and the variety of sources. The list goes on and on with each subject being a massive study in itself. Some things in the Bible can be understood in different ways. For many it is the literal true infallible word of God. This stems from millennia of understanding the texts as divinely inspired. The ancient scribes had a strong tradition of not tampering with sacred texts and leaving them intact. The discovery of the Dead Sea Scrolls demonstrated the astounding accuracy of the transmission of the Biblical texts. For believers, God's word does not change. We may misunderstand or mistranslate, but God's truth remains unchangeable.

The Old Testament was written in Hebrew, with some parts in Aramaic, and the New Testament in Greek (or translated to Greek from Aramaic or Hebrew). These languages have another alphabet and script. Occasionally in this book, words from Scripture will be written in the original language or transliterated. Transliteration is not translating the meaning of a word but rather putting the Hebrew or Greek characters into the English alphabet to make them readable in the English language. When this occurs, it will always be in *italic* except divine names such as God's personal name "Yahweh" and the Hebrew word for God, which is "El" or "Elohim" or other forms of this name. Although there are some exceptions, generally speaking vowels and other markings over and under the letters in Hebrew, Greek and transliterations will not be added to simplify the readings.

THE BOOKS OF THE BIBLE AND THE CANON

The Christian Bible got its name from the Greek word *biblos,* meaning "scroll." Originally, it was a collection of them; each book being one scroll with the exception that all the Minor Prophets were in one scroll. Eventually, the modern-day book form referred to as a codex was adopted, and the Bible became a book, or more accurately, a book containing a collection of books.

The Old Testament was written in Hebrew and is the sacred Scriptures for the Jews. It is also part of the canon for Christians and Jews alike. Many of the Old Testament books were derived from an even earlier oral tradition, finalized and organized in stages. The earliest books were perhaps gathered around 950 B.C., with the Pentateuch (the five books of Moses), achieving its final form around the sixth or fifth century B.C. The Pentateuch is often called the Torah and includes Genesis, Exodus, Leviticus, Numbers and Deuteronomy. Later the books of the Prophets were added in approximately the third century B.C. These are the earlier Prophets: Joshua, Judges, 1&2 Samuel, 1&2 Kings, and the later: Isaiah, Jeremiah, Ezekiel, Hosea, Joel, Amos, Obadiah, Jonah, Micah, Nahum, Habakkuk, Zephaniah, Haggai, Zachariah and Malachi. Then came the Writings: Psalms, Proverbs, Job, Song of Songs, Ruth, Lamentations, Ecclesiastes, Esther, Daniel, Ezra, Nehemiah, 1&2 Chronicles, estimated at around 90 B.C.

The Hebrew Scriptures (the Old Testament) were originally written in Hebrew with a few sections in Aramaic. It was assembled over several hundred years and covering accounts from over two millennia. The Hebrew Scriptures that most Old Testament texts are translated from today is a manuscript that was fixed by the Masoretes of the Ben-Asher family dated 1009 A.D. and referred to as the Masoretic text.[1] The Masoretes were Jewish scribes located in today's Israel and Iraq (former Babylon) between the sixth and ninth century A.D.[2] The name "Masoretes" comes from the word Masorah, which means "tradition" reflecting their goal to record the traditionally correct reading of the texts. According to prominent scholars the Masoretic text represents the grammar of the Hebrew used during the Biblical period."[3]

Hebrew as a language has been around since 1400-1200 B.C.[4] The script itself has changed over time from Paleo-Hebrew to an Aramaic form, from which the Jewish "Square" characters used today evolved sometime after the Babylonian exile 586 B.C.[5] It is read and written from right to left. Originally, there were no divisions for chapters and verses. These came much later during the Middle Ages. On occasion it is questioned if divisions of chapters and verses are in line with the original intent. Additionally, the Hebrew text only had consonants,[6] no vowels and no punctuations. When the Masoretes carefully copied the text, they invented a written system for vowels, accent marks, and marginal notes that were added for clarification. The added vowels came in the form of small inserted dots and lines under, over, and in the letters, which made it possible to leave the consonants intact the way they had been originally handed down. This is of utmost importance, because one word in Hebrew can have the same consonants as another word with the difference lying only in the added vowels. One single letter can change into another letter, depending on where a single inserted dot is placed. An illustration of this is the Hebrew letter *shin*, שׁ while *sin*, שׂ is another. As you can see they are identical aside from the dot over the right on *shin* and over the left on *sin*. Because these markings were inserted several hundred years later it is yet another cause for discussion of various words and passages as to what the original meaning was.

There are also letters in Hebrew that are nearly identical such as *dalet,* ד and *resh,* ר. After years of transmission it can sometimes be dubious whether the letter was copied or not. Words can change depending on one single letter; it can affect an entire passage. What is more, there are several very old translations from Hebrew sources that have some minor variations from the now standard Masoretic one. For instance, the Septuagint is the earliest Greek translation of the Hebrew Scriptures.[7] Scholars believe the Gospel writers had the Septuagint as at least one of their sources, because in the New Testament it sometimes shows Jesus and others quoting Scripture that match up precisely to the Greek Septuagint. For example, in Acts 2:19, Peter quotes the prophet Joel regarding the last days and says in one verse, "blood, and fire, and vapor of smoke." This agrees with the Septuagint; whereas in the Hebrew, it instead says "blood and fire and columns of smoke."[8] Sometimes though, Old Testament quotes in the New Testament correspond directly with the Hebrew Masoretic text and sometimes with Aramaic Targums.[9] These different correlations reveal early New Testament authors had several different sources available and used a variety of them.

Other examples of old texts are the Samaritan version of the first five books of Moses called the Pentateuch,[10] the Targums,[11] and those that include the New Testament like Codex Sinaiticus,[12] the Latin Vulgate,[13] Codex Vaticanus,[14] and the Peshitta.[15] The oldest texts of the Hebrew Bible ever found are the hundreds of scrolls discovered in caves near the Dead Sea, commonly referred to as "the Dead Sea Scrolls." The first ones were found in 1947, and they date to approximately 250 B.C. to 70 A.D. Among the hundreds of scrolls, all the Biblical books were found except Esther. Some scrolls were discovered just in fragments while others nearly complete, some scrolls had multiple copies and others in only one. The vast majority of the texts were written in

Hebrew, but old Hebrew, Aramaic and Greek were also present.

Some of the scrolls are nearly, or exactly, identical to the Masoretic text, others with the Septuagint and the Samaritan Pentateuch. Yet others have textual variations unlike anything we have preserved, showing there were more ancient variations of the Biblical texts in circulation at that time.[16] It again reveals that multiple sources of the sacred Hebrew Scriptures were used. There was not one single standard version utilized before or during the time of Jesus.

The New Testament was also collected in stages, albeit during a much shorter time. There are quotations from the Gospels by church fathers from as early as the second century showing that the New Testament Gospels were already in circulation by at least that time. Around the end of the 4th century A.D., the 27 books currently combined in the New Testament were considered authoritative.[17] The New Testament in most translations is a compilation from literally thousands of different manuscripts that have survived, sometimes just in fragments. In each verse, scholars have determined which is the likeliest to be most like the original wording, because all the sources we have are copies of older texts. None of the original manuscripts have been found to date. The books of the New Testament are believed by most scholars to have first been written in Greek. There are critics who challenge this all-Greek position and assert one or more books were first penned in Hebrew or Aramaic. It is thought the New Testament scriptures were written approximately 50-115 A.D.[18] Some scholars believe it could be even earlier, and aside from genealogies and apocalyptic prophecies, the writers describe what happened during a few decades.

The various texts that make up the Bible are a vast topic with innumerable books and articles written on the subject. The official name for the accepted manuscripts of the

Bible is "canon" which esteemed men of the day agreed upon to be inspired and authoritative. While the belief in Christianity is that God has inspired both the texts and which books are in the canon, it should be acknowledged that Catholics, Protestants and Orthodox Christians have some variations regarding which texts are in their Bible. The Apocrypha, which means "hidden," is an example of writings that are not accepted by all Christian denominations today. Roman Catholics and some Orthodox have the Apocrypha in their Bible, while some Protestants and other Orthodox do not. Each denomination will naturally defend their selection regarded disputed books.

In order to understand today's Bible canon, one needs to examine the history of the Bible in the English language. The first Bible passage translated into English, after being circulated orally, may have been as early as the 8th century. It was done by the Venerable Bede (died 735 A.D.) who translated the Gospel of John into Anglo-Saxon.[19] The first entire Bible to be translated into English, from Latin, was done by John Wycliffe (1320-1384) with perhaps several men under his guidance, during the late 14th century. The Bible translated into English was a precursor to the Protestant Reformation, as it was illegal to translate the Bible without approval from the Catholic Church. This was before the printed press, so these Bibles were handwritten. It was the belief of Wycliffe that everyone should be able to read the Bible.

The first English Bible translated directly from Hebrew and Greek sources was done by William Tyndale (1494-1536) who likewise wanted to make the Bible available to everyone. He studied at Oxford and Cambridge and was not given permission to translate the Bible by the bishop in London. He left England to translate the Bible with a plan to smuggle copies back, which he did. By this time the printed press, invented by Johann Gutenberg in the late 1430's, existed. This made Tyndale's new translation of the New Testament available in a whole new way, just by the sheer number of copies that could be printed. King Henry VIII offered Tyndale sanctuary, as his writer and scholar. Tyndale refused unless it would become legal to translate the Bible into English. The King's men searched for him, and while he was working on translating the Old Testament in Belgium, he was found and jailed. After a year and a half in prison, he was strangled while burned at the stake for heresy. His last prayer was that the King of England's eyes would be opened. Three years later, his prayer was answered. The King of England commanded that every parish in England should have an English copy of the Bible. The version the king promoted was called "the Great Bible." This book included much of Tyndale's translations and work from Myles Coverdale.

The next important Bible produced was the Geneva Bible, published in 1560. This was the Bible of the pilgrims on the Mayflower and Shakespeare. The Geneva Bible had a significant difference from previous versions; it did not include the Apocrypha. It also had marginal notes explaining most things, which angered King James 1. In response, he ordered the 1611 King James Version of the English Bible to replace it. The Wycliffe Bible, the Great Bible, and the original (1611) King James Version of the Bible, all included the Apocrypha. In the original King James Bible, the Apocrypha was situated between the Old and New Testament. A little over two hundred years later, it was taken out King James Version.

The Reformation was the Christian response to a lot of abuse enabled by the religious monopoly and power the Roman Church had. The core theological belief Martin Luther promoted during the Reformation was that Christianity should rely solely on Scripture and not tradition. He firmly rejected things like the sale of indulgences and understood salvation to come only through faith, grace and Jesus. As part of Protestant Reformation's desire to distance itself from the Roman Catholic Church, the Church of England officially denied the Apocrypha canonical authority in 1562.

The Apocrypha, also referred to as deutero-canonical books, are listed below:

- 1-2 Esdras
- Tobit
- Judith
- Additions to Esther
- Wisdom of Solomon
- Baruch, (also called Ecclestiaticus)
- Letter of Jeremiah
- Prayer of Azariah and the Song of the Three Young Men (addition to Daniel)
- Susanna (addition to Daniel)
- Bel and the Dragon (addition to Daniel)
- Prayer of Manasseh
- 1 and 2 Maccabees.

There were a few reasons why these texts were taken out of the canon during the Protestant Reformation and questioned. One is that they were not part of the traditional Jewish collection of books. Jewish historian Flavius Josephus who lived in the first century A.D. wrote this about the Hebrew canon,

> For we have not an innumerable multitude of books among us, disagreeing from, and contradicting one another, [as the Greeks have], but only twenty-two books, {g} which contain the records of all the past times; which are justly believed to be divine; and of

them five belong to Moses, which contain his laws
and the traditions of the origin of mankind till his
death. This interval of time was little short of three
thousand years; but as to the time from the death of
Moses till the reign of Artaxerxes, king of Persia, who
reigned after Xerxes, the prophets, who were after
Moses, wrote down what was done in their times in
thirteen books. The remaining four books contain
hymns to God, and precepts for the conduct of
human life. It is true, our history has been written
since Artaxerxes very particularly, but has not been
esteemed of the like authority with the former by our
forefathers, because there has not been an exact
succession of prophets since that time; and how
firmly we have given credit to these books of our own
nation, is evident by what we do; for, during so many
ages as have already passed, no one has been so bold
as either to add anything to them, to take any thing
from them, or to make any change in them; but it is
becomes natural to all Jews, immediately and from
their very birth, to esteem these books to contain
divine doctrines, and to persist in them, and, if
occasion be, willingly to die for them.[20]

Josephus' work likely demonstrates what most Jews
understood as Holy Scripture at the time. Additionally, there
are some passages in the Apocrypha that many claim are
false teachings, not prophetic. Thus, the argument was the
Apocrypha should not be part of the proper canon.

It should be noted the Apocrypha is included in the
earliest complete New Testament that we still have today:
Codex Sianiaticus. It is from the 4th century and was found
at the St. Catherine monastery on Mount Sinai in Egypt.[21] It
has also been found in some early Greek manuscripts and in
the Greek text of Codex Vaticanus. The Vatican Codex is

handwritten from the 4th century and considered to be the oldest surviving copy of the Bible. The Old Testament in it is based on the Greek Septuagint. Though all New Testament manuscripts after Hebrews[22] are missing, the Apocrypha, except for 1-2 Maccabees and the Prayer of Manasseh, is present.

The Apocrypha was included in the Bible in the Septuagint, which is the Greek translation of the Hebrew Scriptures. The Septuagint is the first translation of the Hebrew Bible into another language. The Torah was translated ca. 250 B.C., Prophets ca. 200 B.C., and Writings ca. 150 B.C. This is a strong indication that the Apocrypha was not just a group of side note scrolls. It implies that they were valued before, and during, the time of Jesus. Additionally, Jerome (347-420 A.D.) translated the Bible to Latin (Latin Vulgate) in the late 300's and early 400's. He excluded the Apocrypha from canonical status but did translate Tobit and Judith from Old Latin. Jerome separated the Apocrypha and understood them as ecclesiastical books, meaning they were church books good for spiritual reading and circulated by the church.

Some theologians accuse the Apocryphal texts of being non-Scriptural because they were only preserved in Greek and Aramaic, not the Hebrew language. Ben Sirach, was found in Hebrew among the Dead Sea Scrolls. Likewise fragments of Tobit in Aramaic were found at Qumran.[23]

Essentially, early Christians understood the Apocrypha as canonical and authoritative. Several synods in the beginning years of the church reveal the Apocrypha held a high status among Christians. The Apocrypha has a long history of being part of the canon for millions of believers and has been for millennia. Not only is it the Roman Catholic Church who deemed the Apocrypha canonical but also the Eastern Orthodox, many in the Oriental Orthodox church, and even a few Protestants. The Apocrypha should never be mixed up with other extra Biblical writings such as Gnostic texts, which have never been understood as divinely inspired by any church.

It is important to understand there is a difference in status among other extra Biblical books. Many manuscripts that circulated the first few hundred years after, during, and before Jesus' time are not, and never have been, part of anyone's sacred canon. Some were considered frauds early on while others had prominence, were encouraged to read, and even on the verge of being deemed canonical. The Shepherd of Hermas, the Epistle of Barnabas, the Apocalypse of Peter and the Didache are in the category of those that had high standing early on. Numerous texts from the New Testament era have been found in the modern era and most are available in various publications, but they are not considered divinely inspired. An example of a collection you can buy is a two-volume set with the title "Pseudepigrapha," which is a word meaning "forgeries," because many of them were considered as such in the early era.[24] Thus, when we discuss scripts outside of the Bible, it is important to know that there is a major distinction between the Apocrypha and extra Biblical texts. The latter had a wide range in standing with regards to legitimacy.

The Bible's long transmission, how the Hebrew language changed over time, and how it got to be the text we have today is no small undertaking to learn. An English reader today will note that Bible translations sometimes differ slightly because no one will translate everything exactly the same. On top of that, no matter how good a translator is, sometimes nuances are just lost. This dilemma was acknowledged even before Jesus was born. The grandson of another man by the name of Jesus, the son of Sirach, who translated the book we refer to as "Ben Sirach" from Hebrew to Greek in the 2nd century B.C. described it this way,

> For what was originally expressed in Hebrew does not have exactly the same sense when translated into another language. Not only this work, but even the law itself, the prophecies, and the rest of the books differ not a little as originally expressed.[25]

This is why it is of prime importance to know Hebrew in order to understand Jesus and what he taught.

It is generally accepted within Biblical studies that many of the books in the Hebrew Scriptures had several authors, and often a redactor put it together. Moreover, in both the New and Old Testament, many scholars think it is not always be the claimed author that had written the text. For example, not all the letters ascribed to Paul in the New Testament are deemed by some to have been written by him. This is based on things such as writing style, content, word choices and other linguistic details. While falsely attributing writings to a more known person occurred in antiquity, at the same time, it was normal for ancient authors to use secretaries. Peter, for example, was said to have Mark write for him. Linguistic details could simply be the result of different secretaries, which is an example of counter arguments supporting the authenticity of Paul's letters.

This book will repeatedly from three Wisdom books, specifically Proverbs, Ben Sirach, and Wisdom of Solomon. The Book of Proverbs contains older wisdom literature and is believed to be a compilation of five different books with the last version of Proverbs believed to have arranged following the Babylonian exile in the fifth century B.C. Proverbs, recognized for all Christians as canonical, presents Wisdom personified in chapters one through nine. The next book of Wisdom is Ben Sirach meaning "son of Sirach" whose first name was actually Jesus. Ben Sirach is one of the canonized books of the Apocrypha in the Roman Catholic, Greek, and Russian Orthodox Bibles. The last book referenced is the Wisdom of Solomon. It is thought to have been written by a Greek speaking Jew in Alexandria during the last part of the first century B.C.[26] However, the original was penned in Hebrew as evidenced by Hebrew forms of it being found among the Dead Sea Scrolls. Evidence points to this being an important source for Jesus and the Apostles.[27] Like Ben Sirach, Wisdom of Solomon is one of the Apocrypha books of the Roman Catholic, Greek and Russian Orthodox Bibles.[28]

CONTRADICTIONS & MISUNDERSTANDINGS

With so many different people writing the Bible over such a long stretch of time and with the existence of several versions, it is no wonder it contains a few contradictions here and there. Take for example the death of Judas. In Matthew 27:3-10, it is described that he hung himself after he had repented for betraying Jesus. The chief priests and elders bought a field to bury strangers in with the blood money he had thrown back at them, and it was therefore called the Field of Blood. But, in Acts 1:18-19 it says that Judas bought this field with his reward money, fell "headlong" and "burst open in the middle and all his bowels gushed out." The Acts account states this is why the field is called the Field of Blood. Both stories are told to fulfill a prophecy, the one in Matthew to fulfill Jeremiah, and the one in Acts to fulfill the Psalms. There is a theme throughout the New Testament of inserting Scripture verses from the Hebrew Bible that were fulfilled by Jesus, revealing he was the true promised Messiah.

So, here we can see two different versions of how Judas died and who bought this field. What we can probably derive from these varied accounts is the potter's field was bought and came to be called the Field of Blood, related to

Judas' death and that Judas died shortly after betraying Jesus. The details of who actually bought the potter's field, exactly how Judas died and so forth will have to come from educated guess work. One demonstration of attempting to explain this discrepancy is a proposal that after Judas hanged himself no one could touch his corpse because the Sabbath began. He finally swelled up and fell down and burst open.[29] Once he had died the field was defiled because of his corpse, and the Temple priests could not take it back. For this reason the blood-money thrown back at them were used in Judas' name to make it a cemetery. The two versions were in this way simply two different accounts of the same story.

These are examples of how the Bible challenges us to a deeper understanding of textual complexities. Sometimes the Bible is confused with God. It is sacred for people of faith because it carries the divinely inspired word of God, designed to teach us about God and how to live. But, the Bible is still a medium that leads us *to* God. It is also for this very reason Bible study is so important.

HISTORICAL CONTEXT & INTERPRETATIONS

There is a vast amount of information at the hands of scholars about the larger cultural context from the Bible was written in. This has further validated how much these texts contain accurate historical information. Interpretations can also vary significantly depending on how much historical information you have access to review. Consider the often quoted passage about when Jesus rode on a donkey into Jerusalem.[30] It is often hailed as an example of his humility because nowadays we look at the donkey as a lowly pack-animal. Scripture says in Matthew that Jesus was "humble" and the Greek word used is in transliteration *praus* meaning "considerate," "humble," or "gentle." However, when Matthew says Jesus is humble, the donkey is not a representation of his humility, because kings and other important people in the ancient Near East rode donkeys.[31] I.e. Jesus riding a donkey signaled his kingship. King David himself rode a donkey.[32] When Matthew is describing this scenario, he is quoting the prophet Zechariah to fulfill prophesy.[33] It is even revealed in the quotation that riding the donkey was a sign of kingship, "Tell the daughter of Zion, Behold, your king is coming to you, humble, and mounted on an ass, and on a colt, the foal of an ass."[34] It was also in contrast to riding on a horse, which symbolized war.[35] Plus, if we look at this quote in the Hebrew Scriptures the word used there translated as "humble" from the Greek is the Hebrew word *'ani*, which refers to someone who is humble in the sense of "poor," or "afflicted.[36] In the Hebrew there are also two more words describing the Messiah. The prophecy in Zechariah says, "Lo, your king comes to you; triumphant and victorious is he, humble and riding on an ass, on a colt the foal of an ass.[37] The description of the donkey is a figure of speech which is why it sounds repetitive, but as we can see there are two words added to describe this king.[38] One is *saddiq*, meaning "righteous" and the other *nosha* which is "to be victorious."[39] So, when Matthew used this prophecy, he was possibly saying that Jesus though distressed and having no financial wealth (or backing) rode into Jerusalem triumphantly as a King in the name of peace.

In addition, the title "Son of God," used for Jesus needs to also be understood in its context. It was in direct opposition to the Roman ruler, also referred to as the "son of god," because he was the son of the deified emperor Augustus. Kingship in that era was seen as a divine institution with a divinely chosen ruler. Israel awaited a Messiah that would free them from the ruling foreign power and usher in an era of prosperity, sovereignty, and peace.

Yet, Jesus denounced coming in and changing things by military might. Just before he was killed he said,

> My kingship is not of this world; if my kingship were of this world, my servants would fight, that I might not be handed over to the Jews; but my kingship is not from the world.[40]

Consequently, he received the cruelest punishment of all. Crucifixion was the most torturous way to die and reserved for those who opposed the Roman Empire. Rome did not kill any of its own citizens this way.

Historical context helps us see the interconnectedness with surrounding cultures. For example; ancient wisdom tradition existed before Israel in neighboring lands, the Law of Moses was a reflection of a preceding tradition of legal laws in Mesopotamia, the Psalms had forerunners in older cultures and there were several earlier stories of the flood from the ancient Near East. This and much more, enable us to know that the Hebrew Bible was not an isolated development detached from other cultures. By the same token we can deduce what made Israel and the Biblical texts unique from what was absent in nearby civilizations. A demonstration of this is their devotion to their one God, Yahweh, which stands out in contrast to the surrounding societies where the norm was to worship many gods.[41] Prophecy was a phenomenon that was widespread, but there are no books with prophetic writings of such volume as the ones found in the Bible. Other examples are the books of Ruth and Esther, who so far have no contemporary equals.[42]

Biblical archeology is a field of utmost importance to Biblical studies. It helps validate or invalidate what we know from Biblical texts and give us new information from ancient libraries, thousands of various artifacts, statues, temples, traces of how they lived, and so forth. It can fill many gaps concerning Biblical times and is a vital discipline in Biblical scholarship.

There are often heated debates about the Bible. There are those who accuse people for reading everything literally, as a tool to discredit them. Others dismiss everything as allegorical teachings and fables. There are overwhelming scholarly and archeological evidences proving that the Bible is not made up, but contains vast amounts of accurate history with plenty of verified information. Elements like the Mosaic Law that state rules should not to be confused with Jesus' methods of teaching, which consisted of both parables and speaking in plain language. The Bible is not an allegorical book simply because there are metaphors present. There are things such as Jonah having lived in a whale three days, which literalists will understand as a miracle but others see symbolically. However, the question can be extended to all miracles. If you deny Jesus walking on water or raising people from the dead, why would you accept him being raised from the dead? You eventually reach a point where either you are a Christian or not; you believe the Scriptures or you do not. Atheists will, of course, deny miracles. An example of critically reading the text without dismissing it is discerning where some wars may have been distorted propaganda, because it conflicts with archeological or other contemporary historical information. Some writers may at times have promoted the viewpoint of one angle of a war.

Today Bible scholars have made progress in understanding all the various aspects of Scripture, but some of this knowledge does not reach the general public or even the pulpits. There are a few Biblical scholars trying to bridge that gap though.[43] It is important to note too that in historical research done by academics there are both believers and non-believers alike. This tension is present because the lenses via which we view history matters, and no one is fully objective. Lastly, the many components of studying the Bible do not mean it is a book of confusion. The moral values it teaches are well defined and consistent. Christians throughout history have and do overall agree more than disagree. These are all demonstrations of how other historical documents and further background knowledge gives a fuller understanding of the Bible.

WOMEN PORTRAYED IN THE BIBLE - A DUAL PERSPECTIVE

It was men, most likely exclusively, who wrote and transmitted the Biblical texts, took the crucial decisions about the canon and wrote all the church doctrines and creeds. The Bible itself is a testimony of a patriarchal world and written mostly from a masculine perspective. When women are spoken about it is often specifically mentioned otherwise it was assumed they referred to men. This may not even be noticeable at first glance. Case in point, Matthew 14:21 says in the story about the feeding of the five thousand that, "And those who ate were about five thousand men, besides women and children." Likewise, in Revelation 14:4 when John is talking about the hundred and forty-four thousand who had been redeemed from earth he refers only to men saying, "It is these who have not defiled themselves with women, for they are chaste . . . ."

Critics often accuse the Bible of sexism because men were rulers and scribes even though this is the case for most of global history because women were homebound to raise children. However, it does not mean that Israel devalued women for that reason or committed sexism. That concept is a reflection of modern values. The Bible portrays women as highly revered and cherished.[44]

Case in point is the story of Zelophehad's five daughters. In Numbers 26:1-2, God asked Moses and

Eleazar, a priest and the son of Aaron, to make a census of every male over twenty years of age. However, Zelophehad had no sons, wherefore his daughters: Mahlah, Noah, Hoqlah, Milcah and Tirzah, would not be counted. This mattered because God told Moses that the land should be divided as an inheritance to all those counted in the census.[45] The daughters of Zelophehad stepped forward, before Moses and Eleazar, as well as the rest of the Israel leaders and the congregation, and said,

> Our father died in the wilderness; he was not among the company of those who gathered themselves together against the LORD in the company of Korah, but died for his own sin; and he had no sons. Why should the name of our father be taken away from his family, because he had no son? Give to us a possession among our father's brethren.[46]

So, these daughters pleaded to Moses that they should not be left out of an inheritance because their father did not participate in Korah's rebellion against Moses, and he had no sons. Upon hearing this,

> Moses brought their case before the LORD. And the LORD said to Moses, "The daughters of Zelophehad are right; you shall give them possession of an inheritance among their father's brethren and cause the inheritance of their father to pass to them. And you shall say to the people of Israel, `If a man dies, and has no son, then you shall cause his inheritance to pass to his daughter.[47]

God commanded that this order should continue in the future and if there were no daughters the inheritance should go to others within the family. So, this was no small matter but changed the laws for all the Israelites in women's favor.

The wisdom books are examples of texts that have plenty of praise for women's virtues. Proverbs chapter 31 is said to be, "The words of Lemuel, king of Massa, which his mother taught him" and even tell us that the teachings are from a woman.[48] Her son, king Lemuel, honored her by passing them on and made sure they were attributed to her. The Song of Solomon is a set of love poems clearly praising a woman, as well as praising a man from a woman's perspective, which suggests a female author in this section.[49]

The book of Ruth and the book of Esther are two different books devoted to a story about a woman. In the Hebrew texts we can read about women who were respected female prophets, Hulda, Noadiah, and Deborah for example.[50] Miriam, the sister of Aaron and Moses is featured as a significant figure and also called a "prophetess."[51] There is a strong indication that Isaiah's wife was likewise a prophetess.[52] Anna in the New Testament was referred to as a "prophetess" as well and spoke about Jesus "to all who were looking for the redemption of Jerusalem."[53]

Women prophesying continued to be theologically valid into Jesus' time. Paul says in 1 Corinthians 11:5 that "but any woman who prays or prophesies with her head unveiled dishonors her head . . . ." This is right after he explains in the previous verse that the reverse is true for men. So, it was taken for granted that both men and women were prophets. Prophesy by females is justified in the New Testament through a passage from the prophet Joel. In Acts, Peter quotes him and said,

> And in the last days it shall be, God declares, that I will pour out my Spirit upon all flesh, and your sons and your daughters shall prophesy, and your young men shall see visions, and your old men shall dream dreams; yea, and on my menservants and my maidservants in those days I will pour out my Spirit; and they shall prophesy.[54]

21

So, the Bible supports prophesy to be practiced by women past, present, and future, upholding the spiritual value of women.

Miraculous childbirth is another well-established theme. Illustrations of this are Sarah who bore Isaac, Hannah who gave birth to Samuel, Elisabeth who bore John the Baptist and, of course, Mary's conception of Jesus. Motherhood was highly revered, and one of the Ten Commandments was to honor your father and mother, equally.[55]

It is specifically mentioned in Genesis how God looked out for the Egyptian slave woman Hagar and her son twice, when no one else did. The first time was when she fled from Sarah and the second after Sarah asked Abraham to send her away for good.[56] Ishmael, who was an innocent victim of the situation, was saved by God Himself who named him so because it meant "the LORD has given heed to your affliction."[57] While God heard Ishmael's cry, Hagar both heard and saw Him and therefore called God "Thou art a God of seeing."[58]

Rebekah, wife of Isaac, is notably featured, even if it is not solely in a favorable light as she helped to trick Isaac into giving Jacob his blessing. Nonetheless, she is pictured as strong willed and taking charge. It was her favorite son, Jacob, who became prominent in Israelite history, not Isaac's favorite son, Esau, and much of that was thanks to Rebekah. Rachel was the love of Jacob's life, and he did years of labor to win the right to be with her. Abigail was a wise woman who saved her unwise husband and his household from being killed by King David by negotiating with him.[59]

It was Pilate's wife who had a dream about Jesus and told him to "Have nothing to do with that righteous man . . . ."[60] Several women who were followers of Jesus are repeatedly present in the New Testament. On the morning of the resurrection it was, according to Mark 16:1, three women, among them Mary Magdalene, who first discovered the empty tomb and whom the angel spoke to about Jesus (verses 5-7). We can understand the importance of female disciples in the early church by notes such as those by Paul.

For example, in Romans chapter 16, he references a series of women along with men whom he is very grateful for. In verse one he mentions Phoebe who was a "deaconess of the church at Cen'chre-ae" and in verse three Prisca is one of Paul's "fellow workers in Christ Jesus" who along with a man risked her life for Paul. In verse 6 he remarks on a hardworking Mary and proceeds to mention several more women of importance for the church. There is Lydia who was "a seller of purple goods" who is described to be a "worshiper of God" when Paul arrived in Thyatira, located in modern day Turkey.[61] Lydia was part of a group of women who were praying together when Paul and Silas came and sat down to talk to them. Then "The Lord opened her heart to give heed to what was said by Paul."[62] After that she, and her household, was baptized and she hosted Paul and Silas. They came back to stay with her again after having been imprisoned and set free thanks to an earthquake destroying the prison.[63] She, and those with her, may have been the first to have been converted in the modern day European continent in addition to hosting and protecting Paul. The last of these examples is Eve who is the other key figure alongside Adam in the creation story, and whose name means "mother of all living."[64]

These passages and others like them give us an insight to the complex status women had that was not a black and white one. The case that women did not have "worldly" leading roles like men in the Bible have also been the norm in most parts all across the globe. Most of all, the Bible does not teach that being a ruler of the world is more important than being a mother. That is a worldly way of thinking that Jesus denounced.

Women have always worked in the home/farm, which involved enormous labor that our modern inventions and economic advances have drastically altered. There have been a few queens and other women in positions of political power, but options for higher education for women have historically been much less than those for men. We should also note that roles for men were also vastly less diversified too. The explosion of innumerable various jobs and topics to study is a recent occurrence.

Men and women's roles, though sometimes overlapping, are historically distinct for the fact that we are physically different. Because women carry children, we have been the ones also primarily raising them and caring for the household. The Bible places a high value on this. While over the centuries men have abused some Biblical passages to argue females were less important, those will be examined here from a literal, historical context. Unfortunately it has taken centuries for women to oppose interpretations of Bible passages because they rarely had any opportunity to do so. Once provided with the education, research abilities, and job opportunities, women began offering another perspective on certain paragraphs of Scripture that had been overlooked or dismissed from a male dominating societal opinion.

In the early part of the nineteenth century abolitionist Sarah Grimke wanted women to be able to study the Bible because she believed it had been interpreted unfairly against women in order to maintain the state of their suppression.[65] A few women became trained in Biblical scholarship and at the end of the 19th century the groundbreaking book, "_A Women's Bible_" was published. It was a commentary on Bible passages that concerns women from a female perspective done by twenty different women under the leadership of Elisabeth Cady Stanton.[66] Stanton was a woman of faith and key figure in the early women's suffragette and anti-slavery movement. <u>A Woman's Bible</u> was an instant bestseller but created controversy and was even denounced by some clergy as Satan's work.

An illustration of what was written in <u>A Women's Bible</u> is by one of the other commentators, a lady by the name of Lillie Devereux Blake. She pointed out that the man was told not to eat of the fruit of this Tree before Eve was even created. So, Eve was, as she put it, not told by "the impressive solemnity of a divine Voice, but whispered to her by her husband and equal."[67] Ms. Blake points out that Eve did not just mindlessly take the fruit when offered, but she argued with the snake. She also remarks on the fact that after God found out what they had done and it was time for reckoning,

> Adam endeavors to shield himself behind the gentle being he has declared to be so dear. "The woman thou gavest to be with me, she gave me and I did eat," he whines—trying to shield himself at his wife's expense! Again we are amazed that upon such a story men have built up a theory of their superiority![68]

She emphasized that Adam did not own up to his part of transgressing God's command, but blamed Eve instead, hardly brave or honorable.

As we can note from these early female Bible scholars a woman's perspective on the Bible, in addition to all other factors, can differ from a man's analysis and offer another valuable interpretation to consider. It is of utmost importance here to note that women are not a minority who seek to put forth either an obscure or marginal view. Women constitute half of the earth's population and play key roles in life as well as in the Bible. Humanity cannot exist without both genders, and creation testifies to the equal value of men and women. Interpretations from a woman's perspective are often dismissed as "feminism." Yet, there is no genre called "masculanism" when a perspective is given solely from the masculine point of view. This natural bias is a testimony to how recent changes are in our understanding of Scripture and how deeply rooted sexism has been in our culture and consciousness

FROM THE WORLDLY REALM TO THE DIVINE

It was rather inevitable that the belief in one lone male God with no female in sight, and an all-masculine Trinity would contribute to sexism. In the Christian world, a woman is asked to pray to God the Father, God the Son and God the Holy Spirit. It is not just one "He" she should bow down to, but three. The male heavenly trio is well entrenched in the western psyche, although it is not as Biblical as we have been led to believe.

Though the Bible was written by men and reflects how they ruled society, this was only a partial picture, because it was much more multifaceted. The Bible simultaneously contains plenty of passages that praises women and places her worth at the highest level. Men may have ruled worldly affairs, for the most part, but women governed in the homes. This was, and is, incredibly powerful too, just in a different way. For people of faith, what matters is to detect and understand what God has to say about women. This book, though, is primarily not about Eve and her daughters. It is about who Eve was modeled after: the existence of a feminine force in the celestial realm.

For this reason, it is time to revisit the three persons of the Godhead, as well as the concept of the Trinity itself. There is a Divine Feminine power waiting to be fully revealed and regain her rightful place in both Scripture and the hearts of mankind. Translations often hide her gender, making her hard to detect. She is at other times in plain view. Yet, somehow she is never even mentioned in churches. When it comes to texts about her, those passages are not read literally, only allegorically, or they are simply ignored altogether. This is a curious fact since so many people believe the Bible is God's literal and infallible word. I do not dismiss a literal belief. It is precisely the belief in a literal wording that makes the arguments I present even stronger.

CHAPTER 2

THE HOLY SPIRIT IN THE BIBLE

Jesus answered him, "Truly, truly, I say to you, unless one is born anew, he cannot see the kingdom of God."

The Gospel of John 3:3

"IT IS WRITTEN" – IN HEBREW

HEBREW THE SACRED LANGUAGE:

The importance of the Hebrew language in Israelite theology is central to the topic of the Divine Feminine. Although the Spirit of God has been viewed as masculine for nearly two millennia, most ordinary Christians are not aware that this viewpoint is wrong and much less why. In the Hebrew texts—the Old Testament for Christians and Jesus' Sacred Scriptures—the Spirit of God is grammatically feminine. Likewise, in Jesus' native tongue: Aramaic, which is very closely related to Hebrew, the Spirit of God is feminine as well. In other words, Jesus himself addressed the Spirit with feminine pronouns. This was not a grammatical inconsequential detail but it had vast theological ramifications.

It is popular by many Christians to claim that God has no physical body and is therefore sexless and often phrases like "God is spirit" is used to back this up.[69] I have already stated this but it bears repeating: the Biblical creation story of man and woman, made in the image of God, is all about gender. It is what enables pro-creation, and I would claim, Creation. The mixing of male and female is not a side note; it is the heart of the matter.[70] This concept is wholly intertwined with the Hebrew language which is why you cannot fully understand Israelite theology if you discount it.

In the Hebrew Scriptures the Spirit is mostly referred to as the Spirit of *Elohim* or the Spirit of *Yahweh*."[71] These are respectively translated in English as Spirit of God and Spirit of the Lord. The word for Spirit in Hebrew, *ruah*, is feminine which, as I have shown, presents this term with a feminine/masculine duality. In the New Testament the phrase "Holy Spirit" is used instead of "Spirit of God." In translations from New Testament texts in Syriac, which is a branch of ancient Aramaic, it is translated as "Spirit of Holiness." This change crystallized the Spirit as a more individual force in addition to how Jesus talked about her.[72] She is part of God Yahweh yet distinguishable from Him. Christians are so used to this and most do not notice, or know, that the Holy Spirit is not prominent in Judaism, and though she is present in the Old Testament she has a far more significant role in the New Testament. This reflects a certain theology that Jesus proclaimed which differs from the one contemporary Judaism developed out of. There is one exception to this, which is the Jewish Kabbalistic mystical teachings, which is a branch out of the Jewish/Hebrew religion and will be examined later.

The main reason for why the Holy Spirit's feminine gender has been obscured is the Greek language. The Old Testament was translated to Greek and the New Testament was either written or early on translated to Greek.[73] The Greek word for "Spirit," transliterated as *pneuma*, is neuter (neutral). This grammatical category does not even exist in Hebrew. Thus the translation to Greek inevitably meant that the Spirit of God became void of gender or neutral.[74] The result for us is that the English New Testament does not reflect the original Hebrew language or concepts when it comes to the gender of the Holy Spirit. Hebrew was, and still is, the sacred language of the Jews. Jesus and the ancient Hebrews understood the Holy Spirit as feminine. This is her authentic gender. Most of all, for any follower of Jesus, it is his views on this beyond grammar that truly matters.

Have you ever wondered why the same people who argue that the femininity of the Spirit is not a theological matter, but simply a grammatical one, always refers to God as "He?" The reason they do so is because the Bible, in clear language, declares Yahweh to be male. Yet, they do not apply the same logic to God's Spirit. Instead it is always the Greek form/translations of the Holy Spirit considered to be the proper one. When the major creeds were written in the fourth century, establishing the concept of the Trinity, they had repercussions for the Holy Spirit that were theologically significant.[75] The Holy Spirit became part of the Trinity and went on to be understood as male. This later turned into official doctrine where refuting the Holy Spirit as male constituted heresy and still does today in many churches.

When we devalue the importance of word choices for the early Hebrews (and the people before them) we tread risky territory. The tradition of exact transmission of sacred texts was profound, every word and sentence pondered upon. It is for this reason that the trend to make God gender neutral is wrong. The gender of the words mattered. The Holy Spirit being feminine was not a grammatical accident. The same applies to Wisdom, which is highly relevant here, because she, like the Holy Spirit, is personified in Scripture as a female. It is my thesis that Wisdom is another epithet for the Holy Spirit, which I will illustrate.

The femininity of both Wisdom and the Holy Spirit were fastened deep in people's psyche in for the ancient

Israelites. Every time they recited or read Scripture and came across the Holy Spirit, or Wisdom, she was in the feminine form. The Hebrews used feminine pronouns like "her" and "she." It is impossible that this would not affect their perception any less than that of Yahweh being male. In light of the continual reference to "she," we cannot claim the gender of the words did not matter, especially with something as substantial as the Spirit of God. That is simply not true.

Lastly, part of my research means I examine, and refer to, many extra Biblical sources from both A.D. and B.C. This includes, what is referred to today as, Gnostic texts. Because of how they can be highly controversial I want to emphasize that this does *not* mean I consider them "Biblical" in the sense that they are divinely inspired. They are not the "word of God" and should not be canonized the way the Bible is. It simply means that back in the early Church era, just as now, there were different groups, and ideas, developing within early Christianity. During the time of Jesus, there were different sects within Judaism. Christianity has seen major schisms with the split between the Roman Catholic Church and the Eastern Orthodox year 1054 and the Protestant Reformation in the 16th century, as discussed in the introduction chapter. Today there are also numerous Protestant denominations within Protestantism including "non-denominational ones." Thus, studying early Christian era manuscripts is part of historical research. Gnostic ideas are particularly relevant to this book because the femininity of the Holy Spirit plays a major role in many of the texts under that heading. They are included to illustrate why this did not begin with the "Gnostics," but with Old Testament Holy Scriptures. In this way, the Gnostic texts serve as further evidence for how prevalent, and important, the femininity of the Spirit was in ancient Israel and the early Christian era.

Additionally, it is important to know that "Gnosticism" is an overarching term that Scholars apply for certain texts but it is not what they were called back then. "Gnostics" were merely one of many off-shoot sects in the first few hundred years after Christ. The term "Gnostics" was picked to represent texts that had similar themes that relate to what that word gnostic means. It is derived from the word *gnosis,* which is a Greek feminine noun that means "knowledge."

YAHWEH

While this book is about the theological significance of the femininity of the Holy Spirit, one thing has to be recognized first. While the Spirit of God is feminine it is equally true that the Bible describes *Yahweh* as a male Deity. Words in Hebrew have a gender and are either masculine or feminine. There is no neuter (neutral) form. His personal name is *Yahweh,* while the word mostly used for "God" is *Elohim.*[76] In addition, He has physical form which humans, created in His image, reflect.

I want to give some illustrations of this but first I need to say a few words about how modern ideas work against what this book is about: the Divine Feminine. I would also dare to claim that modern feminism is in direct opposition to what the Bible says. There has been a movement since the early 1970's to have gender-neutral language for God in Bible translations, which started during the feminist movement. The argument was gender neutrality would value femininity by being gender inclusive. This is unfortunately gravely misleading. Feminism should never be about neutering women and men into becoming "its" in order to make us have the same worth.[77] This is counterfeit to fighting sexism, which rests on recognizing that women are *different* but have *equal value*. If you can only value women by denying their femininity, you have accomplished the exact opposite, i.e. the ultimate suppression of women. If the gender of God is not accurately translated, we simultaneously lose the Divine Feminine presence that exists in Scripture and complements the male Yahweh.

Most of all, it is profoundly unethical to alter sacred texts for any reason. Everyone is free to disagree with the Bible, but translations should *always* stay as true as possible to the original language and intent, which we find via accurate translations aided by an understanding of the historical contexts when originally written in. The long held tradition of copying texts truthfully protects what the Hebrews wrote, which, for believers, is the inspired word of God. "Inspired" means "in Spirit" so it is specifically the Holy Spirit's presence that makes the Bible come alive and guides us to the truth.

Naturally, translators will have to make some interpretive decisions to certain degrees, such as when a word can mean two things, but something as profound as the gender of God is not a subject that belongs in the category of dubious interpretations. Jesus referred to God as "our Father," and this has deep theological meanings.[78] The same applies to God's Spirit. Instead of neutering God, it is time to recognize and highlight that, in the Hebrew Scriptures: Yahweh is male, but the Holy Spirit is feminine. This should decisively matter for Christians, because Jesus' sacred language was Hebrew, not Greek. Jesus was Jewish, not Gentile.

Some illustrations of Yahweh being male can be seen in the prophetic books. This is because prophets, in particular, had visions of God revealing Him as the archetype for humans. A case in point is when Jeremiah said he did not know how to speak because he was only a child. Yahweh then reached out His "hand" to touch Jeremiah's mouth and put His words there.[79] Likewise, when Isaiah received his calling, he saw "the LORD sitting upon a throne, high and lifted up; and his train filled the temple" and the Seraphim covered his face and his feet and "with two he flew."[80] Another example from the Hebrew Scriptures is the prophecy of Micai'ah. Speaking to the King of Israel he said, "I saw the LORD sitting on his throne, and all the host of heaven standing beside him on his right hand and on his left…"[81]

Aside from prophetic visions, passages such as Genesis 3:8 depict God walking around in the Garden of Eden in the cool of the day, while Adam and Eve hid from Him among the trees. Maybe the most famous theophany is in Exodus 33:11 where it says that *Yahweh* used to speak to Moses "face to face, as a man speaks to his friend." In the New Testament, Jesus is repeatedly described to be sitting on the right hand of God in the hereafter. In the Book of Revelation God is on His throne and people will finally see His face.[82] So, from Genesis to Revelation, Yahweh is described in *anthropomorphic* male terms. This matters a great deal, because man and woman were created in God's image. The human form replicates God's form. Remember this when you later read the section about the creation story in Genesis 1.

REVEALING THE PRESENCE OF THE HOLY SPIRIT'S GENDER

I want to show you some literal translations, from Hebrew, of the Holy Spirit, which will give a window into how the ancient Israelites viewed her. The other feminine force in the Bible, who is personified in the same way that the Holy Spirit is in the New Testament, is Wisdom. For all intents and purposes, these two are one and the same feminine Power. I will explain why later, but first I want you to understand how the gender of the Spirit has been obscured in the translations from the original Hebrew. As a result, we do not get a clear picture of just how explicit her presence is and likewise was to the Israelites.

The first example is from Isaiah at a part where he speaks about God's Spirit as "his holy Spirit."[83] A few verses down in this chapter it is reinforced that the Holy Spirit is feminine. If you translate all the Hebrew grammatical pronouns Isaiah 63:14 says this,

> Like the cattle in the plain, **she** goes down, the **Spirit** of Yahweh, **she** gave rest to him, thus you guided your people for the glory of your name.[84]

Here, **"she"** going down and **"she"** giving rest is referring to the Spirit of Yahweh. This gives us a better understanding of how the gender inevitably had theological consequences. The Spirit's femininity would be clear not only when they wrote but while reading Scriptures both privately and aloud. The Israelites thought and talked about the Spirit of God as a feminine force.

Another example is from Job 32:8 where it literally says,

> but the **Spirit**, **she** is in man, and the **breath** of Shadday, **she** gives understanding to them.

Compare this to an English translation, which goes as follows, "But it is the spirit in a man, the breath of the Almighty, that makes him understand." The English translation is quite different from the original Hebrew. In addition, we have another example here of how it is the Spirit that gives understanding. As previously mentioned, the Spirit understands the will of God, and it is **she** who makes humans understand God as well. We can also here see the ideas of the Holy Spirit are intertwined with Wisdom, because it says that the Spirit **takes her place** in humans and **she is the breath of God**. We already know that one of the Holy Spirit's roles is to enter into people and fill them with divine understanding, and that Wisdom did this too. For example, Wisdom of Solomon 7:25 says about Wisdom,

> For **she** is a **breath** of the power of God.[85]

Both the Spirit of God and Wisdom are manifest as the breath of God, indicating they are one and the same force.

An additional demonstration of this duality is from Job 33:4. In a regular English translation it says, "The spirit of God has made me, and the breath of the Almighty gives me life." Translating the Hebrew pronouns this passage would read like this,

> **Spirit** of El, **she** made me, and the **breath** of Shadday **she** gives life to me.

Talking about the Spirit of God this way places the presence of the Divine Feminine deeply into the reader's consciousness. This clear description is lost today in our translations; wherefore we, wrongfully tend to think she was not an important part of the Hebrew faith.

Another prophet who spoke repeatedly about the Spirit as a Divine Feminine force was Ezekiel. Looking again at a literal translation one short line in Ezekiel 2:2 would read as follows,

> **she** came into me, the **Spirit**.

The common English translation is "the Spirit entered into me." As we can see, the fact that the Spirit is feminine is lost in English. The verb "came" or "entered" has the prefixed feminine pronoun and agrees in gender and number with the Spirit in this sentence. Yes, the author followed the Hebrew grammatical rules, and because the Spirit is feminine, the attached pronoun had to agree. However, we cannot dismiss this as simply grammar that has no theological meaning, or impact. As we continue, I will show how it had utmost significance for many, especially Jesus.

Later in Ezekiel we have an even clearer example of both the femininity of the Spirit as well as her role. It is literally written,

> and **she** came upon me, the **Spirit** of Yahweh, and **He** spoke to me.[86]

Here we are presented with the clear duality of the feminine Spirit entering into the human, but yet Yahweh, who is male, is the one speaking. Perhaps this signaled the way a human is not ready to perceive the word of God unless the Spirit has first entered. In this sense, the Spirit is the conduit between God and man. In the regular English translation the verse reads, "And the Spirit of the LORD fell upon me, and he said to me." In English, the male-female presence is eliminated.

In Ezekiel 37:1 it literally says,

> **She** was upon me, the **hand** of Yahweh, and He brought me out by the **Spirit** of Yahweh and He set me down in the middle of the valley, and she was full of bones.

Here, translating the pronouns has another result. Yahweh's hand is described as not only God's instrument, but feminine too. This is because the Hebrew word for "hand" is a feminine word and so the pronoun agrees with it, just as the valley here is feminine which is why translating it "she was full of bones" reflects that. It is of course easy to argue that this in fact shows that the femininity of the Holy Spirit does not mean anything because here, the hand is feminine, and even the valley.[87] Yet, even the hand here seems to have layers of meanings. Not only is the hand tied to the same role as that of the Spirit, but Yahweh brought Ezekiel out "by" the Spirit and as the "hand" of God was "upon" him he was saved. The hand displays the protection of God, a very masculine attribute. God is protective, but the force He uses as His instrument is here feminine.

Another example of the hand having a similar role to the Holy Spirit is in Ezra 7:28 where it says in the latter part of the verse, "for the hand of the LORD my God was upon me." The literal translation would be "for the hand of Yahweh my God (was) upon me." Aside from God's name not being translated these versions are virtually identical. It is because the hand is here in construct with Yahweh and no pronouns are present. Thus, it is not always the case that the gender of a word like hand is clearly displayed. The Holy Spirit who inspired the written scripture had a reason for using feminine pronouns when describing the hand in Ezekiel. That reason was to emphasize a Divine Feminine nature.

It is worth mentioning too that though the "hand of God" is mostly referred to as something positive like an instrument of His protection. But, His hand was also used to carry out punishments. When the Philistines had captured the Ark of the Covenant, God was angry and through His "hand" He caused them much harm. For example in 1 Samuel 5:6 it literally says that,

> The **hand** of Yahweh, **she** was heavy on the Ashdodites and He brought desolation and He afflicted them with tumors, Ashdod and her vicinities.

This rhetoric continues in Samuel. While the "hand" shows an interesting noteworthy parallel to the Spirit of God, the hand being in feminine form may not be a sustainable argument alone to understand it as a separate force. Rather, this could potentially be where the idea of the laying on of hands originated from, which is directly tied together to

Wisdom and the Holy Spirit's presence by invoking her presence via the laying on of hands.[88]

It can simultaneously reflect the modern saying that when you have someone you rely on very much, this person is almost an extension of you, and you therefore refer to that individual as your "right arm" or "right hand." The significance of the Spirit of God, and Wisdom, being feminine clearly exhibit much more meanings than mere grammatical features and strongly indicates a continuation of God's feminine part/partner taking the form of Lady Wisdom and the Holy Spirit.

Translating the pronouns from Hebrew exposes the prominent presence of the feminine Spirit in the Hebrew faith that has been lost in translation. A literal translation reveals more of how the ancient Israelites saw and understood the features of God, instead of what amounts to a more interpretive approach that have decided that the femininity of the Spirit is not important. The Spirit of God is a fundamental part of the Hebraic faith. Humans have souls (*nephesh*), and God is the Creator of all. But, it is only when we are given God's Spirit (*ruah*) that we change from within. His presence on earth—the Holy Spirit—can permeate humans. In this way God has a living relationship with mankind. This duality is undeniable, because Yahweh is masculine and the presence of His Spirit on earth is feminine.

The above quotes are all from the Hebrew Scriptures where the Spirit and Wisdom are both feminine. Translating the pronouns from Hebrew exposes, as you can see, the prominent presence of the feminine Spirit in the Hebrew faith that has been lost in translation. The Holy Spirit figures as Yahweh's instrument, the active force landing on and entering into humans, guiding them, while He is Source of the information, the Power and the One who speaks, albeit, through the Spirit.[89]

THE HOLY SPIRIT & WISDOM IN THE OLD TESTAMENT AND THE APOCRYPHA

IN THE BEGINNING...

The word "Genesis" comes from the Greek and means "origin," which in turn is a translation from the Hebrew word "beginning." This is the word that opens the first book of Moses, together with the prefix "in." The Spirit of God appears in Genesis 1:1-2 where it says,

> In the beginning God created the heavens and the earth. The earth was without form and void, and darkness was upon the face of the deep; and the Spirit of God was moving over the face of the waters.

These lines are loaded with meanings, and I cannot go into all of them here. What I want to point out now is that the Spirit of God was present "In the beginning." Take a mental note of this as we go forward. The Hebrew word for Spirit is *ruah,* which can also mean "wind." *Ruah* is grammatically feminine.

Another reason why I want to offer for why Wisdom and the Holy Spirit are one and the same is that they are both present in the beginning. While we explicitly see that the Spirit of God was present "In the beginning" in Genesis 1:1, the Bible also talks about who was present in the book of Proverbs. Proverbs 8:22-23 says about Wisdom,

> The LORD created me at the beginning of his work, the first of his acts of old. Ages ago I was set up, at the first, before the beginning of the earth.

The word for "beginning" here is in transliteration *re'sheyt.* It is the exact same word, together with a prefixed preposition, as the very first word in Genesis 1:1.⁹⁰ As already noted by many, the use of *re'sheyt* in Proverbs is alluding to a connection with Genesis 1:1, thus making a theological statement. Proverbs continues to describe a list of creations that Wisdom preceded and follows by saying that she was next to God and partook in creation itself. By these Scriptural words, we can right here see a link to the feminine presence in the creation story of Genesis 1:26-27. Furthermore, a few verses later Scripture says,

> when he assigned to the sea its limit, so that the waters might not transgress his command, when he marked out the foundations of the earth, then I was beside him, like a master workman . . . [91]

Wisdom is described as nothing less than a co-Creator with God in the beginning.

Ben Sirach also ties Wisdom to the Spirit of God when Wisdom says, "I came forth from the mouth of the Most High, and covered the earth like a mist."[92] This is undoubtedly paralleling the line in chapter two before God creates Adam which says,

> but a mist went up from the earth and watered the whole face of the ground - then the LORD God formed man of dust from the ground, and breathed into his nostrils the breath of life; and man became a living being.

Wisdom being the breath of God and the Holy Spirit described as transmitted via breath makes them one and the same. Additionally, this verse simultaneously links Wisdom to the Spirit moving over the face of the waters in the opening scene in Genesis. It says that, "darkness was upon the face of the deep; and the Spirit of God was moving over the face of the waters."[93] The word "Spirit," is in Hebrew a feminine word transliterated as *ruah* and it also means "breath" and "wind." Wisdom hovering as mist over the earth and the Spirit hovering over the waters of the earth, and both being described as the breath of God which is the meaning of *ruah*, ties the Spirit and Wisdom together as the dual manifestations of the Divine Feminine. It also declares her presence *"in the beginning"* before the creation of mankind.

One occasion explains the Holy Spirit's two fold meaning; Spirit and breath, with the latter reminding us of Wisdom as breath, is when Jesus breathed on his disciples and said "Receive the Holy Spirit."[94] We can see this concept echoed in Proverbs 2:6 too where it says, "For the LORD gives wisdom; from his mouth come knowledge and understanding . . . ." Wisdom personified, described as "breath" which in Hebrew is a synonym to "Spirit,"[95] acting as a co-creator with God present "in the beginning" of Creation, are all indications that the Spirit of God and Wisdom are one and the same Power. These are rather profound connections, but there is more confirming that they are one and the same.

The book of Ben Sirach opens up with continuing the ideas of Proverbs and declares this,

All wisdom comes from the LORD and is with him for ever. The sand of the sea, the drops of rain, and the days of eternity–who can count them? The height of heaven, the breadth of the earth, the abyss, and wisdom–who can search them out? Wisdom was created before all things, and prudent understanding from eternity. The root of wisdom–to whom has it been revealed? Her clever devices–who knows them? There is One who is wise, greatly to be feared, sitting upon his throne. The LORD himself created wisdom; he saw her and appointed her, he poured her out upon all his works. She dwells with all flesh according to his gift, and he supplied her to those who love him.[96]

This verse declares that Wisdom is not just an inherent attribute of God but a separate entity created by Him. The line that Wisdom was created "before all things" testifies that it was His first creation reflecting what is written in Proverbs. When it says that all wisdom is with Him forever, it can be understood as a roundabout way of declaring that she is co-eternal with Him. Important to observe is the statement regarding it has not been revealed to anyone how she came to be. Finally, the way she "dwells with all flesh according to his gift" certainly fits the description of how the Holy Spirit functions.[97]

In Ben Sirach 24:8, Wisdom is described again as created by God saying, "Then the Creator of all things gave me a commandment, and the one who created me assigned a place for my tent." In the next verse it continues, "From eternity, in the beginning, he created me, and for eternity I shall not cease to exist." So, Wisdom is both personified and eternal, a divine trait, suggesting she is a divinity.

In Wisdom of Solomon she is similarly described to have been present since the beginning of creation and comprehends the will of God. It is explained this way,

> With thee is wisdom, who knows thy works and was present when thou didst make the world, and who understands what is pleasing in thy sight and what is right according to thy commandments. Send her forth from the holy heavens, and from the throne of thy glory send her, that she may be with me and toil, and that I may learn what is pleasing to thee. For she knows and understands all things, and she will guide me wisely in my actions and guard me with her glory.[98]

Note here Wisdom is a she portrayed to live in heaven with God, and not just that, but at God's own throne. This is mentioned twice in this chapter. Earlier it says, "give me the wisdom that sits by thy throne."[99] Lady Wisdom sits by God at His throne. This adds to how the Holy Spirit was personified in the New Testament, because she is depicted as sitting by God's throne. It could strongly indicate Jesus read and supported these Wisdom teachings.

Wisdom is also portrayed to have been specifically present at the creation of mankind again when it says,

> O God of my fathers and LORD of mercy, who hast made all things by thy word, and by thy wisdom hast formed man.[100]

Reading just these lines alone does not indicate that Wisdom is personified here but immediately following she is. So, the context declares her presence during the creation of humans.

This is how Wisdom of Solomon additionally describes this feminine force,

> For she is a breath of the power of God, and a pure emanation of the glory of the Almighty; therefore nothing defiled gains entrance into her. For she is a reflection of eternal light, a spotless mirror of the working of God, and an image of his goodness.[101]

Wisdom parallels the Spirit of God here again because she is called "breath of the power of God." As stated earlier, "breath" and "Spirit" in Hebrew are interchangeable. She is also connected to light. Something that is undetectable in the English rendition is that the word "reflection," in Greek *avpau, gasma* is really not the correct translation.[102] This noun is active, not passive, which would make the word mean "radiance" instead. It is translated as "reflection" to parallel the next sentence where she is described as a "mirror" and "image." This then could correspond to the concept of the moon reflecting the sun's light. But, if the writer meant the word to be in the grammatical form it actually was written in, it signifies that Wisdom/the Spirit is more than a mirror image of God's light. She herself is light, radiating from God and part of His eternal light. She is the rays of God's light that goes out and touches people, causing warmth, growth, healing and transformation. The words "spotless mirror" could suggest that she simultaneously His counterpart, is reflecting His presence on earth. In fact, the previous line here about Wisdom stating that she is a "pure emanation of the glory of the Almighty" supports that she radiates.

Apart from how it does not say "reflection," this was written at a time when the knowledge about the moon's light being a reflection of the sun was fairly recent. Though Greek and Chinese thinkers knew of it in the 5th and 4th century B.C.,[103] it is unclear how widely known this was, but later in Ben Sirach the moon is specifically mentioned. It says,

> He made the moon also, to serve in its season to mark the times and to be an everlasting sign. From the moon comes the sign for feast days, a light that wanes when it has reached the full. The month is named for the moon, increasing marvelously in its phases, an instrument of the hosts on high shining forth in the firmament of heaven.[104]

The moon played a significant role in their lives, and, as we can see, the Hebrews followed a lunar calendar. These descriptions may suggest they saw the moon as emitting its own light not reflecting the sun.[105] By having "reflection" instead of radiance, there is an allusion that Wisdom was likened to the moon. If the author of Wisdom meant to make that connection, and the Israelites indeed knew that the moon reflected the sun she is a reflection precisely in the sense that the rays of the sun causes the moon to shine.[106] She is the rays, not the fireless moon. Either way you look at this, it all implies that she is not a receiver of God's eternal light, but despite being personified and distinct, she is simultaneously an intrinsic part of God.[107]

Wisdom of Solomon further elaborates about Wisdom that, "She glorifies her noble birth by living with God, and the LORD of all loves her. For she is an initiate in the knowledge of God, and an associate in his works."[108] This again declares her as separate from God as well as His partner in all of what He does. She is closer to Him than anyone else. In some places Lady Wisdom is explicitly connected to the feminine Spirit of God. In Wisdom of Solomon 7:22-23 it says,

> for wisdom, the fashioner of all things, taught me. For in her there is a spirit that is intelligent, holy, unique, manifold, subtle, mobile, clear, unpolluted, distinct, invulnerable, loving the good, keen, irresistible, beneficent, humane, steadfast, sure, free from anxiety, all-powerful, overseeing all, and penetrating through all spirits that are intelligent and pure and most subtle...

This passage claims that Wisdom is not just a spirit, but a Holy Spirit. She is well defined, and the way she penetrates certain people is wholly in line with how the Holy Spirit functions. Just a little later in the same book, Wisdom of Solomon 9:17, it states about God that,

> Who has learned thy counsel, unless thou hast given wisdom and sent thy holy Spirit from on high?

Again, we detect a connection between Wisdom and the Holy Spirit.

Wisdom is repeatedly depicted to be entering into people causing them to do great things. In Wisdom of Solomon 7:27 it says,

> Though she is but one, she can do all things, and while remaining in herself, she renews all things; in

46

every generation she passes into holy souls and
makes them friends of God, and prophets . . .

Note also that her ability to "renew all things" resonates
with the New Testament notion of being "born again." The
same sentiments are continued in Wisdom of Solomon 10:16
where it says,

> She entered the soul of a servant of the LORD, and
> withstood dread kings with wonders and signs.

This verse describes how Wisdom was present and worked
throughout Israel's history, and specifically in righteous
people. It is for example explained that it was she who
caused the parting of the Red Sea along with several more
deeds.[109]

Wisdom does not only enter people but she is the one
who is sent out to answers prayers. In Wisdom chapter 7:7 it
says,

> Therefore I prayed, and understanding was given me;
> I called upon God, and the spirit of wisdom came to
> me.

Again, the idea of Wisdom coming internally to a human to
reveal truth and guide the person is exactly the same way
the Holy Spirit operates. One illustration from the New
Testament is when the hand of God was said to be upon
John the Baptist, "And his father Zechari'ah was filled with
the Holy Spirit, and prophesied . . . ."[110] Another is at
Pentecost when "they were all filled with the Holy Spirit and
began to speak in other tongues . . . ."[111] The active roles of the
Holy Spirit and Wisdom were not just deeply intertwined
but identical and played a significant part of the Hebrew
faith before the word "Christian" even existed.

The Holy Spirit is for the most part called the Spirit of
God in the Hebrew Scriptures but there are occasions where

she is referred to as the Holy Spirit too. In Psalm 51:6, 10-11, the author writes,

> Behold, thou desirest truth in the inward being; therefore teach me wisdom in my secret heart . . . Create in me a clean heart, O God, and put a new and right spirit within me. Cast me not away from thy presence, and take not thy holy Spirit from me.

Here we see Wisdom yet again tied to the Holy Spirit and changing someone from the inside. Metaphorically speaking, the Spirit changes someone's heart.

In the book of Daniel, it is "the spirit of the holy gods" that is mentioned.[112] In Daniel 5:11-12, this is what king Belshaz'zar's wife said about Daniel when they needed someone to interpret the legendary writing on the wall,

> There is in your kingdom a man in whom is the spirit of the holy gods. In the days of your father light and understanding and wisdom, like the wisdom of the gods, were found in him, and king Nebuchadnez'zar, your father, made him chief of the magicians, enchanters, Chalde'ans, and astrologers, because an excellent spirit, knowledge, and understanding to interpret dreams, explain riddles, and solve problems were found in this Daniel, whom the king named Belteshaz'zar.

This emphasizes the excellent traits that Daniel had because of having the Holy Spirit, and how the concept itself was recognized not only by Israelites. The Holy Spirit gave "light," "understanding" and "wisdom."[113] Moreover, this wisdom is divine.

What stands out in Daniel, as noted earlier, is that it says "gods" instead of "God." The Hebrew word used is in the masculine plural from the root *Elah*. It is translated as such because not only is *Elah* in the plural but "holy" which it is in construct with is likewise in the masculine plural.[114]

It also opens up a whole new topic, because the plural adjectives or verbs accompany the word for Elohim, when it clearly refers to "God," in many places in the Hebrew Scriptures but is not translated that way in English. Let me give an example from Proverbs, which relates directly to the topic here. In chapter 9:10 it states,

> The fear of the LORD is the beginning of wisdom, and the knowledge of the Holy One is insight.

"Knowledge" is singular and in construct with "Holy," but "Holy" is in the plural making it literally "the Holy Ones," instead. Without the pointed vowels, this could have originally been in the dual; meaning "the *two* Holy Ones." Another instance is Gen 35:7 when Jacob builds an altar at El-Bethel. The usual translation is, "there God had revealed himself to him." But, the Hebrew literally reads "the Gods had revealed themselves to him." *Elohim* is always plural but the accompanying verb, "reveal," is also plural which then suggests a plural meaning of *Elohim*. Since it is not consistent that the plural *Elohim,* when referring to "God," is supported by plural adjectives and verbs, this presents a problem explaining it. Two other quick illustrations are first Joshua 24:19 that where he speaks about Yahweh saying that He is a "holy God." However, the Hebrew says אלהים קדשים meaning "holy Gods." This is understandably translated as "a holy God" because it speaks of Yahweh. Nevertheless, a literal translation is "holy gods." The second found in Ecclesiastes 12:1 has in Hebrew "your Creators" not "your Creator," which is the standard English translation.[115]

Though Exodus is not part of the Wisdom books, there is one passage I want to mention in this context. In chapter 28:3 where Yahweh is speaking to Moses about all the things He wants him to do, He mentions that Moses should make holy garments. God tells him, "to all who have ability, whom I have endowed with an . . . ." However, "able mind" is in transliteration from the Hebrew *ruah hokmah*, which is literally "the Spirit of Wisdom." "Endowed" also means "fill," which is perfectly in line with how the Spirit fills a believer up. So, the latter part is more accurately translated, "whom I have filled with the Spirit of Wisdom. . . ." As we can see, different translations can make a big difference. Here, "able mind" is an interpretation more than a translation and can unfortunately obscure a belief that the Spirit of Yahweh was feminine and related to Wisdom. As such, she is a divine Power from God. The word choices are interesting because "wisdom" did not have to be accompanied by "spirit." If it truly referred to just an "able mind" *ruah* is unnecessary. It is precisely such details that reveal how the Israelites viewed Wisdom as more than a personal attribute.

It is described at the end of Deuteronomy that right before Moses died he laid his hands on Joshua and proclaimed that he was "full of the spirit of wisdom."[116] It was God Himself who had directed that Moses should do so, because Joshua had "the spirit."[117] The priest Elea'zar also laid his hands on Joshua after Moses had died.[118] The laying on of hands was an early Christian practice, and in Deuteronomy and Numbers we see its ancient roots. Jesus practiced the laying on of hands, and it is described in the letter to the Hebrews to be part of the early church's core beliefs along with baptism, resurrection, and the last judgment.[119] The laying on of hands is directly related to the Holy Spirit. For instance, this instance is described in Acts 8:14-20,

> Now when the apostles at Jerusalem heard that Sama'ria had received the word of God, they sent to them Peter and John, who came down and prayed for them that they might receive the Holy Spirit; for it

had not yet fallen on any of them, but they had only been baptized in the name of the Lord Jesus. Then they laid their hands on them and they received the Holy Spirit. Now when Simon saw that the Spirit was given through the laying on of the apostles' hands, he offered them money, saying "Give me also this power, that any one on whom I lay my hands may receive the Holy Spirit." But Peter said to him, "Your silver perish with you, because you thought you could obtain the gift of God with money! You have neither part nor lot in this matter, for your heart is not right before God.

The continuation of this ritual, going back from at least millennia into Jesus' time, ties the "Spirit of Wisdom" and the "Holy Spirit" together as one and the same.

In Wisdom of Solomon there are also some thoughts about everlasting life along with yet another reminder that Wisdom was present from the beginning. In Wisdom 6:17-22 it says,

The beginning of wisdom is the most sincere desire for instruction, and concern for instruction is love of her, and love of her is keeping of her laws, and giving heed to her laws is assurance of immortality, and immortality brings one near to God; so the desire for wisdom leads to a kingdom. Therefore if you delight in thrones and scepters, O monarchs over the peoples, honor wisdom, that you may reign forever. I will tell you what wisdom is and how she came to be, and I will hide no secrets from you, but I will trace her course from beginning of creation, and make the knowledge of her clear, and I will not pass by the truth . . .

These passages talking about "her Laws" refer to the Torah, which is yet another feminine word in Hebrew. Keeping the laws means staying in sync with Wisdom and leads to eternal life. Additionally, this is another segment talking about Wisdom being present at the "beginning of creation."

The book of Baruch is one of the texts along with Wisdom of Solomon, Ben Sirach and a few others that were taken out of the Bible during the Protestant Reformation, but are still intact in the Catholic and Eastern Orthodox canon. Baruch was said to be Jeremiah's friend and secretary and claims to have written in the Babylonian captivity. This Greek text was originally written in Hebrew. Internal evidence suggests it has more than one author. Final redaction is estimated to been about 150-60 B.C.[120]

Baruch is interesting for us because he spends quite some time speaking about Wisdom. In Baruch 3:29-4:4 he says,

> Who has gone up into heaven, and taken her, and brought her down from the clouds? Who has gone over the sea, and found her, and will buy her for pure gold? No one knows the way to her, or is concerned about the path to her. But he who knows all things knows her, he found her by his understanding. He who prepared the earth for all time filled it with four-footed creatures; he who sends forth the light, and it goes, called it, and it obeyed him in fear; the stars shone in their watches, and were glad; he called them, and they said, "Here we are!" They shone with gladness for him who made them. This is our God; no other can be compared to him! He found the whole way to knowledge, and gave her to Jacob his servant and to Israel whom he loved. Afterward she appeared upon earth and lived among men. She is the book of the commandments of God, and the law that endures for ever. All who hold her fast will live, and those

who forsake her will die. Turn, O Jacob, and take her; walk toward the shining of her light. Do not give your glory to another, or your advantages to an alien people. Happy are we, O Israel, for we know what is pleasing to God.

Wisdom is identified with the Torah, and in this way, she appeared on earth. Not for the first time though, because she was given early on to Jacob and Israel too. She is also described here as a shining light, as well as "glory."[121] In addition she is depicted again to have her home in heaven, which, of course, is where God resides.[122] In Job we can see there is a trace of this age-old idea when Yahweh answers Job out of a whirlwind and questions him about his limited understanding and asks where he was during creation "when the morning stars sang together, and all the sons of God shouted for joy?"[123]

Something else worth noting in the block quotation above is the end of the third and beginning of the fourth line where it says God founded Wisdom "by his understanding." The word "understanding" is often parallel to Wisdom and this echoes some passages elsewhere. In Proverbs where Wisdom is personified, it says that "The LORD by wisdom founded the earth; by understanding he established the heavens."[124] Jeremiah said about God that, "It is he who made the earth by his power, who established the world by his wisdom, and by his understanding stretched out the heavens. . . ."[125] Though this is not evidence that Jeremiah understood Wisdom to be a distinct force present with God in the beginning, we should at least consider it possible. This idea was clearly present with other writers like Baruch, Jeremiah's secretary.

Both the passage from Baruch and the previous verse from Wisdom of Solomon connect Wisdom to life. Having Wisdom leads to life, but it alludes to more than the one on earth. It suggests that Wisdom leads to eternal life. In this sense, the female Law / Wisdom also has allusions to the Tree of Life in the Garden of Eden, promising it would cause humans to live forever if they ate its fruit. Following her, by obeying the Torah, lets one gain Wisdom, which leads to everlasting life.

As shown, there is ample scriptural evidence for Wisdom and the Holy Spirit functioning as one and the same divine force and being understood as such by the Hebrews. Furthermore, she was even said to be seated by God at His throne, partook in the creation of the world, and she alone was present in the "beginning" with God. These are all compelling evidences of a Divine Feminine presence by the side of Yahweh. She is the Holy Spirit, also known as Wisdom, but, there is more.

WISDOM – IN PROVERBS 8:30

I want to go back for just a little to Proverbs 8:30 that was discussed earlier and expand on one word in that verse because of its relevance to this subject. The pertinent passage is about Wisdom and goes like this, "then I was beside him, like a master workman; and I was daily his delight, rejoicing before him always. . . ."[126] It is the word "master workman" that is of interest to this topic. In Hebrew it is אמון and in transliteration *amon*. Where this passage takes us, gives yet another interesting insight into this topic.

This word "master workman" is a masculine noun and also translated as "artisan" or "architect." In the feminine form of the noun it means "faithfulness." It is a word used with this particular translation only twice in the Hebrew Scriptures. The other occasion is in Jeremiah 52:15 as a description of some of the groups taken captive when Nebuchadnezzar conquered Jerusalem. This is the same word as the name Amon, who was a king of Judah ruling 642-640 B.C. after his father Manasseh.[127] He was the grandson of Hezekiah who ruled 716-687 B.C.[128] It was Manasseh who reversed the religious reforms his father Hezekiah had done and put a statue of Asherah in the Temple among other things.[129] It is also the name of an Egyptian god.

The root of *amon* consists of the Hebrew letters *aleph, mem, nun*, which are the same as those in the word "Amen" used today by Christians, meaning "verily" or "truly." This root with other vowel markings also means "confirm" or "support" and occurs one time in 2 Kings 18:16 with the meaning "pillars" or "supporters of the door."[130] Noteworthy, in this context it is also the fact that this word in Kings is in the feminine form. It is often translated there as "doorposts." The question is what is a doorpost? In English dictionaries this can refer to a doorjamb, a doorframe, or a part of the frame. But, it is not the same word used for "doorframes," being *mezuzah*, which we can find in Deuteronomy 6:9 and 11:20 where the Jewish tradition of putting a piece of parchment affixed to the doorframes (*mezuzah*) in houses comes from. Neither is it the usual word for pillars. In all other instances the word *'ammud* or *massebot* (really meaning large stone) are used to designate this. It is likely not a doorjamb because it is about how the gold was stripped from it. It may specifically mean the hinges and the "pillars" that enable a door to open and some translate it that way.

The passage in Kings where this word for these "pillars" occurs is during Hezekiah's reign late 7th and early 6th century B.C. who was known for making sweeping reforms such as getting rid of the high places, the pillars (*massebot*), the Asherah and the bronze serpent Moses had made.[131] He also built a tunnel for water, which still exists today. It is described that in the fourteenth year of his reign the Assyrians came to Judah and upon this Hezekiah said to the king of Assyria, "I have done wrong; withdraw from me; whatever you impose on me I will bear."[132] Consequently Hezekiah pays a fine to the Assyrian king, and strips the gold off of the "doors of the temple" and the "doorposts" supporting these doors to give him the gold as part of the payment.[133] It is here the word "doorposts" appear that has the same root as "master workman" in Proverbs 8:30. Whatever the word exactly meant, it described something covered with gold.

This passage accidently gives a glimpse of something we may have never otherwise known about. Though it was the gold here that was of value, the unusual name for the doorposts/pillars, so closely related to the word in Proverbs 8:30 with the root for these two words having the meaning of "support," "confirm," "faithful," "trust" and such, is perhaps a possible connection to Wisdom and her place at the gateway, represented as pillars on each side of the door, into the Temple.[134]

There are a few passages in Proverbs that mention Wisdom speaking at the "gates." Proverbs 1:20-21 imparts, "Wisdom cries aloud in the street; in the markets she raises her voice; on top of the walls she cries out; at the entrance of the city gates she speaks." Later in chapter 8:1-3 it states,

> Does not Wisdom call, does not understanding raise her voice? On the heights beside the way, in the paths she takes her stand; beside the gates in front of the town, at the entrance of the portals she cries aloud.

In the same chapter in verse 34, it says, "Happy is the man who listens to me, watching daily at my gates, waiting beside my doors."[135] Later we can read that "Wisdom is too high for a fool; in the gate he does not open his mouth."[136] Finally, it praises a good wife and mentions that, "Her husband is known in the gates, when he sits among the elders of the land."[137] The very last verse of Proverbs declares about a good woman that, "Give her of the fruit of her hands, and let her works praise her in the gates."[138]

Considering Wisdom and her presence at the gates, which are flanked by pillars, there is something here that supports Proverbs 8:30 relating to Wisdom. Looking at the early translation of this passage in Proverbs from Hebrew to the Greek Septuagint from around the third century B.C. we can see another perspective of how they read this Scripture. The Greek translation of "master workman" is a feminine participle literally meaning to "join or give in marriage" or "betroth." It is a word specifically used in terms of matrimony, ἁρμόζω, which the word "harmony" comes from. Other verbal forms of this word are, "fit together" or "put together" or "join" and it was generally used as such.[139] We find the same word in 2 Corinthians 11:2 for example where Paul speaks to the church in Corinth being "betrothed" to the Messiah. By using this term in the Septuagint, it gives the word in Proverbs 8:30 a much more intimate interpretation than what is expressed in the word "master workman." It appears the translator accentuated togetherness with undertones of a marriage between God and Wisdom. While *amon* in Hebrew is a masculine noun, hence the word Masterwork-*man* is used, the passage in Proverbs defined Wisdom as having an active role in Creation. We can thereby conclude that we can see the parallel between Wisdom in both the Hebrew and Greek texts. They both testify to God creating the world with Wisdom by His side.

THE CREATION OF MAN AND WOMAN MIRRORS HEAVEN

Some people are unaware that there are two creation stories of how God created mankind. The first one is in chapter one and the other one follows in chapter two. Many see the second as giving details on the first, whereas these are not two different accounts but two versions of the same story.[140] For academic research, this indicates a likelihood that Genesis was written by more than one author, and at least one redactor who weaved it all together, which is a topic well covered by scholars. This section is about the first story—chapter one—in Genesis. There are passages in the Bible that are enigmatic and demand deeper insights. The creation account of man and woman, on the sixth day, belongs in this category.

As stated earlier, Genesis literally opens up with first mentioning God and then right after the Holy Spirit. She was present before the creation of mankind. Genesis 1:1-2 says,

> "In the beginning God created the heavens and the earth. The earth was without form and void, and darkness was upon the face of the deep; and the Spirit of God was moving over the face of the waters."

In verse two, the text could have just said God (*Elohim*), or *Yahweh*, was hovering over the face of the waters, but it does not. It specifies that the "Spirit of God" was hovering over the waters. She was present, and she was moving. Only following the movement of the Holy Spirit, it explicitly states that God starts speaking. In verse three we read, "And God said, 'Let there be light;' and there was light."

God proceeds to create and calls everything good. On the sixth day it describes man and woman being made in the image of God, which is what sets them apart from all the rest of creation. In Genesis 1:26-27 it says;

> Then God said, "Let **us** make man in **our** image, after **our** likeness" . . . So God created man in his own image, in the image of God he created him; male and female he created them.

The dilemma in these passages is that God is quoted using the plural "us" and "our" leading any reader to wonder whom aside from God was this referring? The other problem relates to the word "image." In Hebrew transliteration, it is *selem,* and refers to a physical resemblance, not a psychological or spiritual one. Since Yahweh is male, and the text is referring to a tangible physical resemblance for both male and female, in whose image was woman made?

Usually this question is ignored or explained by way of God either lacking gender or encompassing both sexes. Though God in many parables can seemingly have various roles with female metaphors; Yahweh/El is grammatically solidly referred to as a male, and neither does such an answer explain why the plural pronouns were used.[141] Some Christians going back to the early church fathers explained the plurality as referring to the Trinity. However, since the Trinity concept is all male, it still does not answer the question of who the woman was physically modeled after. St. Ambrose, who became bishop of Milan in 374 A.D., explained it this way,

> But let us consider the precise order of our creation: "Let us make mankind," He said, "in our image and likeness." Who says this? Was it not God who made you? What is God: flesh or spirit? Surely not flesh, but spirit, which has no similarity to flesh. This is material, whereas the spirit is incorporeal and invisible. To whom does He speak? Surely not to Himself, because He does not say: "I shall make" but "let us make." He does not speak to the angels, because they are servers, and servants cannot have a part in a work along with their Master and Creator. He speaks rather, to the Son . . .[142]

We can see St. Ambrose thought God was talking to Jesus and that humans were created in both God's and Jesus' image, because it was a spiritual image, not a physical image. However, the word "likeness," *demut*, just like "image" refers to how something looks. Other meanings of this word are "pattern," "form," and "shape." It is interesting to note the Hebrew words used in the phrase, "in our image, after our likeness" are respectively *selem* (image), a masculine word, and *demut* (likeness), a feminine word. In a sense these word choices themselves reflect that there were two different creations, one male and one female.

When Adam and Eve ate of the forbidden fruit, their innocence was taken away, and they gained a new understanding. God said that they had become, "like one of us, knowing good and evil."[143] God had warned Adam that if they ate the fruit, they would "die." Adam and Eve were expelled in order to stop them from eating of the Tree of Life and living forever in a state of sin.[144] So, at that time, death and the ability to understand and choose between good and evil—a divine characteristic—were introduced to humans. This new capacity directly contradicts the notion that mankind was inherently created in the spiritual image of God.[145]

> St. Ambrose went on to say about this topic that,
> The "image" of God is virtue, not infirmity. The "image" of God is wisdom. The "image" of God is He alone who has said: "I and the Father are one," thus possessing the likeness of the Father so as to have a unity of divinity and of plentitude. When He says "let us make," how can there be inequality? When, again, He says "to our likeness," where is the dissimilitude?[146]

St. Ambrose makes the claim that Adam and Eve were created in the image of Jesus, not God. Ambrose creates a duality out of the line, "in the image of God" where the "image" represents Jesus.[147] The problem is that this is not what the Scripture says, because there is a plurality in the phrase "our image" not a singularity.[148] St. Ambrose assumption is a good representation of the way many Christians have understood the first creation story for nearly two millennia, even though it is not biblically accurate.

The Royal plural has been another explanation for the plural pronouns in the first creation story. As the name reveals, important people such as royalty were addressed in the plural instead of singular, and sometimes they referred to themselves in this manner as well. This was used in Europe in the early second millennium A.D. and onwards. However, it is a tenuous argument to claim that the Hebrew God referred to Himself in the way kings addressed themselves over two millennia later in Europe.[149]

Because the influence of Canaan is rather noticeable, the generally accepted scholarly interpretation is that the creation story was originally Canaanite and that the plural pronouns referred to the ancient Canaanite pantheon.[150] Canaan was the name of Israel before the Israelites conquered it following the exodus from Egypt. Prior to that, the Hebrew people were just one of many peoples in that area. It is claimed that the Canaanites, who already lived there when Abraham came, strongly influenced the Hebrew faith. Aside from the numerous references to the Canaanites in the Bible itself, there was a major discovery in Ras Shamra on the Syrian coast in 1928 where thousands of Canaanite texts (cuneiform tablets) were found dating from the 14th century B.C. They have since shed light on much in the Hebrew Scriptures because of numerous parallels between the two involving Yahweh's character, the Psalms and much more. However, while the information from Ras Shamra puts forth a theory of a Canaanite origin to the first creation story in Genesis, the particular explanation of the plural pronouns referring to the ancient Canaanite pantheon of gods has major flaws.

From a scholarly perspective, traces of the Canaanite council of minor gods are present in plain view in Scripture. An example of this would be is Job 38:7, where God questioned Job about where he was when He laid the foundation of the earth and "the morning stars sang together, and all the sons of God shouted for joy?" It is not the existence of the "sons of God" that is the problem with regards to the creation story, but the role scholars suggest they had. The Canaanites had a supreme god and goddess: El and Asherah, who were the Creators of everyone. Asherah was also referred to as Elat, which is the grammatically feminine form of El. The Canaanite texts reveal that the entire pantheon collectively never had the role of being Creators; this was the exclusive titles reserved for the top couple. Asherah was the Mother, and El the Father. Two epithets for Asherah were "the mother of the gods" and "the creatress of the gods," while El was called "the father of mankind."[151] For this reason, if you are going to assert that the creation story is originally Canaanite, it is illogical that the plural pronouns in the creation account of Genesis 1 would refer to anyone else but the chief pair, El and Asherah.[152]

> Let us look at the first creation story of humans again, "Then God said, "Let us make man in our image, after our likeness" . . . So God created man in his own image, in the image of God he created him; male and female he created them."[153]

The opening "Let us make man in our image" suggests it was God's idea. God is also the one pronouncing those words of creation, and in the last verse (27) the text switches between plural and singular in a particular way. Let me put the relevant words in italics to show what I am getting at, "So God created *man* in *his* own image, in the image of God he created *him*; male and female he created *them*." Although

He created both man and woman, it was only specified that the man was in the "image" of God. This alone could be a subtle indication that the woman did not resemble God, but a feminine divinity.[154] For scholars putting forth the Canaanite thesis, this ought to be Asherah, not an entire council.

The plural pronouns in Genesis 1:26 staying intact clearly displaying that God was talking to someone else in the heavenly realm was not an isolated incident and appears again shortly thereafter. In Genesis 3:22, Yahweh expresses concern after the man and woman have eaten the forbidden fruit and proclaims, "the man has become like one of **us**, knowing good and evil." Likewise in Genesis 11:7, with regards to the tower of Babel, God says,

Come, let **us** go down, and there confuse their language.

Isaiah 6:8, in what is referred to as "the calling of Isaiah" there is a passage alluding to God not being alone as well. Right after Isaiah's vision of God, Isaiah hears Him say,

Whom shall I send, and who will go for **us**?[155]

In other words, God included someone else, apparently quite close to Him, when He was speaking about mankind on several occasions. Hebrew scribes had a strong tradition of copying texts meticulously as they were handed down; yet even after Moses introduced monotheism, these passages have stayed the same. There would have been innumerable chances for editors to change those plural pronouns posing a challenge to God being the only one in male form present, but no one did.

This is crucial to the creation story, in Genesis 1:26-27 of man and woman. It means the blue print for women, the one in whose image we were created in, is a Divine Feminine power. This heavenly force is the Spirit of God whom Jesus talked about as the Holy Spirit. She is present in the beginning with the Divine Yahweh. She is the only feminine power in sight, and she is our Mother.

The first creation story does not support man's superiority over the woman. Instead, it shows man and woman being created at the same time, equal in worth. I propose it mirrors the prototype 'couple' (for lack of a better word) in heaven that are One.[156] The man was not more important because he looked like the One he was created after. The woman was patterned after the One as well. God, along with the Spirit, were both mentioned in this creation, *together*. The best way to understand how Yahweh, who is male, and His Spirit, who is feminine, can represent *Elohim* (God), is via the Biblical understanding of marriage, which makes them One. This is how marriage is explained in Genesis chapter two and may refer to the Heavenly prototype for marriage. The old saying, "a marriage made in heaven" has a new profound meaning if instead it relayed a feminine complementary power that God was talking to in the first Creation story.

Naturally, Christians, as well as Jews, are not going to accept the scholarly explanation given of Asherah, as the one by God's side if the creation story of man and woman is originally a Canaanite story. In the Bible, she was an ousted Canaanite goddess, and the wife of El, which would constitute heresy. This entire topic will be thoroughly examined in another book. Suffice to say the argument I have presented which places Asherah as the one next to El, if the story is originally Canaanite, is directed to scholars to refute the idea that the plurality in the creation of human beings refers to a council of minor gods instead of a Divine Feminine aspect of the One. Those who claim that it was the divine council that God referred in Genesis are not proposing a logical argument. Instead, it should be asked why they have overlooked the most logical conclusion for whom God is talking to when the passage clearly describes men and women being created in the physical image and likeness of God? Why do they think it is the divine council and not the Divine feminine counterpart?

Second, I want my Christian audience to understand why the plural pronouns in the creation story do not refer to Jesus and Yahweh, since that is the standard way to rationalize the plural presence of Scripture in the Church. To reiterate, the creation story speaks of humans being created in the image of God. The Hebrew word for image relates to how we look. The creation story is not about a spiritual "likeness," but refers to who humans are physically modeled after. The creation story of mankind is about how people are set apart from other living beings, and moreover, it is about the difference between men and women.

This does not mean that a Christian should believe in paganism or deny Jesus as the Messiah. Again, the Bible itself testifies to the feminine Spirit being present before the creation of humans. Jesus existing before the world and being involved with creation, does not mean he was the blueprint for women. Jesus is male.

Before we continue with the Holy Spirit's role in creation, I want to go over the story of when God made Adam and Eve in the second chapter of Genesis because it is relevant to so many of the discussions to come. It also complements what was just examined in Genesis' first chapter, because it likewise reflects the presence of the Divine Feminine hidden within the male. In essence, the creation of man and woman, in both chapter one and two, plus what happened in the Garden, sets the stage for everything else that follows in the Bible.

ADAM & EVE

The second Creation account starts at Genesis 2:4 where the first one ends. The story of Adam and Eve in Genesis has unfortunately, for the last couple of millennia, more often than not been used as a justification for the idea that women have less worth and resulted in treating them as such. There are two prime reasons, derived from twisting Scripture, which have been used against women. First, Eve was understood as created with inherently less worth because she did not mirror God the way Adam did. Instead of being a new independent creation from the ground she wasfashioned from his rib or side (Hebrew uncertain) and made for the purpose of being a helper to Adam.[157] Secondly, after the fall of man, God said that part of the punishment Eve would receive was that her man would rule over her.

This naturally presents a problem for those who believe the Bible is the inspired word of God, meaning the texts do not become outdated. Jesus himself said, "Scripture cannot be broken."[158] One should of course not invent something that is not there in order to make it politically correct for today. Distorting or censuring Biblical texts have throughout Biblical history constituted the gravest sin. For this reason female scholars have challenged the traditional interpretation of the second narrative that have, for the most part, been seen as saying that men are superior. I will show examples of alternate readings that endorse equality between the sexes and highlight women being portrayed in a positive light.[159]

In the second chapter of Genesis, Adam was formed from the dust of the earth the very same day as earth and heaven were created. God breathed life into Adam's nostrils and placed him in the Garden of Eden.[160] He then declared that it was not good for Adam to be alone and fashioned all the animals, from the ground as well, specifically for this purpose. Yet, none of them turned out to be the "helper fit for him" that God had intended. This is where Eve enters the story.[161] However, she was not created out of the earth but from Adam's own body. Adam even called her woman, because she was taken out of him. This is reflected in the Hebrew term for woman, *'ishshah* which has the same root as the one for man, *'iysh*, but with an added ending, which is the Hebrew feminine ending *–ah* which is the letter *he* plus a vowel.[162] Thus *'ishshah* contains both the masculine and feminine, while the word for man stands alone, reflecting the state of man in the Garden before Eve was added. In the first creation story the words "woman" and "man" are not used for the division of gender, instead "male" and "female," are used, in Hebrew *zakar* and *neqebah*, a designation also used for animals, which further illustrates this point.[163]

Traditionally Eve has been seen as less than "whole" for being taken out of Adam. It has been pointed out though that the same logic can be used to understand Adam as equally less than "whole" if he is missing the part that God took to make Eve. Furthermore, the fact that Eve was created from his "side" can be perceived as symbolic for a couple who are to live and walk through life together side by side. God did not take a part from Adam's foot or head, but his side implying Eve is an equal.

Adam has also been interpreted as having more worth because he was created first. This line of thinking has likewise been challenged by women. In the first account animals were created before Adam. With the logic of first creation has more value, then animals would have more value than human beings. While humans have traditionally been understood as the crown of creation in the first creation story, very few would ever see Eve, in the second story, as more important than Adam, because she was God's final creation. The focus has instead always been on her being made out of Adam, not the ground, fueling the argument that she has lesser worth. Adam though, shared his origin with animals that were also created out of the ground. This can be understood as either positive or negative, depending on your outlook. But, if Eve is denied equal value with Adam because she was not created from the ground, then Adam could be said to share identical worth with the animals that were likewise made from the soil. Yet, this is rarely understood to be the case by those who place Adam higher than Eve. Lastly, if the substance that Eve was fashioned from was secondary in worth it must mean that Adam was too, since it was taken from his body. However you look at it, the argument for Eve being inferior to Adam can, and has been countered with these arguments by female scholars.

Scholar Trible sees the creation of Adam and Eve as simultaneous because Adam's sexuality depends on Eve and vice versa. She believes that before Eve's creation sexuality and gender did not exist and in this sense Adam and Eve were both new creations at the same time.[164] They both came from the same source; the one flesh of humanity, *ha-adam*. The Hebrew word *adam*, which is the name of the first man, means "ground" or "soil" when you add a feminine ending to it.

One of the key passages that has made Adam look like he is more important than Eve is the sentence quoted above usually translated as, "I will make him a helper fit for him" in Genesis 2:18. This is not the best translation though. In the original language the preposition *ke* means "as" and *neged* "in front of" or "opposite" are together used for what is here translated as "fit for." However, when these prepositions are joined, the word indicates "corresponding to," which implies that Eve is "equal and adequate" to Adam.[165] Therefore, this passage would be better translated, "I will make for him a helper, matching him."[166] This gives Eve's role a different tone and meaning from the other

English translation where she sounds more like a servant, and not a counterpart, who is there to *share* life with Adam.[167] Adam and Eve complement each other.

The wording "fit for" has now been modified in some Bibles, and instead we can for example find "a helper suitable for him."[168] In a very literal translation from the Latin Vulgate from 1899 it says, "a help like unto himself."[169] Unfortunately this last translation is not quite the best and has caused considerable damage and still continues to do so.[171] It is important to understand here that the term *'ezer* translated as "helper" is in the Hebrew Scriptures not a derogatory term. For instance, it is used to described God in Psalm 54:4 where it says, "Behold, God is my helper; the LORD is the upholder of my life."[172]

Eve being created for Adam as a suitable companion has also been understood as if this was her only function in life, and, on top of that, it was a submissive and weaker role. Yet, it is never suggested that men are frail because Adam was so lonely without Eve that she was created specifically to be his mate. The one who was expressively needy in this story was Adam, not Eve. Additionally, having one purpose does not exclude another. The Bible explains that after the fall God ordained Adam to take care of Eden and "till it and keep it."[173] Yet, men have never been relegated to only being farmers. In the same way, there is no reason to think that women's sole role was to be Adam's companion and have children. Though this is central and good, she is well equipped to do more and has always done more in life.

Though some continue to see Eve as an afterthought, looking at it from another angle is all that is needed to appreciate her having the same value as Adam. Furthermore, Eve was not only Adam's counterpart, but she enabled humans to procreate. In fact, the necessity for a male and female to be together in order to reproduce reinforces the notion that they both have inherently equal worth. The creation of Adam and Eve is a story of separation followed by a re-unification, which is the origin of marriage where a man and a woman come together again to become "one flesh."[174]

In addition to Adam and Eve becoming One in marriage, the idea of "one flesh" can also be understood how a new human is created. In the human body the cells has the full DNA, forty-six chromosomes, except in each egg and sperm, which has half the number: twenty-three. So, when a woman and man come together they each supply half of the DNA needed for a new life. Since all human life depends on man and woman uniting and contributing exactly half the genetic code for a new human, this too is evidence of their equal value.

The Bible is clear about one thing: all the riches of Eden did not benefit Adam without Eve. He was lonely without her. God Himself said, "It is not good that the man should be alone."[175] He even first created animals for that reason, but there was still no one complementing him. All this can reflect something about God and why Yahweh is masculine yet His Spirit is feminine. Let us remember here what Wisdom, who by all accounts is another epithet for the Holy Spirit, says when she is speaking about herself in Proverbs 8:22-23. She says,

> The LORD created me at the beginning of his work, the first of his acts of old. Ages ago I was set up, at the first, before the beginning of the earth.

She then proceeds to describe how she came about before the creation of the world, as narrated in Genesis. The culmination comes when she finally says,

> . . . then I was beside him, like a master workman; and I was daily his delight, rejoicing before him always, rejoicing in his inhabited world and delighting in the sons of men.[176]

Wisdom was by the side of Yahweh during the creation. She is part of Him, just like Eve was part of Adam, and together they are One. Adam needing someone that complemented him, and ended his loneliness, may reflect Wisdom/Holy Spirit's role in relation to Yahweh.

THE FALL

I want to just briefly go over the Fall of Man since this event, just like the creation account, has so often been misunderstood. Eve's role in the fall is also relevant because it is intrinsically related to how we view both women and the Divine Feminine.

Eve's punishment that her husband should rule over her by implication means that Adam did not rule over Eve prior to this. It was a kind of reversal in what had just happened. The snake tempted Eve, and Eve in turn tempted Adam. He listened to Eve over following God's command. God had told Adam before Eve was even created to not eat the forbidden fruit. In a way, Eve ruled over Adam in that instance. Eve's punishment, understood to be passed on to all women, was to be ruled by men. However, after the coming of Christ, this cannot be reconciled with notions of freedom, being forgiven and able to walk in the newness of life. What Jesus offered as far as freedom from the curse is incompatible with women being ruled by men. Paul later expounded on that as well, and it is all tied to the Holy Spirit.

Jesus gives redemption from the Fall of Man. Our human tale started in Garden of Eden: we were expelled from there, and the rest is a story of how to find our way back in a world where our knowledge of good and evil has allowed sin to enter. Jesus' message to us is all about how we can gain access to the Kingdom of Heaven. According to

John 8:31-32 Jesus declared that, "If you continue in my word, you are truly my disciples, and you will know the truth, and the truth will make you free." The very definition of the word freedom is in contradiction to what it means to be "ruled over" by another human. Jesus also said that, "every one who commits sin is a slave to sin"[177] and "if the Son makes you free you will be free indeed."[178] He did not discriminate between men and women because being free has to do with how you live. We all have a choice because of free will, and for that reason freedom is applicable to everyone. The Holy Spirit is the Spirit of Truth, so the Holy Spirit is an instrumental part of this process because it is via the Holy Spirit we know the truth.[179] The Holy Spirit is Wisdom from above.

Paul elaborates on the Fall of Man in Romans chapter 5 and talks about Jesus' grace versus the Law and that we are all redeemed through the resurrection of Christ. In verses 18-19 he says,

> Then as one man's trespass led to condemnation for all men, so one man's act of righteousness leads to acquittal and life for all men. For as by one man's disobedience many were made sinners, so by one man's obedience many will be made righteous.

Paul points out that all people were condemned in the Fall of Man and similarly, everyone is made righteous again through Christ. Here, these words of Jesus, in John's Gospel 14:6, apply, "I am the way, and the truth, and the life; no one comes to the Father, but by me.

Additionally, Paul is well known for promoting the idea of acquired equality through faith, and the way to this is via the Holy Spirit. In 1 Corinthians 12:13, he said, "For by one Spirit we were all baptized into one body–Jews or Greeks, slaves or free–and all were made to drink of one Spirit." In Galatians 3:26, 28 he wrote this,

> for in Christ Jesus you are all sons of God, through
> faith . . . There is neither Jew nor Greek, there is
> neither slave nor free, *there is neither male nor
> female*; for you are all one in Christ Jesus.

He again declares women and men as having equal worth.
In Colossians 3:11 the same thing is echoed,

> Here there cannot be Greek and Jew, circumcised and
> uncircumcised, barbarian, Scyth'ian, slave, free man,
> but Christ is all, and in all.

Paul taught that all who come to the faith, and by doing so
reject sin, are automatically equal. The body of Christ
included slaves, women and Gentiles equally.

In Romans 6:4 Paul said, "as Christ was raised from
the dead by the glory of the Father, we too might walk in
newness of life." This idea developed from the concept of
forgiveness, which was one of Jesus' main messages
emphasized just before he died. For example, during the
Last Supper Jesus said, "this is my blood of the covenant,
which is poured out for many for the forgiveness of sins."[180]
The prophesied legacy Jesus would leave was that,
"repentance and forgiveness of sins should be preached in
his name to all nations, beginning from Jerusalem."[181] Jesus
taught what was earlier foretold by Jeremiah who spoke
about the days coming when there would be a new covenant
where God would write His Law in the hearts of His people.
It ended with these words from Yahweh, "for I will forgive
their iniquity, and I will remember their sin no more."[182] This
is what Jesus announced to be implemented, and it suggests
once you are forgiven, you start with a clean slate. Earthly
consequences for sin are sometimes inevitable, and we still
live in a fallen world, but lingering punishment and being
cursed is not in agreement with salvation. Therefore, a
sound theology means that all humans have access to be

free, even though we live in a fallen world, through the forgiveness of sins. John the Baptist preached repentance from sin and baptized in water of repentance. He was the one who said that Jesus "will baptize you with the Holy Spirit and with fire" in Matthew 3:11. So, becoming free entails repentance, and once you have done that you can receive the Holy Spirit. This is what sets you free from sin.

MARRIAGE

What Jesus essentially taught about forgiveness was also in many ways a reversal of what happened in the Garden of Eden. The institution of marriage has its origin in the second description of the creation of man and woman. This happened before the fall, when Adam and Eve had no knowledge of sin, necessarily meaning they were innocent. The language used to describe marriage, "one flesh,"[184] infers a full unity and equality between the sexes. Jesus imparted a return to the original state of innocence in the sense that forgiveness renders you no longer guilty. This time though, it was a conscious decision, both given and chosen. The reason Adam and Eve were expelled from Eden was not because they tasted the forbidden fruit. It was because after they had eaten it, they were not allowed access to the Tree of Life since it would let them live forever in Paradise in a sinful state. The way back had to include consciously rejecting evil and Jesus showed humans how to find eternal life. By following his teachings, repent from sin and be forgiven, you could then receive the Holy Spirit. Being born again via the Holy Spirit is synonymous to eating the fruit from the Tree of Life. Additionally, because access to freedom from sin represented a return to innocence, it inevitably suggests that Jesus led the way to restoring the original equality between the sexes that existed before the Fall.

If humans were to be irreversibly cursed since the "fall of man" the logical conclusion must be that Jesus died in vain. He did not. Another thing is for sure: Jesus did not differentiate between women and men when he spoke of forgiveness of sins. He did not die just for men, and he never stated or even suggested that women were inferior. He spoke of marriage (quoted earlier) in Matthew 19:3-9,

> And Pharisees came up to him and tested him by asking, "Is it lawful to divorce one's wife for any cause?" He answered, "Have you not read that he who made them from the beginning made them male and female, and said, 'For this reason a man shall leave his father and mother and be joined to his wife, and the two shall become one flesh'? So they are no longer two but one flesh. What therefore God has joined together, let not man put asunder." They said to him, "Why then did Moses command one to give a certificate of divorce, and to put her away?" He said to them, "For your hardness of heart Moses allowed you to divorce your wives, but from the beginning it was not so. And I say to you: whoever divorces his wife, except for unchastity, and marries another, commits adultery."[185]

Jesus cited both the first and the second creation story in here, but there was no hint of women having lesser worth. Instead, his chastisement is directed not only to Pharisaic men, but the hardness of the heart of men overall. Jesus concedes that Moses allowed divorce, but his concern is about God's original intent with marriage. He says that the only thing that invalidates a marriage is if sexual immorality occurs, because it severs them being "one" which takes place in the sexual union, which is confined for marriage.[186]

Paul said of marriage, "This mystery is a profound one . . . ."[187] He added that it mirrored Jesus' relationship with the church, and because of that, the man was "the head of the wife."[188] This marriage metaphor was not odd for Paul to use, because in Hebrew Scripture Israel was often spoken about as the wife of God.[189] For Paul, Jesus and the church formed a marriage in the same way that God and the Israelites did.

It should also be noted that the word "head" in Hebrew is *rosh*, and this is the same word as "beginning" used in Genesis 1:1 "In the beginning." This is important in order to understand why Paul said that in marriage, the man is the head of the wife. The word "head" does not suggest a master and slave relationship. Instead, it alludes to Eve originating/being created, by God, out of Adam. Adam was the beginning of Eve. He is not worth more, but in the marital male-female dynamic, he has a leadership position.

Leadership should not be confused with control. When God punished Eve in the Garden of Eden after taking the fruit and then giving it to Adam, God told her, "… yet your desire shall be for your husband, and he shall rule over you." This sets a tone of negative submission, which is not what leadership is. This is why it would be a punishment. When Jesus discussed rulers he told his disciples in Matthew 20:25-26,

> But Jesus called them to him and said, "You know that the rulers of the Gentiles lord it over them, and their great men exercise authority over them. It shall not be so among you; but whoever would be great among you must be your servant.

Jesus said that to be great in the kingdom of God is not to control but to serve. Likewise, Paul wrote in Ephesians 5:25, 28,

> "Husbands, love your wives, as Christ loved the church and gave himself up for her, … Even so

husbands should love their wives as their own bodies. He who loves his wife loves himself."

This is not negative submission but mutual sacrifice and service in love. Throughout history men have been the warriors and protectors because they are physically stronger and women carry children. They have different roles, but the same worth.

In order to understand the punishment over Eve though we need to look a little deeper into what this means now so we can separate women being ruled by men and the leadership position men have that Paul referred to.

NO CURSE

I want to give some concluding points about the fall and the curse. First, there is an interesting line in Genesis 5:29 when Lamech became the father of Noah and said, "Out of the ground which the LORD has cursed this one shall bring us relief from our work and from the toil of our hands." This suggests an early belief that, in fact, Noah saved the people from the curse pronounced in Eden. When God saved him because he was righteous and he took the animals, his wife, his sons and their wives on the Ark, everything started from scratch and the curse of the ground was no longer valid. Despite Man's wickedness God said, "I will never again curse the ground."[190]

Second and lastly, in a literal reading of the Fall of Man it was actually only the snake and the ground that God explicitly cursed. Although it is easy to infer this to include the man and the woman when God listed the punishments, at a closer look it never specifically states that. Here is what God said,

The LORD God said *to the serpent*, "Because you have done this, *cursed are you* above all cattle, and above all wild animals; upon your belly you shall go, and dust you shall eat all the days of your life. I will put enmity between you and the woman, and between your seed and her seed; he shall bruise your head, and you shall bruise his heel."

To the woman he said, "I will greatly multiply your pain in childbearing; in pain you shall bring forth children, yet your desire shall be for your husband, and he shall rule over you."

And *to Adam* he said, "Because you have listened to the voice of your wife, and have eaten of the tree of which I commanded you, 'You shall not eat of it,' *cursed is the ground* because of you; in toil you shall eat of it all the days of your life; thorns and thistles it shall bring forth to you; and you shall eat the plants of the field. In the sweat of your face you shall eat bread till you return to the ground, for out of it you were taken; you are dust, and to dust you shall return."[191]

The *bold italics* are mine in order to highlight that when God explicitly talks to the woman, no curse is mentioned. Likewise, when God addresses the man, only the ground is cursed. The reason the ground was cursed was *because* of Adam, perhaps signifying that God avoided cursing Adam directly. Instead He took it out on the ground from which Adam was made, while reminding him that he would return to it. Death had now been introduced.

However, Adam and Eve were punished. In most people's minds the difference between curse and punishment is probably that a punishment is less severe, and more temporary, than a curse, even though a curse can be lifted. The specific punishments God gave to Adam and Eve matched their respective transgressions. Eve listened, and believed, what the serpent said instead of Adam who, we can deduce, told her what God said. On top of that she asked Adam to eat of the fruit too. Adam listened, and believed, what his wife said instead of following, and thus believing, God's instructions about the forbidden fruit.

Let us go back to the cursing of the ground for a minute. Following the flood, this is what it says in Genesis 8:21 after Noah made offerings to God,

> And when the LORD smelled the pleasing odor, the LORD said in his heart, "I will never again curse the ground because of man, for the imagination of man's heart is evil from his youth; neither will I ever again destroy every living creature as I have done."

As mentioned above, the curse on the ground is by every indication no longer in place.[192] God seemingly lifted it because man's propensity for evil was so strong that He stopped taking it out on the ground. It is important here that God ended the curse after the ground had been cleansed by the flood. It parallels baptism that washes us clean from the sins of the past in our personal lives. Once you are washed clean, you can receive forgiveness for your sins.

Even though the word "curse" is a harsher word, the effects of The Fall, over men and women, may have lasted longer than the curse on the ground because it is up to each man and woman to repent and approach God to be forgiven. A curse pronounced by God can also be lifted by God, and He did just that. The ground, in contrast to humans, cannot ask for forgiveness.

The only one still cursed, from the Garden, is the serpent. He is the Tempter who represents the Devil, whose goal is to lead us away from God. He tempts us to disobey

God by persuasion into believing his lies. Sometimes he lies outright, sometimes by twisting the truth or lying by omission. Adam and Eve were expelled from Eden because they were not allowed to eat from the Tree of Life in a state of unrepented sin, as the knowledge of good and evil had now been introduced to humanity. Though physical death, and sin, remains, God provided a way to eternal life, where good will finally triumph over evil, via repentance and forgiveness of sins.

Paul words in Romans 6:4 are relevant here,

We were buried therefore with him by baptism into death, so that as Christ was raised from the dead by the glory of the Father, we too might walk in newness of life.

We cannot walk in the newness of life if we are not free. Jesus specified in John 8:34 that "Truly, truly, I say to you, every one who commits sin is a slave to sin." True freedom means being freed from sin. From all this we can deduce that if women stay in a state of sin, it means we remain under the punishment of being ruled by men. Likewise, men cannot walk in the newness of life and rule over women. The very existence of the human race depends on the union of a woman and man as one, which in itself signifies equal worth. Men and women *complement* each other, and the love Jesus taught was *sacrificial* not self-seeking.

WISDOM – THE HOLY SPIRIT & WATER

Before we leave the examination of the Holy Spirit/Wisdom in the Old Testament we will examine one more aspect associated with the Holy Spirit and Wisdom: Water. It has significant and deep connections to the feminine, which deserves a separate heading. Let us start in Ben Sirach 24:5-8 where Wisdom herself utters these words,

> Alone I have made the circuit of the vault of heaven and have walked in the depths of the abyss. In the waves of the sea, in the whole earth, and in every people and nation I have gotten a possession. Among all these I sought a resting place; I sought in whose territory I might lodge. Then the Creator of all things gave me a commandment, and the one who created me assigned a place for my tent. And he said, "Make your dwelling in Jacob, and in Israel receive your inheritance.

This could describe Wisdom's descent into the human sphere and her role here, which Christians are familiar with as the Holy Spirit. The fact that Wisdom herself is speaking is also a strong indication of her as distinct and personified force from the celestial realm.

Ben Sirach says that the man who fears God and keeps the Law will gain Wisdom, and "She will feed him with the bread of understanding, and give him the water of wisdom to drink."[193] This line ties Jesus directly to the Wisdom teachings when he declared being the "bread of life"[194] and his statement to the women from Samaria that he met at Jacob's well. He told her, "whoever drinks of the water that I shall give him will never thirst; the water that I shall give him will become in him a spring of water welling up to eternal life."[195] Jesus' words about the key to eternal life symbolized by "water" and his teachings about the bread of life were both declarations that he had the Spirit of Wisdom.[196]

Wisdom is furthermore described to take her place inside people, literally like water. She fills men with water from different rivers, which makes them full of understanding. While being identified with the Torah, it says about her that she, as such,

> fills men with wisdom, like the Pishon, and like the Tigris at the time of the first fruits. It makes them full of understanding, like the Euphrates, and like the Jordan at harvest time.[197]

Her associations with three out of the four rivers in the Garden of Eden, the Jordan replacing Gihon,[198] simultaneously point to her presence in the Garden of Eden and the beginning of creation.

The connection of Wisdom to "the first fruits" symbolizes her fertility and how she produces results (fruit).[199] She fills people with the water that causes insight. This leads to bearing fruit, which in metaphoric language declares that her teachings lead to life. In the next segment we will see how this is linked to the Book of Revelation.

Ben Sirach repeatedly links water to Wisdom and states that,

> Just as the first man did not know her perfectly, the last one has not fathomed her; for her thought is more abundant than the sea, and her counsel deeper than the great abyss.[200]

The text proceeds with more allegories between Wisdom and water strengthening this bond.[201] Isaiah too used water as a spiritual metaphor and linked it to the Holy Spirit. In Isaiah 44:3 God speaks to Israel saying,

> For I will pour water on the thirsty land, and streams on the dry ground; I will pour my spirit upon your descendants, and my blessing on your offspring. They shall spring up like grass amid waters, like willows by flowing streams.

Blessings and water are both associated with God's Spirit, and the symbolism of water is used as a metaphor to what causes God's people to flourish.[202] As evident, there is no shortage of passages that make it clear that Wisdom and the Holy Spirit serve the exact same role and both were present in the beginning. This does not mean they are two competing forces. As we turn to the New Testament, it will only strengthen the assertion that they are one and the same personified divine power revealed to us by two epithets.

THE HOLY SPIRIT & WISDOM IN THE NEW TESTAMENT

THE CONNECTION TO WATER

The New Testament texts, in our modern Bibles, are translated from ancient Greek. In Greek, Wisdom is still grammatically feminine, but the Spirit has gone from feminine to neuter. The translations from Greek obscure the fact that Jesus himself would have addressed the Spirit as a feminine power because he spoke Aramaic and Hebrew. However, in some places we can see the Spirit's femininity anyway via context.

The water-theme continues in the New Testament where the Holy Spirit is also described to fill people. As that happens a new spiritual understanding takes place. You are changed on the inside. An illustration of this is Paul's conversion, which did not take place on the road to Damascus but afterwards when Jesus sent Anani'as to lay his hands on Paul to restore his sight and let him "be filled with the Holy Spirit . . . ."[203] Anani'as was told by Jesus to go to Paul because, "behold, he is praying, and he has seen a man named Anani'as come in and lay his hands on him so that he might regain his sight."[204] It does not say Paul had been converted yet, but he was "praying." Likely perplexed and asking to get his sight back, he was given a vision about who was to come and lay his hands on him to restore his sight. The fact that Paul lost his sight and regained it when he was given the Holy Spirit makes a parallel between physically seeing and spiritual insight. Paul gained both when Anani'as performed the laying on of hands on him, which is a ritual that invokes the presence of the Holy Spirit.

In the Book of Revelation the reoccurring theme of water plays a key role. Jesus talked about the water of life, which leads to eternal life.[205] This water of life is now present in the new heaven and earth as is the Tree of Life, which was previously situated in the Garden of Eden. Both the water of life and the Tree of Life are synonymous to the Holy Spirit and Wisdom. It was because of the Tree of Life that Adam and Eve were expelled from Eden and now those who gain entrance to the Tree of Life are those that have been washed clean and forgiven.

In the very last chapter John says he saw,

the river of the water of life, bright as crystal, flowing from the throne of God and of the Lamb through the middle of the street of the city; also, on either side of the river, the tree of life with its twelve kinds of fruit, yielding its fruit each month; and the leaves of the tree were for the healing of the nations.[206]

This river of water flows from the throne of God and we can deduce that it is this water that gives life to the Tree of Life. In turn, the fertile Tree of Life yields fruit each month for the healing of the nations. These are clear references to feminine traits that the Tree of Life has which undoubtedly links it to the only kosher Divine Feminine power: the Holy Spirit/Wisdom. It is here appropriate to do a little deeper examination on this part of the book of Revelation to better understand what is says because it greatly matters.

For starters, it sounds like John saw two trees, one on each side of the river. But, the Tree of Life, mentioned twice, is in the singular. The word for "on either side," in Greek εντευθεν, is an adverb meaning "from here." It would mean "on each side" if it were repeated which it was not.[207] Instead it is combined with another word, in Greek εκειθεν, which has a similar meaning, "from there," making the translation "from here and from there" which is why it has been translated "on either side." Perhaps the "from here and from there" means something different though. The last word εκειθεν can mean "from that place." It is a compound word where the first two letters εκ refer to something "out of." The first adverb is also a compound word where the first two letters εν point to something that is "in." When these words are used alone there are flexibilities for how they can be translated. All this to say that there is only one Tree of Life and the odd wording, which I just parsed, may signal something important about the placement of the Tree.

Let us think for a minute about the context. The river is flowing out of the throne and into the middle of the street of Jerusalem. The verb "to be" is not present but in Greek it is not necessary and can be implied, wherefore we can concur that the Tree of Life is in Jerusalem. But, there cannot be one single Tree that simultaneously stands on each side of the river which begs for another meaning for "on either side of the river" and leads to the question of where the later punctuations were set. Additionally, there is a feminine personal pronoun in the genitive meaning "of her" which is translated above as "the city" because it clearly refers to Jerusalem. However, when it is translated "the city" instead of the literal translation "of her" it obscures the presence of the feminine. This is yet another case where this is not a purely grammatical detail because Jerusalem is in Revelation called "the Bride," signaling that her gender is important.

With all this in mind I have done another slightly more literal translation with explanations in the parenthesis in order to better understand what John may have meant in Revelation 22:1-2,

> I was shown the river of the water of life, shining like crystal, coming out of the throne of God and of the Son. In the middle the street of Her (Jerusalem) and of the river, from here (Jerusalem) and from there (the throne) (was) The Tree of Life bearing twelve fruits each month, giving away its fruit and the leaves of the Tree in order for healing of the nations.

The Tree of Life was situated in the New Jerusalem in the middle of both the street and the river. The river was running through the main street because the meaning is spiritual not physical. The Tree of Life was not situated on either side of the river but in the center of Jerusalem, which is scripturally important.

A few lines prior it says of the city that "its gates shall never be shut by day–and there shall be no night there . . . ."[208] This last passage is a reversal of what happened in Eden. Adam and Eve were driven out of the Garden and God placed the cherubim and a flaming sword to "guard the way to the tree of life."[209] Not only that, but when God planted trees in the Garden of Eden it is explicitly stated that the Tree of Life was "in the midst of the garden . . . ."[210] The Book of Revelation corresponds to this placement by likewise positioning the Tree of Life in the heart of the New Jerusalem. The river surrounds the Tree of Life and as we know water is necessary for a tree to grow, so the Tree and water are intrinsically interconnected emphasized by the ability of the Tree of Life to bear fruit.

The river coming from God's throne can even be understood as the conduit between God and the Tree of Life because the water of life is not meant to refer to a physical river but symbolically indicate the agent for eternal spiritual life. As stated earlier, Jesus said at Jacob's well to the woman from Samaria,

> "whoever drinks of the water that I shall give him will never thirst; the water that I shall give him will become in him a spring of water welling up to eternal life."[211]

Jesus juxtaposed this water to physical water, and it is this spiritual water Revelation is communicating. The "street" of Jerusalem could be another pun aiming at Genesis where the cherubim guarded "the way" to the Tree of Life. Here in the New Jerusalem the destination of both "the river" and "the street"[212] (i.e. the way) is eternal life, embodied in the fruit that the Tree of Life bears.

When the New Jerusalem came down out of heaven God would dwell with men, and it proclaims "death shall be no more" making the contrast between death and life abundantly clear.[213] Death and night are banished. Life and light are forever present. The presence of the Divine Feminine is explicit and important in the Book of Revelation. The Water of Life and the Tree of Life are symbolic representations of the Holy Spirit whose fruit brings healing in the everlasting life.[214] Proverbs repeatedly mentions the Tree of Life and it is relevant here to cite 11:30 where it says, "The fruit of the righteous is a tree of life, but lawlessness takes away lives."[215] The implication of the Tree of Life being in the midst of Jerusalem tells us that she is in the heart of the people who have gained entrance to the heavenly Jerusalem. With the water of life flowing out of the Father's throne, He is now dwelling with His people. This is depicted as the union of the divine male and female power within God via God's reunification with the humans who have chosen the Way of Life.

The "water of life" plays an important part in the last chapter of the Book of Revelation, which concludes by describing the testimony of Jesus saying, "The Spirit and the Bride say, 'Come.' And let him who hears say, 'Come.' And let him who is thirsty come, let him who desires take the water of life without price."[216] Following this there are stern warnings for anyone who would in any way change this text, saying, "God will take away his share in the tree of life and in the holy city . . . ."[217] So, John's Revelation basically ends on the note of the Spirit, paralleled with the Bride, inviting everyone to drink from the water of life, which is freely available to all mankind. Salvation does not depend on any worldly status or means. But, you have to choose it and if you do you will get your share in the Tree of Life that was lost to us in the Garden of Eden.

What is of essence, for us regarding the book of Revelation, is that we can see how John knew the *theological significance* of the Holy Spirit's feminine gender. The Spirit is the Bride who provides a feminine counterpart to the Father and The Son.[218] She connects us with God. The Bride, present in Jerusalem, is said to be "the wife of the Lamb."[219] When this heavenly capital is introduced it says,

> And I saw the holy city, new Jerusalem, coming down out of heaven from God, prepared *as a bride adorned for her husband*; and I heard a loud voice from the throne saying, "Behold, the dwelling of God is with men. He will dwell with them, and they shall be his people . . ."[220]

The Bride coming "down of out of heaven from God" and God now dwelling "with men" portrays a picture we find repeatedly in the Old Testament where Israel is described as the wife of God.[221] It is a marriage—where the presence of the Holy Spirit is *the Bride*—precisely *because the Holy Spirit is feminine.* She is present within the people of God represented by Israel. It is via her that we know God. Jesus—the Messiah—is *anointed by the Holy Spirit* whom God chose to testify to the truth and pass it on to the nations of the world.[222] In all these ways, the Book of Revelation provides irrefutable evidence for the significance of the Holy Spirit's feminine gender.

In the New Testament John the Baptist was on the scene before Jesus and baptized people in water. This was a practice rooted in ritual purity and demanded an inner conversion to have any effect.[223] Jesus asked to be baptized in the Jordan by John, and following his baptism, the Holy Spirit descended on Jesus in the form of a dove.[224] John said, "I have baptized you with water; but he will baptize you with the Holy Spirit"[225] differentiating between two forms of baptisms, indicating baptism with water only had a cleansing effect after repentance and in fact lacking the Holy Spirit. As water is physically used for cleaning, baptism is the symbolic act of cleansing the inner spiritual part after one has turned away from sin, which prepares the way for the Holy Spirit.

In the Gospel of John Jesus said, "Truly, truly, I say to you, unless one is born of water and the Spirit, he cannot enter the kingdom of God."[226] This was in response to the question of the Pharisee Nicodemus about what it means to be "born anew"[227] when he did not understand that Jesus was not talking about being born again physically. Jesus tied water and Spirit together. One goes with the other, just like John preceded Jesus, water enables the way for the Spirit to enter.

At one point Jesus celebrated the Feast of Tabernacles in Judea, and on the last day this took place,

> . . . Jesus stood up and proclaimed, "if any one thirst, let him come to me and drink. He who believes in me, as the scripture has said, 'Out of his heart shall flow rivers of living water.' " Now this he said about the

Spirit, which those who believed in him were to receive; for as yet the Spirit had not been given, because Jesus was not yet glorified.[228]

We have the metaphor explained to us here by John in plain language: when Jesus used the term "living water' he meant the Holy Spirit.

THE PROMINENCE OF THE HOLY SPIRIT

It is important to take a look at some highlights of the Holy Spirit's role in Jesus, his family and follower's life. As remarked on earlier, there is a marked difference between how the Holy Spirit is described in the Old and the New Testament. Though she is feminine in the Hebrew Scriptures, she was nearly always part of the phrase "Spirit of God/Lord." In the New Testament, she is almost at all times called "the Holy Spirit" making her role more individualized. This is why her legacy in the ensuing Christian faith granted a separate persona in the Nicene Creed. Right at the outset of Jesus' ministry, it was his mission to baptize in the Holy Spirit, which set him apart from John. The teachings about the Holy Spirit were a huge vitally important part of Jesus' birth, mission, role, and teachings. She was not a side note but took center stage in the faith. Wisdom is present too, but just not as pronounced as the Holy Spirit.

In the first chapter of Luke an angel is telling John the Baptist's father Zechariah, that John will be "filled with the Holy Spirit, even from his mother's womb."[229] Likewise, Zechariah is filled with the Holy Spirit when he prophesied about his son.[230] One of the most famous occasions where the Holy Spirit is present is when Mary is told how she will get pregnant without having a husband. The angel told her that,

> "The Holy Spirit will come upon you, and the power of the Most High will overshadow you; therefore the child to be born will be called holy, the Son of God."[231]

The first line in this passage can be read in two ways. One is that the Holy Spirit and Power are two synonymous words for God. Another is to see these as two divine titles complementing each other as in, the Holy Spirit *and* the Most High. Both will partake in the creation of the Holy One of God.

Before Jesus was born there was a man called Simeon, and it says,

> "the Holy Spirit was upon him. And it had been revealed to him by the Holy Spirit that he should not see death before he had seen the LORD's Christ."[232]

Simeon was "inspired by the Spirit"[233] when he came to the Temple where Joseph and Mary had brought Jesus to do the rituals according to the Law of purification as tradition prescribed. This story was not only to show that Jesus was the awaited Messiah, but the key role the Holy Spirit played in this revelation. Mary and Joseph raised Jesus in Nazareth, and it says that the child Jesus "grew and became strong, filled with wisdom . . . ."[234] As we have seen earlier, Wisdom and the Holy Spirit, could be seen as one and the same. To be filled with Wisdom equals being filled with the Holy Spirit, which then implies Jesus was so long before his baptism. The dove landing on Jesus at his baptism meant he was the selected and crowned Messiah, but it may not necessarily exclude him from having the Holy Spirit prior to that event, particularly not because of how Jesus was conceived. The angel who gave the news to Mary said,

> "The Holy Spirit will come upon you, and the power of the Most High will overshadow you; therefore the child to be born will be called holy, the Son of God."[235]

It is hard to think Jesus did not have the Spirit his whole life for that reason.

The tale about Jesus, twelve years old, staying behind in the Temple after celebrating Passover in Jerusalem, ends with the family's return to Nazareth, and it says, "Jesus increased in wisdom and in stature, and in favor with God and man."[236] With Luke being the only Gospel that has a few rare passages about Jesus' childhood, it is worth noting that Wisdom is mentioned in this context. Indeed, when Jesus grew up, he became known for his wisdom, and many of his teachings can be traced directly to the wisdom books. Mark documented that when Jesus came back to his own country after having been away, he was teaching on the Sabbath in the Synagogue, and people were astonished and asked, "Where did this man get all this? What is the wisdom given to him?"[237] Afterwards they were offended because they discovered that they knew him, his mother, brothers and sisters. This was the time Jesus proclaimed that a prophet is honored everywhere except among his own. Josephus, the first-century Jewish historian, described Jesus as a "wise man" suggesting this was part of his reputation among some non-Christians.[238]

In Luke 7:35 Jesus says, "Yet wisdom is justified by all her children" and later in 11:49,

> Therefore also the Wisdom of God said, "I will send them prophets and apostles, some of whom they will kill and persecute."

The Greek word for Wisdom, in transliteration *Sophia,* is grammatically feminine just like it is in Hebrew. Moreover, Jesus is here quoting an unknown Scripture. It is thus possible that Jesus had a wisdom text considered sacred that could have described the Holy Spirit as a "Mother" while giving her strong ties to Wisdom since she has children. By the very least, the way he talked about Wisdom reveals that he adhered to the personified divine Wisdom tradition by quoting what she "said."

John the Baptist said that Jesus would baptize with the Holy Spirit[239] and Matthew 3:16-17 tells us,

> And when Jesus was baptized, he went up immediately from the water, and behold, the heavens were opened and he saw the Spirit of God descending like a dove, and alighting on him; and lo, a voice from heaven, saying, "This is my beloved Son, with whom I am well pleased."

In this well-known story the Spirit of God took the form of a dove. The parallel passage of this in Luke says that the Holy Spirit descended in the "bodily form" of a dove.[240] There was also a light that shone on Jesus. Note too that the voice did not come from the dove but from heaven, the recognized abode of the Father, making the distinction between the Spirit and Father-God clearer. Immediately after Jesus' baptism according to Matthew, Mark and Luke, it was the Spirit that led him into the wilderness. Luke described Jesus as being, "full of the Holy Spirit . . . ."[241] Following the forty days and nights in the wilderness of fasting and resisting the Devil, Jesus began his ministry.

One interesting passage that all three synoptic Gospels have is about the grave sin of speaking against the Holy Spirit. Jesus, who preached forgiveness in a radical way; turning the other cheek, forgiving seventy-seven times instead of seven, even asking God, from the cross, to forgive his persecutors also said something drastic in light of this and it had to do with the Holy Spirit. In Matthew he is quoted this way,

> He who is not with me is against me, and he who does not gather with me scatters. Therefore I tell you, every sin and blasphemy will be forgiven men, but

the blasphemy against the Spirit will not be forgiven. And whoever says a word against the Son of man will be forgiven; but whoever speaks against the Holy Spirit will not be forgiven, either in this age or in the age to come.[242]

We can elaborate endlessly about what this means, but one thing is certain: Jesus was not mincing words when it came to protecting the Holy Spirit. He reserves the worst possible punishment to whoever commits this violation.

Another renowned occasion of the Holy Spirit in the New Testament is Pentecost. It is described that on that day,

"suddenly a sound came from heaven like the rush of a mighty wind, and it filled all the house where they were sitting."[243]

The entrance of the Holy Spirit was like a wind, which is the other meaning of the Hebrew word for "Spirit," in transliteration *ruah*. Peter interpreted the event to be fulfillment of prophecy by the prophet Joel who talked about the outpouring of God's Spirit on his people at the end times.[244]

In some instances we can detect a slight connection between the Holy Spirit and Wisdom in the New Testament the way we can, albeit much more profoundly, in the Hebrew Scriptures and the Apocrypha. For example, after Pentecost when the disciples face persecution and are organizing, they appoint seven of them to preach the word of God. These people were reportedly "full of the Spirit and of wisdom . . . ."[245] Additionally, the first martyr Stephen, while arguing with opponents, is described as winning the dispute. It says, "But they could not withstand the wisdom and the Spirit with which he spoke."[246] Wisdom entails the Holy Spirit and vice versa.

Paul also discussed the difference between the wisdom of the world and the Wisdom of God. In the first letter to the Corinthians he elaborated on this and called Christ "the power of God and the wisdom of God."[247] We here have the duality; power (*El* means "power" and is grammatically male) and wisdom (*Sophia* grammatically female), and Jesus had both. Later, Paul said that God made Jesus "our wisdom, our righteousness and sanctification and redemption . . . ."[248] He said, "we impart a secret and hidden wisdom of God, which God decreed before the ages for our glorification."[249] Wisdom is additionally described by Paul as one of the gifts of the Spirit.[250]

Though Jesus came to baptize with the Holy Spirit, it was these passages by Paul about Wisdom that later helped foster the idea that Jesus was Wisdom, instead of having Divine Wisdom. This fused Jesus as Wisdom, and in doing so, further concealed the prominent role of Wisdom as a distinct feminine power of God.[251]

In Ephesians Paul is praying for his fellow Christians, "that the God of our Lord Jesus Christ, the Father of glory, may give you a spirit of wisdom . . . ."[252] He states later that, "through the church the manifold wisdom of God might now be made known to the principalities and powers in the heavenly places."[253] This acknowledges that the Wisdom of God appears in different ways.

There is something relevant to this we can learn from Philo who lived at the same time as Jesus. Philo was a Jewish Greek-speaking Biblical philosopher who lived in Alexandria, Egypt. He wrote about the symbolic significance of the dove, and how it was linked to Wisdom. While examining Genesis 15:9 about some sacrifices God asked of Abraham He wrote,

> Besides all these things, "a turtle dove and a pigeon," that is to say, divine and human wisdom, both of them being winged, and being animals accustomed to

> soar on high, still different from one another, as much
> as genus differs from species or a copy from the
> model; for divine wisdom is fond of lonely places,
> loving solitude, on account of the only God, whose
> possession she is; and this is called a turtle-dove,
> symbolically; but the other is quiet and tame, and
> gregarious, haunting the cities of men, and rejoicing
> in its abode among mortals, and so they liken her to a
> pigeon.[254]

This tells us that there was a Jewish understanding of divine
Wisdom symbolized by a turtledove. Philo also talked about
the dove as a "she" who belonged to God. This reinforces
the premise I have presented that Wisdom and the Holy
Spirit, who settled on Jesus in the form of a dove, was at this
time understood to be one and the same Divine Feminine
character of God.

In the book of John before Jesus gets arrested, he talks
to the disciples about the "Counselor" that is to come when
he leaves.[255] This Counselor is synonymous with "the Spirit of
truth" and "proceeds from the Father," reflecting the trait of
both Wisdom and the Holy Spirit.[256] The Greek word for the
counselor can also be translated as "helper," "comforter,"
"advocate." "Helper" undeniably reminds us of Eve's role as
a helper, in Hebrew transliteration *ezer*, to Adam. As such, it
is a link to Eve being fashioned after the Divine Feminine
role model. Jesus stated that the Counselor will be sent in his
name and coming when he leaves.[257] He even claimed that
the "Spirit of truth" could not come unless he leaves. In John
16:13-15, Jesus goes on to say that,

> When the Spirit of truth comes, he will guide you into
> all the truth; for he will not speak on his own
> authority, but whatever he hears he will speak, and
> he will declare to you the things that are to come. He
> will glorify me, for he will take what is mine and

declare it to you. All that the Father has is mine; therefore I said that he will take what is mine and declare it to you.

The masculine pronouns are used here because they apply to the word for "Counselor" present prior to this quote, which in Greek is a masculine word.[258] Consequently, the writer follows grammatical rules calling the Counselor "he."[259] But, Jesus was not speaking Greek. If the Hebrew word Jesus used was the same as the word for "counselor" that is present in Isaiah 9:6, it is a feminine noun.[260] Because Jesus said that the Counselor did not speak on his (her) own authority it necessarily means that the Spirit of Truth is subject to the authority of God.[261] She is a recipient and a transmitter of God's word and a Counselor to humans. Likewise, the Hebrew word for "truth"—*emet*—is like the Hebrew word for "Spirit"—*ruah*—feminine. "Truth" is feminine in Greek too.[262]

This all tells us that when Jesus spoke about "the Spirit of truth" and "the Counselor" the Greek translations portrays the gender inaccurately. For Jesus, the divine Spirit of truth/Counselor was feminine which is lost in English.
Jesus' last farewell commands included the Holy Spirit. The closing passages in Matthew says,

And Jesus came and said to them, "All authority in heaven and on earth has been given to me. Go therefore and make disciples of all nations, baptizing them in the name of the Father and of the Son and of the Holy Spirit, teaching them to observe all that I have commanded you; and lo, I am with you always, to the close of the age."[263]

This is often thought to have been added later because of the seemingly Trinitarian formula. However, mentioning all three need not entail a masculine Trinity that was decreed around three-hundred years later at the council of Nicaea. Jesus was specifically announced by John the Baptist to come in order to baptize with the Holy Spirit according to all four Gospels, plus the Book of Acts records Jesus declaring that the disciples will be baptized with the Spirit.[264] The Holy Spirit was understood as part of God yet distinct. This was a prime feature of Jesus' teachings. For him to ask the disciples to include God *and* the Holy Spirit while baptizing is therefore not farfetched.[265] He also included himself because he is the promised Messiah—the anointed one—who was to come and bring salvation.

I earlier mentioned that by context we could detect how important the feminine gender of the Holy Spirit is. One of these occasions is in the Gospel of John where Jesus said, "Truly, truly, I say to you, unless one is born of water and the Spirit, he cannot enter the kingdom of God."[266] Jesus was answering the Pharisee Nicodemus about of how you become "born anew."[267] It is also often translated as "born again" because Nicodemus did not understand at first what Jesus said. He told him, "How can a man be born when he is old? Can he enter a second time into his mother's womb and be born?"[268] The whole reason that Jesus gives the illustration of being born again is because the Spirit is feminine. Women give birth, and likewise the Spirit gives birth. One birth is earthly, and the other one is spiritual. We are spiritually "born" *through* the Spirit while we are simultaneously born *of* God.[269] He is the source, and when we become believers He is our Father because the seed comes from Him. That is why Jesus so often used the seed in parables about believers.[270] Although Jesus does not call the Spirit his Mother in this verse, this is exactly the role he describes her to have by describing us gaining the Spirit it as a birth. This is a feminine reference. The Holy Spirit is our spiritual Mother via whom we are born in a new way once we believe. This is synonymous with what the Prologue of the Gospel of John describes when those who believe are born by God. It says about Jesus that,

> But to all who received him, who believed in his name, he gave power to become children of God; who were born, not of blood nor of the will of the flesh nor of the will of man, but of God.[271]

This birth analogy mirrors what Jesus said to Nicodemus, although here the emphasis is being born of God, whereas Jesus talked about being born again via the Holy Spirit. There is a parentage because this is how you become a "child" of God. We can go back to the creation story of man and woman and see how it ties into all this. Since the Spirit is feminine and we are born through her, by logical conclusion, that makes her our Mother. Earthly parents mirror our heavenly ones.

One major instance in the New Testament where we can see that the Holy Spirit is feminine, via context, is in the concept of "the bride and the bridegroom." Let us look in the Gospel of John where this story unfolds after John first saw Jesus,

> The next day he saw Jesus coming toward him, and said, "Behold, the Lamb of God, who takes away the sin of the world! This is he of whom I said, 'After me comes a man who ranks before me, for he was before me. I myself did not know him; but for this I came baptizing with water, that he might be revealed to Israel." And John bore witness, "I saw the Spirit descend as a dove from heaven, and it remained on him. I myself did not know him; but he who sent me to baptize with water said to me, 'He on whom you see the Spirit descend and remain, this is he who baptizes with the Holy Spirit.' And I have seen and have borne witness that this is the Son of God."[272]

Shortly following this, it is recorded twice that Jesus, along with the apostles, baptized people.[273] This is understood as the beginning of Jesus' ministry. A little later it says that Jesus did not baptize, only the disciples did.[274] However, three claims for and one against, may leave that single comment to lose out. The important part of the story is that it is suggested here that Jesus and the disciples distinguished themselves by baptizing with the Holy Spirit.

While Jesus and his apostles were baptizing, some tensions began between the two parties. The text says,

> Now a discussion arose between John's disciples and a Jew over purifying. And they came to John, and said to him, "Rabbi, he who was with you beyond the Jordan, to whom you bore witness, here he is, baptizing, and all are going to him." John answered, "No one can receive anything except what is given him from heaven."[275]

John declared Jesus' authority to be from heaven, which means he justified it. Since the discussion was about "purifying," it could also have entailed what forms of baptism would count; water, or water and oil, or even just oil. John continues his answer by going into a long line of defense for Jesus and reiterates among other things that,

> You yourselves bear me witness, that I said, I am not the Christ, but I have been sent before him. He who has the bride is the bridegroom; the friend of the bridegroom, who stands and hears him, rejoices greatly at the bridegroom's voice . . . [276]

Here we see the concept of bride and bridegroom. John repeats that he is not the Messiah, Jesus is. He does not say so plainly, but speaks in symbolic terms about a sacred heavenly marriage. The reason Jesus is the Messiah is because he has the "bride." The bride is of course the Holy

Spirit, which is exactly what John proclaimed Jesus would baptize people in. The word *messiah,* in translation being "anointed," means Jesus himself had the presence of the Holy Spirit, which constituted a form of sacred marriage. It joins the heavenly and earthly, God and His people by way of the Holy Spirit. John declaring himself as the "friend of the bridegroom" was his way of saying Jesus was the awaited Messiah. John also said, "For he whom God has sent utters the words of God, for it is not by measure that he gives the Spirit."[277] This suggests that God did not withhold the Spirit but gave her in full to Jesus. Jesus has complete access to divine knowledge from the Father through the Spirit.

In essence, when John defends Jesus he does so by affirming that Jesus has the Holy Spirit. Moreover, these quotations from the Gospel of John are yet more displays of John the Baptist adhering to beliefs that elevated the feminine Holy Spirit in that he referred to her as "the Bride."

It is described in all three synoptic Gospels that a discussion about fasting came up because the disciples of John and the Pharisees both fasted unlike Jesus and his disciples who did not. Jesus was asked why, and he answered,

> And Jesus said to them, "Can the wedding guests fast while the bridegroom is with them? As long as they have the bridegroom with them, they cannot fast. The days will come, when the bridegroom is taken away from them, and then they will fast in that day."[278]

Here then, Jesus himself uses this marriage metaphor and applies the role of the bridegroom to himself, supporting what John said. Moreover, the word translated as "wedding guests" is in the Greek literally, "sons of the bridal chamber." This then, refers to the disciples in a much more intimate way signaling a closer relation to the Bride, i.e. the Holy Spirit.

Jesus used another parable consisting of a wedding and a bridegroom in the story about the ten bridesmaids. Five were foolish and five wise. The foolish were not ready for the wedding because they had no oil for their lamps. The wise were ready, because they had oil. The bridegroom came unexpected in the night and the foolish ones were not prepared. While five foolish bridesmaids hurried to get oil, the door was shut, and they consequently could not come in. The lesson was to always be ready.[279] This story, only found in Matthew, concerned the end times. Having the lamps ready represented being filled with the Holy Spirit (oil and light). In the second coming, Jesus is the bridegroom, and he said that this is what the Kingdom of Heaven would be like. So, the Kingdom of Heaven is where the bridegroom and the maids with their oil-filled lamps are present. Here, just like the other parable, the bride is not mentioned. But, the language and symbolism used make it necessary for the bride to be present and the feminine Holy Spirit is the only likely candidate. The Kingdom of Heaven then is likened to a wedding: the union of the masculine and the feminine.

The Book of Revelation uses the imagery of the bride and bridegroom repeatedly. Jesus, the lamb, is the bridegroom, and his bride (also referred to as wife) is Jerusalem.[280] Additionally, Jerusalem is often called "daughter," wherefore Israel is "Mother."[281] It is from here the modern idea of the church as the bride began. Israel and Jerusalem refer to God's chosen people, but the bridal concept entails more than humans as we have seen. The bride applies to believers in God but the reason is because they have the Holy Spirit who is The Heavenly Bride. If you do not understand that the Spirit is feminine, you miss the entire point of why the word "bride" is used in these illustrations, and sadly most Christians unfortunately do.

There is a part of the Book of Revelation illustrating this point, which is the vision described in chapter 12. It opens up with an account of a great sign appearing in heaven, which is

> "a woman clothed with the sun, with the moon under her feet, and on her head a crown of twelve stars; she was with child and cried out in her pangs of birth, in anguish for delivery."[282]

Following this, the red dragon, who is the Devil, waited and wanted to devour the child. She gave birth to a male child, clearly referring to Christ, who was swept up in heaven before Satan could take him. The woman then fled to the wilderness where she had a place prepared for her by God and was nourished for a certain amount of days. This prophecy alludes to the last chapter in Isaiah, which talks about the end times and God's judgment on the world with fire.[283] Zion, synonymous to Jerusalem in Revelation, represents the bride and as we have seen, is also understood as the Holy Spirit.[284] Here she is plainly portrayed as a woman, which should leave the reader without any doubt about her femininity and the significance of it.

Returning to the Wisdom books for a minute because we can trace this concept of the Bride to the Holy Spirit in believers. They were written before Jesus' time and possibly books he considered sacred. By the very least, they represent a take on the Divine Feminine in Book of Proverbs, which circulated at that time. In the book "Wisdom of Solomon," Wisdom is described as a bride. It says,

> I loved her and sought her from my youth, and I desired to take her for my bride, and I became enamored of her beauty. She glorifies her noble birth by living with God, and the LORD of all loves her. For she is an initiate in the knowledge of God, and an associate in his works.[285]

Here we can see a source for the bride imagery from Wisdom texts: who the bride is and how she functions as a bride to believers. More support for the bridal concept in Revelation originating from the Wisdom books can be seen in Ben Sirach too. There we find the passage,

> From eternity, in the beginning, he created me, and for eternity I shall not cease to exist. In the holy tabernacle I ministered before him, and so I was established in Zion. In the beloved city likewise he gave me a resting place, and in Jerusalem was my dominion.[286]

Wisdom was described and understood as the bride who resided in Jerusalem. When the believer in Ben Sirach talked about her as a bride, it was a figure of speech. She was still the consort of God.[287] Wisdom is the bride and was understood as the Holy Spirit by Jesus and John the Baptist, making them one and the same. The presence of the Holy Spirit, symbolized as the bride, is what sets God's people apart from the rest of the world, and her capitol is Jerusalem. Going back to the Old Testament for a second, Isaiah prophesied about Zion's vindication and speaking on behalf of God he said,

> For Zion's sake I will not keep silent, and for Jerusalem's sake I will not rest, until her vindication goes forth as brightness, and her salvation as a burning torch. The nations shall see your vindication, and all the kings your glory; and you shall be called by a new name which the mouth of the LORD will give. You shall be a crown of beauty in the hand of the LORD, and a royal diadem in the hand of your God. You shall no more be termed Forsaken, and your land shall no more be termed Desolate; but you shall be called My delight is in her, and your land

> Married; for the LORD delights in you, and your land
> shall be married. For as a young man marries a virgin,
> so shall your sons marry you, and as the bridegroom
> rejoices over the bride, so shall your God rejoice over
> you.[288]

This paragraph is loaded with the symbolism of marriage. Zion is God's Bride. By the same token it says, "your sons shall marry you" indicating union with God's people and Zion, His Bride. These are the two concepts we see continued with Jesus and John the Baptist. Jesus the bridegroom is the anointed one, the one who has the Holy Spirit, i.e. Zion. Jesus in turn anoints his followers, who then also receive the Holy Spirit and become God's people. The very last metaphor used here is God as the Bridegroom and Zion/the Holy Spirit as His Bride.

The bridal concept was found in the Dead Sea Scrolls as well. Here is an excerpt from a Wisdom text praising God looking out for His people, "Like a man comforted by his mother, so will He comfort them in Jerusal[em. Like a bridegroom] with the bride, so will He dwel[l] with her [for e]ver."[289]

God and His Wife Jerusalem, symbolizing His people who have the Holy Spirit, were an essential part of ancient Israelite theology.

The bride, as used in Christian rhetoric to mean "the Church" misses the full meaning if it is not understood that the title, "the bride," is specifically feminine because the Holy Spirit is feminine and she resides in the Church. Most of all, she is God's Bride. This verifies and underscores yet again how important the Holy Spirit's femininity was in the early church.

Furthermore, when we see the concept of the bride and the bridegroom found in what is today labeled a "gnostic" text, this concept is not heretical, but to put it in a modern terms, it is "Biblical." The canonical Gospels, let us know just how important this imagery was for Jesus, John the Baptist, their predecessors and followers. The imagery of the bride and bridegroom is about the bridal chamber. Marriage was the ultimate symbol for the presence of God.

We can conclude that Wisdom and the Holy Spirit/Spirit of Truth/Counselor, were intimately tied to Jesus and by all indication they are the same force. This was God's power present in believers. She was presented as an individual strong divinity who is part of God, yet yields to God's authority. Add to this that Jesus' native tongue was Aramaic/Hebrew and that the earliest texts possibly written in Hebrew/Aramaic and the evidence for Jesus referring to the Holy Spirit as a feminine Power are conclusive. She is the one through whom we are born again.

We have now gone through numerous passages in both the Old and New Testament that shows the prominence of the Holy Spirit by revealing how the ancient Israelites would have known her feminine gender via the Hebrew/Aramaic language. We have seen how and why the personified Wisdom is one and the same feminine power as the Holy Spirit and the role she plays in the salvation of mankind. Most importantly, Jesus' teachings reveal how the Holy Spirit and Wisdom are feminine and why it matters.

JESUS' INTERACTION WITH WOMEN

Because the Holy Spirit is feminine, it is pertinent to take a look at how the canonical Gospels portray Jesus' interactions with women. Are his views of the feminine in line with a character that would understand and praise the Holy Spirit as feminine? Let us therefore take a look passages telling us something about Jesus' view.

In Matthew 5:28 Jesus clarified that adultery began in the heart, and he directed his chastisement to men looking lustfully at women. When a woman was caught in adultery, Jesus publicly defended her and told the scribes and Pharisees that the one without sin should be the first to throw a stone. Everyone left, and Jesus said, "Neither do I condemn you; go, and do not sin again."[308] On one occasion Jesus spoke to a woman from Samaria even though it was not custom for a Rabbi to engage in a conversation with someone from Samaria, much less a female. Not only that, but Jesus revealed that he was the Messiah to the Samarian woman, which was something he was quite selective in doing. It also shows how he extended salvation to those considered outside of the circle.[309] He healed many women and brought one girl back to life.[310] When a woman anointed his head with a costly ointment, the disciples were upset, because the money could be spent on helping the poor, but Jesus defended her.[311]

When asked if it was lawful to divorce, Jesus said Moses allowed it due to the hardness of our hearts, but from the beginning of creation, this was not the Father's plan. He quoted the creation of male and female in Genesis and how they become one flesh in marriage to back his view of marriage. Then Jesus followed it up with the famous line used today in Christian marriage ceremonies, "What therefore God has joined together, let not man put asunder."[312] The way he quoted the creation account revealed no sign of inequality between the sexes. Furthermore, when Jesus expounded on marriage, at the disciples' urging, he first noted that a man who divorces his wife commits adultery "against her."[313] Following that he says that a woman who divorces her husband and marries someone else also commits adultery. In other words, he chastised both sexes equally, but if anything, the man a little more, because his lecturing was consistently directed at men first.

At one point Jesus reprimanded some scribes and Pharisees who wanted him to show them a sign. Recognizing their cynical attempt to trap him, he claimed no sign would be given to this "evil and adulterous generation. . . ."[314] He then said the only one that would be given would be that of Jonah. Jesus drew a parallel between Jonah's three days and nights in the belly of the whale and his own impending three days and three nights in the grave before rising from the dead. He pointed out that the men of Nineveh would rise up in judgment, because even they believed Jonah. Next he states that "The queen of the South" will also arise at the judgment of this generation and likewise condemn it.[315] She travelled from the ends of the world to see Solomon because she recognized his greatness, but now when someone superior was present, it was not acknowledged. In Jesus' two examples, one being the men of Nineveh, and the other the queen of Sheba, he made the woman's recognition of what was from God equally important to the men's. She, who was not even a Hebrew, would be in a position now to judge those very men that did not believe Jesus was sent by God.

Jesus used parables to explain God's joy for one single sinner turning his life around and one of them portrayed a woman who had ten silver coins and lost one.[316] It is interwoven between the story of the lost sheep and the prodigal son. The lead character being a woman in the middle story reveals the depth of Jesus' awareness and inclusiveness of women. A female was likewise the center of the parable about the woman who kept bothering an evil judge to give her justice against a man who had done her wrong. It was told by Jesus as an example of how much more God, who is good, would hear His people when they cry out to him.[317] This saying was to encourage the disciples to keep praying and not tire, and Jesus chose a woman to serve as a role model for the disciples. Not only that, but the example was about a woman who had been unjustly treated by a man.[318] In doing so, Jesus effectively made another subtle point that a woman should be treated right and will be heard by God if she is not. At another instance Jesus saw the rich putting their gifts in the treasury and a poor widow two copper coins. He used this occasion to teach and said that the poor widow gave more than the rich men who gave out of their abundance, while she gave all she had to make a living.[319] Jesus contrasted these men against a poor woman whose husband had died.[320]

The controversial passage describing Jesus' mother and brothers wanting to speak to him whereby he stretched out his hands over his disciples and said, "Here are my mother and my brothers! For whoever does the will of my Father in heaven is my brother, and sister, and mother" has often puzzled believers.[321] Jesus who firmly adhered to the Commandments would surely never break "Honor your father and your mother."[322] In fact he did not denounce his family. He simply used this occasion to teach something specific about what would make someone his true brother, sister, and mother. Though it was his mother and brothers who wanted to speak to him, he included "sister" in his teaching or real family, again showing his sensitivity to women. Jesus made the argument that true kinship comes from doing the will of our Heavenly Father and not necessarily of your earthly parents because they can be wrong. This may not sound so revolutionary now, but it was then. There were different social and economic classes and religious and ethnic classes as well, and Jesus declared that anyone who believes in Yahweh and adheres to His precepts is on equal footing with himself even though he was the Messiah. In essence, Jesus publicly stated equal opportunity for everyone to be a child of God, not just Jews. If anyone teaches what is contrary to Yahweh's Law, your responsibility is to follow what is true and right no matter whom you go against.

This was exemplified in another teaching too though it is sometimes distorted to suggest it promotes violence. Jesus said,

> "Do not think that I have come to bring peace on earth; I have not come to bring peace, but a sword. For I have come to set a man against his father, and a daughter against her mother, and a daughter-in-law against her mother-in-law; and a man's foes will be those of his own household. He who loves father or mother more than me is not worthy of me; and he who loves son or daughter more than me is not worthy of me; and he who does not take his cross and follow me is not worthy of me. He who finds his life will lose it, and he who loses his life for my sake will find it." [323]

Jesus is using the "sword" as a metaphor to represent division not violence. If one or more people support false teachings, you should not doubt or give it your stamp of approval to avoid conflict. It does not matter who it is, even if it is someone as close to you as can be. An allegiance to Jesus' teachings, because they present the truth, is what the first commandment to have no other gods next to Yahweh is about. It will inevitably cost you conflicts with the world, and you must expect it and be strong. It was a prophetic warning to prepare his followers that the price of faith is sometimes even their lives. It was also fulfilled not long after Jesus left with countless martyrs following in his footsteps. This is about keeping the faith and the sacrifices it entails.

Paul declared ideas along the same lines when he emphasized that the hand of salvation is for anyone who had faith in Jesus. He said, for in Christ Jesus you are all sons of God, through faith. For as many of you as were baptized into Christ have put on Christ. There is neither Jew nor Greek, there is neither slave nor free, there is neither male nor female; for you are all one in Christ Jesus. And if you are Christ's, then you are Abraham's offspring, heirs according to promise.[324]

Paul did not invent these ideas. Jesus, in essence, taught the same principles, which was in turn in line with the original Hebrew Scriptures. Jesus said adhering to the truth sets you free and makes you Abraham's heir. Yahweh is the God of all the earth and living right—following God's commands—is what makes you a child of God. Jesus did not condemn his family but taught the crowd what it means to have him as a brother. It was unrelated to bloodlines, economic status or ethnicity, and centered on following the will of God. This opportunity was offered equally to men and women.

One story about Jesus and a woman that may at first glance seem to contradict this story and demands a closer look. A Canaanite woman followed Jesus and pleaded with him to heal her daughter from a demon, but the disciples begged him to send her away. At first Jesus was silent. When she persisted, he said he was sent to the lost sheep of the house of Israel. She then kneeled, asking him to help her again, and he said "it is not fair to take the children's bread and throw it to the dogs."[325] He was clearly making a difference between the Jews and infidels, and as we know bread stands for teachings. Then,

She said, "Yes, Lord, yet even the dogs eat the crumbs that fall from their masters' table." Then Jesus answered her, "O woman, great is your faith! Be it done for you as you desire." And her daughter was healed instantly.[326]

This story does show that Jesus' primary mission was giving the true teachings to the Hebrew nation. Jesus calling the Jews "children" and non-Jews "dogs" was a way to draw a distinction between those who worshipped Yahweh and followed His commandments and those who did not. It was a rejection of idolatrous practices. However, this woman persisted and said that she would take what she could of the teachings (bread) and miracles trickling down to others from the Hebrew God through Jesus, whom she also referred to as "Lord."[327] Jesus then granted her wish because of her faith and commended her for it. This was a woman whom the disciples thought should be turned away; yet she understood and acknowledged the Hebrew God and recognized that Jesus was sent by Him. When she did, Jesus likewise recognized her. This tale did not degrade this Canaanite woman, quite the opposite. It was one among several strands of stories showing that it was not always the ones expected to have faith or recognize the truth that did. In this situation it was an outsider, a woman, who rightly believed, and Jesus praised her. It simultaneously uncovers the pattern of who to reach in his mission: first the Jews, then the Gentiles.

During Jesus' final week, it was the many women who had come with Jesus, all the way from Galilee, which stayed present with him during the persecution, execution, burial and resurrection. When Jesus had been sentenced to death and was walking on his way toward Golgotha, he had a large following of people. Luke specifically mentions that it was "women who bewailed and lamented him."[328] Upon this Jesus gave a particular warning of future sorrows for women.[329] All three Synoptic Gospels say that several women were looking on from afar when Jesus was crucified.[330] The accounts of who exactly was in the core group of women that stayed with him differ in the Gospel accounts, although the one person that all claim were present was Mary

Magdalene.³³¹ After his burial, the women came to the grave to take care of the body on the first day, first thing in the morning, following the Sabbath.³³²

According to Luke, when the women had come at sunrise on the first day of the week (Sunday), they found the tomb empty. Two angels appeared and told them Jesus was resurrected, so they went back to tell the eleven Apostles and the other followers. Luke writes,

> Now it was Mary Mag'dalene and Jo-an'na and Mary the mother of James and the other women with them who told this to the apostles; but these words seemed to them an idle tale, and they did not believe them.³³³

Mark verifies nearly the same story as Luke, except it was only one angel in the tomb, and he adds that Jesus appeared as risen to Mary Magdalene first. He additionally confirms that when she told the disciples, they did not believe her. After Jesus showed himself to Mary, he became visible to two other disciples. When he was finally seen by the eleven Apostles, "he upbraided them for their unbelief and hardness of heart, because they had not believed those who saw him after he had risen."³³⁴ This necessarily means he admonished them for disbelieving Mary Magdalene.³³⁵

Matthew's story says it was one angel in the tomb when Mary Magdalene and another Mary came on that Sunday morning. The angel told them to quickly go and tell the disciples, and they ran back to do so. While on their way they met Jesus.³³⁶ John's version of this tale corroborates the others that indeed Mary Magdalene came to the tomb first and found it empty, but there was no angel, and she did not know what had happened to Jesus. As she ran to tell the disciples, Simon Peter and John respond by running to the tomb.³³⁷ John outran Peter and reached the tomb first, and likewise, John entered the tomb before anyone else where he "saw and believed."³³⁸ It also says that they still did not understand the Scriptural prophecy that Jesus was to rise. Both John and Peter left immediately after this, but Mary stayed at the tomb. She there met two angels and asked them where Jesus was. She then turned around and saw Jesus himself although she did not recognize him at first. Then,

> Jesus said to her, "Mary." She turned and said to him in Hebrew "Rab-bo'ni!" (which means Teacher). Jesus said to her, "Do not hold me, for I have not yet ascended to the Father; but go to my brethren and say to them, I am ascending to my Father and your Father, to my God and your God." Mary Mag'dalene went and said to the disciples, "I have seen the Lord"; and she told them that he had said these things to her.[339]

It is only recorded in John that he ran to the tomb as soon as he heard the news, entered it, and believed first. It raises some suspicions wherefore some people think this was added later. Whether or not that is true, John still grants Mary her proper place in that historic moment. She not only followed Jesus and stood by him when he died, but she was the first to come to the tomb and meet him resurrected.

All the Gospel details reveals that women, and in particular Mary from Magdala, were not only followers of Jesus but faithful to him all the way until the end. Seemingly it was the men, even the disciples (save John according to John's Gospel) who initially scattered. They would have had valid reasons to fear for their lives more than the women, but the women were still at risk too. The canonical Gospels' passion narratives strongly suggest that Jesus was particularly close to Mary Magdalene because of how prominently she is featured in the resurrection story. Additionally, we see throughout the Gospels how Jesus honored and cared for women.

SUMMARY OF JESUS' VIEW OF THE DIVINE FEMININE

We can see the New Testament repeatedly shows Jesus had very inclusive and positive interactions with women, sometimes even to the bafflement of his own disciples. When they protested, Jesus reprimanded them. There are no passages to the contrary.[340] He defended and emphasized the feminine Holy Spirit in an utmost way. His ministry started when the Holy Spirit descended on him in the form of a dove anointing him as the Messiah, and he taught that you have to be born again via the Holy Spirit. Because of this, and more, we get a clear picture of Jesus' positive stance and defense on the feminine. This could be attributed to his righteousness, but it could also partly stem from an understanding that the Wisdom/Holy Spirit is a Divine Feminine power. Jesus' teachings about the Holy Spirit combined with the fact that John the Baptist said that his specific mission was to baptize with the Holy Spirit would naturally have ripple effects. If the Gospels portray this accurately we should see others pick up where Jesus left off on such a belief. This is exactly what happened in the early Church.

Jesus' mother had her own profound story of his conception. One that made men hold her in the highest reverence, so much so that she was later called the "mother of God." Jesus was not only surrounded by highly spiritual women but also raised by one, who remained close to him until the very end. The story of his birth in Luke describes Mary set aside as "favored" and gives her significant attention.[341] Her stance when she said, "Behold, I am the handmaid of the Lord; let it be to me according to your word"[342] changed history for millions upon millions of people. She represents the Mother-element: safe, warm, approachable, loving, interceding for believers' behalf to God. The other significant woman in Jesus' life was Mary Magdalene who is featured as a prominent disciple, and the one who, along with some other women, first discovered the empty tomb and saw him resurrected. This is no small matter. Given that all this information is included, it is a solid sign that Mary the mother of Jesus and Mary Magdalene gave their personal testimony, which was then recorded by the Gospel writers.

In sum, we have seen how Jesus understood the Spirit as feminine and how Wisdom and the Holy Spirit were both personified. They have the same function and converge in same roles; hence, this tells us they are one and the same Divine Feminine power. Lastly, we find evidence for the word "mother" being applied to both Wisdom and the Spirit.

CHAPTER 3

JESUS AND OUR MOTHER IN THE FIRST GOSPEL

My mother, the Holy Spirit

Jesus in *the Gospel of the Hebrews*

JESUS CALLS THE HOLY SPIRIT, MY MOTHER

This section centers around a Gospel referred to as "The Gospel to the Hebrews." I am going to only give a very brief introduction to this Gospel here but you should know that it is profoundly important for many reasons. It will be explained in a forthcoming book that examines this Hebrew Gospel and the background in depth. For here and now, I want to let you know that numerous ancient sources testify to the existence of the Gospel of the Hebrews. It was well known, among the early church fathers, to be the original Gospel written by the Apostle Matthew in Hebrew. The fact that it was first composed in Hebrew is of vital importance. As you know now, the Holy Spirit is feminine in Hebrew, but we cannot see that in our modern English translations. This is because every copy of the New Testament found so far is in Greek where the Spirit is neuter which our translations then reflect. But, thanks to the ancient church

Fathers writings we have many quotes from the Gospel to the Hebrews. So, let us now take a look at this.

Church Father Origen of Alexandria (ca. 185-254 A.D.) elaborated in one of his writings on Jeremiah 15:10, where the prophet calls out to his mother, wondering why things are so hard for him. Origen examines this passage and goes into detail about the word "mother" and what it may refer to in this context. He wrote,

> *Woe is me, mother, as what kind of man did you bear me?* What *mother* does he speak of? Is he not able to declare as women both *soul* and Mary? But if a person accepts these words: *My mother, the Holy Spirit, has recently taken me and carried me up to the great mount Tabor,* and what follows, one is able to see his *mother.*[343]

The first quote is from Jeremiah, but the second is at this instance not referenced. The Holy Spirit is identified as being feminine in line with the Hebrew Scriptures, but additionally, she is called "mother." This suggests a glimpse into an early tradition later lost.

In another homily expounding on the same passage from Jeremiah, Origen further examines what the word "mother" means in this context plus mentions what someone else before him thought of this. He says,

> Therefore he was saying—for I first will discuss the common view—*Woe is me, mother, what kind of man did you bear who is judged and disputed over all of the earth?* But of those before me, someone has pointed out this text by saying that he was saying these things not to his biological mother but to the mother who gives birth to prophets. But who produces prophets other than the wisdom of God? Thus he said, *Woe is me, mother, what did you bear,"* O Wisdom! But the children of wisdom are told also in the Gospel: *And wisdom sends her children.* Thus it may be said, *Woe is me,*

> *mother, my wisdom, what kind of man did you bear who is judged.*[344]

The translator has here made the quotations he is using from another Gospel in italics. Wisdom is referred to as "mother" and combined with the other interpretation; we can see that Wisdom is interchangeable with the Holy Spirit. The passage quoted is almost, but not quite, identical to the line found in Luke saying, "Yet wisdom is justified by all her children."[345] It is also found nearly the same in Matthew who has "deeds" instead of "children."[346] Because the quote by Origen is slightly differently worded having "sends" instead of "justified," it could mean this was a quote from another Gospel considered authoritative. The context of these passages is a debate about John the Baptist and Jesus living so differently discussed earlier in the context of Nazarenes. One was drinking wine, the other not, but despite this they were sent by the same source: Wisdom, also understood as The Holy Spirit, and she is called "mother."

At another occasion Origen refers to the same Gospel passage again that he used when examining Jeremiah 15:10, although the context is now John 1:3. He discusses everything being made through the Word. However, this time Origin reveals who he is quoting and from what Gospel,

> If any one should lend credence to the Gospel according to the Hebrews, where the Saviour Himself says, "My mother, the Holy Spirit took me just now by one of my hairs and carried me off to the great mount Tabor," he will have to face the difficulty of explaining how the Holy Spirit can be the mother of Christ when it was itself brought into existence through the Word. But neither the passage nor this difficulty is hard to explain. For if he who does the will of the Father in heaven is Christ's brother and

sister and mother, and if the name of brother of Christ may be applied, not only to the race of men, but to beings of diviner rank than they, then there is nothing absurd in the Holy Spirit's being His mother, every one being His mother who does the will of the Father in heaven.[347]

Here we learn that not only was this quote from the Gospel of the Hebrews, but Origen, who obviously had this text available to him, testifies that it was Jesus himself who called the Holy Spirit his "mother." This is profound and especially because Origen regards this text as authoritative. Origen was the "greatest teacher of Christian doctrine of his time" which tells us plenty about the status of this Gospel.[348] When confronted with Jesus calling the Holy Spirit "mother" he does not dismiss it but interprets it. Origin thinks this is in line with Jesus calling anyone who did the will of God his sister, brother or mother,[349] which he thought included "beings of diviner rank." Therefore, according to Origen, the Holy Spirit is of divine rank, but not God, and because of that it is perfectly in line with Jesus' teachings to call her "Mother".

Later Origen brings in Wisdom to this discussion. He delves deeper into John's prologue and pondering about Jesus he writes,

The "word" is, as a notion, from "life," and yet we read, "What was made in the Word was life, and the life was the light of men." Now as all things were made through Him, was the life made through Him, which is the light of men, and the other notions under which the Savior is presented to us? Or must we take the "all things were made by Him" subject to the exception of the things which are in Himself? The latter course appears to be the preferable one. For supposing we should concede that the life which is the light of men was made through Him, since it said that the life "was made" the light of men, what are we to say about wisdom, which is conceived as being prior to the Word? That, therefore, which is about the Word (His relations or conditions) was not made by the Word, and the result is that, with the exception of the notions under which Christ is presented, all things were made through the Word of God, the Father making them in wisdom. "In wisdom hast Thou made them all," it says, not *through*, but *in* wisdom.[350]

Origen concludes that, what is "about the Word" "was not made by the Word." He does not equalize Wisdom with Jesus. Instead, he determines that Wisdom according to Scripture existed prior to the Word, and he speaks about Wisdom in a way that corresponds clearly to the Biblical Wisdom traditions where she is personified and present with God in the beginning of everything.[351] This view on Wisdom was a prevalent and orthodox understanding at that time, and even more so before Jesus' time. It could also be when Origen earlier quoted a Gospel with the line "*And wisdom sends her children,*" this was the Gospel of the Hebrews too since it is only slightly different from what we have in Matthew and Luke.[352]

Fourth century church father Jerome is the source most frequently witnessing to the Gospel of the Hebrews having "at least twenty-four references to and quotations" from it according to scholar Edwards who have done a thorough study of it.[353] Jerome does not cite this specific passage about Wisdom sending her children. But, he does quote the part where Jesus calls the Holy Spirit his Mother in his commentaries on Micah, Isaiah and Ezekiel.[354] Furthermore, it is the only non-canonical Scripture Jerome makes references to. Evidently, Jerome thought highly of the Hebrew Gospel.

The quote from Jesus in the Gospel of the Hebrews where he calls the Holy Spirit his Mother could be a clue to why this gospel eventually disappeared entirely from the scene. It was used by Nazarenes and Ebionites, and according to Jerome, it was preserved at the library in Caesarea.[355] This was destroyed around the seventh century by Muslim invading forces, giving us yet another explanation for why many texts are missing today. Jerome and many others were not only well aware of the Gospel of the Hebrews, said to be the original recordings by Matthew, but granted it significant attention and authority. It was important in scholarly circles for quite some time. Jesus calling the Holy Spirit his Mother was not understood as heretical. Instead they discussed what it meant that he called her "my Mother."

While it is not questionable that this line existed in the Gospel of the Hebrews, most modern scholars believe that regardless of these testimonies all texts about Jesus were originally written in Greek including this Gospel of the Hebrews. However, "the Spirit" in Greek is neuter and had this line been written originally in Greek, it would have presented inherent grammatical problems for Jesus to call the Holy Spirit "my Mother." This was exactly why some of the church fathers had to explain this sentence about the Holy Spirit when coming across it. Only a Gospel written in Hebrew (or Aramaic) would reflect the Holy Spirit in her feminine form. Instead, the quote from Jesus about the Holy Spirit is precisely why it makes it a higher probability to originate back to a true saying of Jesus.

Since the evidence we have for the Gospel of the Hebrews comes from ancient personal testimonies, any assessment and analysis of its contents determining it to be an original Matthew in Hebrew or to be based on Greek is inherently limited. Dismissing what so many church fathers claimed should not be done. The deeper problem regarding this Gospel is not that it disappeared despite its prominent place in the first few centuries, but it is the fact that it still, for the most part in Biblical scholarship, is completely ignored. In theological settings, it is even worse. This Gospel and quote by Jesus about the Holy Spirit is entirely unknown among most lay Christians. In Greek, and consequently the languages the New Testament has been translated into, the Holy Spirit has been neutered. This is why the truth of the Holy Spirit began to disappear. Fourth century creeds buried this issue even deeper in darkness. Before God's people Israel, Jesus and the early Christians believers knew about the Holy Spirit's femininity.

THE TITLE "MOTHER"

I want to show some instances where the word "mother" was used as a title applying to the Holy Spirit/Wisdom before Jesus' time, as well as afterwards, in the Bible. If the Holy Spirit is our Mother, which we can infer, it is important to see if we can trace any existing tradition for this concept.

The author of Wisdom of Solomon describes himself praying and while doing so the spirit of Wisdom came to him. Then there is a long series of praises about Wisdom and what she brings. He concludes by saying.

> I rejoiced in them all, because wisdom leads them; but I did not know that she was their mother.[290]

This can be read allegorically, but in light of how Wisdom is personified in these very passages, it probably has a more literal meaning and hints that her title was "mother." In Ben Sirach we read, "he who holds to the law will obtain wisdom. She will come to meet him like a mother and like the wife of his youth she will welcome him."[291] Wisdom is here both "mother" and "wife" and tied to the Torah, which is another feminine word. Proverbs adds the title sister in 7:4, declaring, "Say to wisdom, 'You are my sister,' and call insight your intimate friend . . . ." So, she is not only mother, but sister and wife as well.

Israel and Zion are sometimes portrayed as the wife of Yahweh.[292] The connection to Wisdom inhabiting Israel/Zion can be seen when she chose Israel as Her dwelling. If she inhabited Israel/Zion and is God's wife, she could indirectly be the representation of the Mother of Israel.[293] In this sense, it portrays Yahweh and His wife Wisdom. Supporting this metaphor is a line in 2 Esdras. This is an Apocrypha book believed to have been written sometime in the first century in Hebrew with later Greek additions. In the central part, thought to have been composed early in Hebrew, it says "For Zion, the mother of us all . . . ."[294] This again implies that the concept of a spiritual Mother was present in the first century in Israel. This is evident in the quote earlier brought up where Jesus in Luke's Gospel said, "Yet wisdom is justified by all her children."[295] This necessarily makes Wisdom a mother.

We can further read in Ben Sirach about the earth, another feminine word, as a "mother." It says,

> Much labor was created for every man, and a heavy yoke is upon the sons of Adam, from the day they come forth from their mother's womb till the day they return to the mother of all.[296]

The writer draws a parallel between a human mother who gives physical birth and the earth, whose arms will receive you as a mother in death, echoing Genesis 3:19, "you are dust, and to dust you shall return." Earth is the counterpart to God because His abode is heaven. In this way the "Mother of all" may represent more than the soil we become part of when we die. The earth could parallel heaven and

124

symbolize the divine mother whose spiritual realm you return to once you die.

There is an important early extra Biblical text supporting this notion as well. In the "Dialogue of the Savior," found in Nag Hammadi, we find a nearly identical reference to the "mother of all" in Ben Sirach that matches the meaning suggested there. It is estimated to have reached the final form it has now sometime in the second century. However, because it appears to be a compilation of different textual sources parts of it are believed to have been written as early as "before the end of the first century," making it a significant source for early Christianity.[297] In addition, there are parallels in this text with Matthew, Luke, John, and the gospel of Thomas, and it records sayings between Jesus and three disciples; Matthew, Mary and Judas. So, this is yet another indication of Matthew's importance as well as the female disciple Mary Magdalene. At one point it says,

> [Mary said, "Of what] sort is that [mustard seed]? Is it something from heaven or is it something from earth?" The Lord said, "When the Father established the cosmos for himself, he left much over from the Mother of the All. Therefore, he speaks and he acts."[298]

Here then is a reference to God the Father and Creator of the world/heaven, and His counterpart, the "Mother of all" reflecting earth. By putting them together like this, contrasting and complementing each other, it suggests a deeper meaning, as well as corresponding to what was written in Ben Sirach much earlier.

The phrase "mother of all" with the added word "living" goes back to Genesis where the etymology of Eve's name is explained, "The man called his wife's name Eve, because she was the mother of all living."[299] Eve was created in the image of the divine Mother of All, which is reflected in Eve's name.

We can see precisely this association being drawn in a later relevant fragment except it concerning the Holy Spirit, instead of Wisdom. It was written by an author who was discussing what a Bishop by the name of Methodius (260-312 A.D.) said about the Trinity,

> the innocent and unbegotten Adam being the type and resemblance of God the Father Almighty, who is uncaused, and the cause of all; his begotten son shadowing forth the image of the begotten Son and Word of God; whilst Eve, that proceedeth forth from Adam, signifies the person and procession of the Holy Spirit.[300]

Eve's creation mirrored the Holy Spirit in the same way that the Son reflected Adam and the Father according to this theologian. As such, the Holy Spirit is recognized as a divine Mother, which simultaneously again connects Wisdom and the Holy Spirit as one and the same Divine Feminine. This idea was not a heresy but based on the Hebrew Scriptures.

Deborah was a prophetess and judge of Israel, described in the book of Judges, chapters 4-5. It says that, "until you arose, Deb'orah, arose as a mother in Israel."[301] Her important position as a political leader carried the title "mother." This signals that being a woman in ancient Israel involved more than raising children, cooking meals and other traditionally female chores. Deborah was not famous in Israel because she had children but due to her prominent position as a prophetess and judge, which also suggests that "mother" was an official title for a woman speaking on behalf of God and influencing decisions over the whole nation.

Saint Jerome even mentioned Deborah while commenting on Ezekiel 16:13. Quoting from the Gospel of the Hebrews, which is of the greatest importance, he wrote,

> In the Book of Judges we read "Deborah," which means "bee." Her prophecies are the sweetest honey and refer to the holy spirit, who is called in Hebrew by a feminine noun. In the Gospel of the Hebrews that the Nazarenes read, the Savior indicates this by saying, "Just now my mother, the holy spirit, whisked me away."[302]

This is one of the many instances when Jerome quoted from the Gospel of the Hebrews citing Jesus referring to the Holy Spirit as his Mother. We can speculate that Jerome also drew the conclusion that the prophetess Deborah, a recipient of the Holy Spirit, was called "mother" because it was a reference to the Holy Spirit who was understood by Israel as a the heavenly "Mother."

At another occasion Jerome suggested that the Holy Spirit's femininity was unimportant. In his commentary on Isaiah he had this to say,

> In the Gospel of the Hebrews that the Nazarenes read it says, "Just now my mother, the holy spirit, took me." Now no one should be offended by this, because "spirit" in Hebrew is feminine, while in our language (Latin) it is masculine and in Greek it is neuter. In divinity, however, there is no gender.[303]

Yet, we just saw that when he talked about Deborah on this other occasion it was precisely the Holy Spirit's femininity that was relevant. I doubt anyone would have questioned why Jesus repeatedly called God "my Father" or as he did in the Lord's Prayer, "our Father." The Holy Spirit's gender mattered to Jesus. She also mattered before Jesus' time and in the earliest centuries after him too. It was questioned by Jerome, because the Holy Spirit was a known Divine Feminine, which presented a problem to the developing all-male Trinity. Jerome had to explain it, and tried to defend an all-male Trinity using this particular dismissal of God's feminine aspect. Ironically, Jerome always protected the authority of the Gospel of the Hebrews.

There is something from an extra-Biblical text that must be included here. Cyril of Jerusalem (ca 315-386 A.D.) is recorded in a Coptic text discussing Mary Magdalene and Mary the mother of Jesus, whom he actually claimed was also from the village of Magdalia (Mary Magdalene literally means Mary of Magdalia). After Jesus died, his mother Mary lived with the Apostle John following the two of them adopting each other as mother and son. This was Jesus' way to have his mother taken care of, which he pronounced from the cross.[304] Cyril then describes Mary's last days before she departed to the "Jerusalem of heaven."[305] When Mary prepared for her departure, she called all the virgins to give them ordinances. It says she took the hand of Mary Magdalene, who it says, at this time was very old. According to this text Mary was sixty, and if Mary Magdalene was Jesus' age she would maybe have been in her mid-forties at this time. Mother Mary then announced,

> Behold your mother from this time onwards. Give rest to her spirit, even as she hath given rest to me in my days. Observe the customs which ye arranged to keep with the Christ when ye were with Him.[306]

This reveals a number of things. First, it emphasizes Mary Magdalene's special connection to Jesus. It strongly suggests that there was no other woman, save Mary his mother, closer to Jesus. Not only that, but Mary Magdalene was close to Mary who chose her to inherit her position in this group of devout women. Second, it tells us about a sacred order of women, devoted to the faith and upholding the purity laws, that was instituted by Jesus himself. Thirdly, Mary's position had the title "Mother," which she then passed on to Mary Magdalene. This could have been what eventually developed into the female monasteries where also the title "Mother" is used. This is actually supported in one of Epiphanius' writings where he said that another name of the early Christians was "Jesseans," and according to Jewish Philo of Alexandria (ca 20 B.C.-50 A.D.) there were Jessean monasteries in the first century.[307] This is quite profound. The possibility of Jesus, laying the foundation for a spiritual assembly of women, where the one heading it was called "Mother" speaks volumes about his faith. Aside from showing his support for women, it further enhances the chances of Jesus understanding and believing in the Holy Spirit/Wisdom as a divine Mother.

Jesus calling the Holy Spirit "Mother," as recorded in the Gospel of the Hebrews, does not tell us he used a title grasped out of thin air, which historians therefore can say was unlikely to have happened. Quite the contrary, there is plenty of evidence for where this concept came from. Wisdom and the Holy Spirit were repeatedly linked as one and the same, and calling this feminine power "Mother" was a legitimate aspect of the Hebrew religion. Furthermore, the feminine Hebrew word for "earth" at times served as a symbolic counterpart to God in "heaven." He is Father, and she is Mother. Israel and Zion were figurative manifestations of God's "Wife." Lastly, the feminine word Torah was yet another physical appearance of the feminine counterpart of God manifested on earth.

CHAPTER 4

BELIEFS ABOUT THE
DIVINE FEMININE SPREAD

But there are also many other things which Jesus did; were every
one of them to be written, I suppose that the world itself could not
contain the books that would be written.

John 21:25

RELEVANT EXTRA-BIBLICAL TEXTS

DANIEL, BEN SIRACH, AND DEAD SEA SCROLLS

We have seen how Jesus calling the Holy Spirit his
"Mother" can be traced back to Hebrew Scriptures and
reveal an Israelite traditions for it and, but what happened to
this belief? Did it disappear like the Gospel of the Hebrews,
or did it continue? Was it developed and expanded? Let us
see how interrelated different groups and their manuscripts
were. This is relevant because in the same way, later
Christian texts can be traced back to what Jesus said.
Important to remember in this context is that the Jewish
canon was not closed until sometime in the later first or
second century A.D., and the Christian canon even later as
mentioned in the introduction chapter.

All the books from the Hebrew Bible were found in
the Dead Sea Scrolls except Esther and there were also a vast

amount of other texts. In some of these texts, we can see specific common themes and ideas within early Christianity. A minor example is the expression "tongues of fire" in Acts 2:3. This concept was found in the Dead Sea Scrolls.[356] Another relevant find among the Scrolls was the Book of Ben Sirach written in Hebrew. This book, which belongs to the Apocrypha for Protestants and canon for Catholics, had only been found in the Greek prior to this discovery. It is a crucial book when it comes to elaborating on a personified feminine divine Wisdom. It is also an example of a Greek text where the original Hebrew was not found until the 20th century.

Other noteworthy scripts found were Aramaic fragments from the Books of Enoch dated from between ca 200 B.C. until the start of the new era. Enoch is comprised of several books composed in different times.[357] The first Book of Enoch, which is the oldest, is preserved in its entirety in Ethiopic.[358] The originals were written in Hebrew and/or Aramaic, as found in Qumran.[359] The Books of Enoch entails much about the concept of "the Son of Man," which is frequently found in the New Testament in reference to Jesus. The title "Son of Man" is also present in the Hebrew Scriptures, predominantly in Ezekiel where the prophet himself is referred to in this way. In transliteration the phrase is *ben adam* and simply refers to a human being. Daniel makes use of this title twice, but there is a distinction that is not noticeable in English. Once Daniel refers to himself as *ben adam* just like Ezekiel.[360] However, when he describes the man he saw in his apocalyptic visions, it is in transliteration *bar enosh* and refers to a very particular being.[361] The idea of this heavenly man is also found in the Books of Enoch. Though the specific parts about "the Son of Man" (*bar enosh*) in Enoch correlating to Daniel were not found at Qumran, there is a later Coptic version where the whole book was preserved. It is well recognized by scholars how influential this text was for the Jesus and his followers.

Let me illustrate with an example how the Book of Daniel clearly inspired the Books of Enoch as well Jesus and his followers. Daniel 7:13-14 says,

> I saw in the night visions, and behold, with the clouds of heaven there came one like a son of man, and he came to the Ancient of Days and was presented before him. And to him was given dominion and glory and kingdom, that all peoples, nations, and languages should serve him; his dominion is an everlasting dominion, which shall not pass away, and his kingdom one that shall not be destroyed.

It is not too hard to see how Jesus was understood as the one Daniel described to be "like a son of man."

Here is the Ethiopic version of the first Book of Enoch, chapter 48, "the book of the Similitudes," dated 105-64 B.C.[362] in this we can see more of how ideas originating from Daniel developed in Enoch and how both influenced Jesus and the disciples,

> At that hour, the Son of Man was given a name, in the presence of the Lord of the Spirits, the Before-Time; even before the creation of the sun and the moon, before the creation of the stars, he was given a name in the presence of the Lord of the Spirits. He will become a staff for the righteous ones in order that they may lean on him and not fall. He is the light of the gentiles and he will become the hope of those who are sick in their hearts.[363]

> For this purpose he became the Chosen One; he was concealed in the presence of (the Lord of the Spirits) prior to the creation of the world, and for eternity. And he has revealed the wisdom of the Lord of the Spirits to the righteous and the holy ones, for he has preserved the portion of the righteous because they

> have hated and despised this world of oppression
> (together with) all its ways of life . . . [364]

> In those days, the kings of the earth and the mighty
> landowners shall be humiliated on account of the
> deeds of their hands . . . they shall fall on their faces;
> and they shall not rise up (again), nor anyone (be
> found) who will take them with his hands and raise
> them up. For they have denied the Lord of the Spirits
> and his Messiah. [365]

Daniel calling God "Ancient of Days" correlates with
Enoch's title "Before-Time." The one who is "like the son of
man" in Daniel is given dominion over all people who will
serve him and his kingdom will never be destroyed. In
Enoch those who deny the Messiah/Son of Man (and God)
will not be resurrected. The Enoch texts are Messianic and
proclaim that the Son of Man is the Anointed (Messiah) who
was chosen and existed before the creation of the world. He
was a comforter to the troubled, the righteous, and the
gentiles, while opposing kings and oppressors. This
certainly parallels Jesus.

Some precise similarities exist between beliefs in the
first book of Enoch and the Gospels, because this text also
talks about Wisdom. As we just saw in the second above
cited passage the Son of Man revealed "the wisdom of the
Lord of Spirits" to good people. When "the book of
Similitudes" in the first book of Enoch opens it says,

> The vision which Enoch saw the second time—the
> vision of wisdom which Enoch, son of Jared, son of
> Mahalalel, son of Kenan, son of Enosh, son of Seth,
> son of Adam, saw. This is the beginning of the words
> of wisdom which I commenced to propound . . . [366]

Here is a description of Enoch having an actual vision of Wisdom. In other words, if Enoch could see Wisdom it means she had a shape and was personified. With the way he goes on to describe the "words of wisdom" that he has "received" it further strengthens the description of a divine entity that gave them to him.[367]

In a section of Enoch describing how Wisdom could not find a place to dwell it echoes Ben Sirach where Wisdom wandered, could not find a resting place, and finally God assigned her place to be in Jacob.[368] Here though, Wisdom settled in the heavens, and Iniquity went out. In this same part we can also see where the idea of Wisdom and her children could have derived from. One line goes "Then Wisdom went out to dwell with the children of the people."[369] Luke has, "Yet wisdom is justified by all her children," and Matthew has the almost identical phrase.[370]

Another example of Wisdom in Enoch correlating with Ben Sirach is in the opening of the Son of Man section where it says,

> I saw the fountain of righteousness, which does not become depleted and is surrounded completely by numerous fountains of wisdom. All the thirsty ones drink (of the water) and become filled with wisdom. (Then) their dwelling places become with the holy, righteous, and elect ones.[371]

Compare this with Ben Sirach 15:3 for example where it says of Wisdom, "She will feed him with the bread of understanding, and give him the water of wisdom to drink." This is the same idea about Wisdom and water. We can also see how the idea of Wisdom and her children came from 1 Enoch.

So, the Book of Enoch reveals a relation with the slightly earlier book of Ben Sirach about a personified Wisdom, and this was all written before the time of Jesus.

Because there are clear parallels between the Son of Man in Enoch, Daniel, and the canonical Gospels, this tells us that a belief in a personified Wisdom would likely have been adopted by Jesus and the disciples too.

THE THIRD BOOK OF ENOCH AND SHEKINAH

The third book of Enoch was also written in Hebrew but much later. It is part of Merkabah texts, which was a form of early Jewish mysticism. It has been dated vastly differently by scholars, ranging from parts being from the first century to the entire book being composed in ninth and tenth century.[372] It is attributed to a Rabbi Ishmael who lived in the late first and early second century. In this text, there is a Divine Feminine force called Shekinah. This is a feminine word meaning "divine presence." It is derived from the Hebrew root שכן being škn in transliteration, which means "settle down," "dwell," "abide."[373] In the noun it means "dwelling" and with an added *mem* in front, משכן, it is the name for the tabernacle of God used extensively in Exodus and Numbers.

An illustration of a passage where we find this word is Exodus 40:34. It reads, "Then the cloud covered the tent of meeting, and the glory of the LORD filled the tabernacle." It is the word "tabernacle" that Shekinah is derived from. "Tabernacle," as well as the word "glory," are both masculine words, while Shekinah referring to God's divine presence is the feminine form from the root for "tabernacle." This Hebrew feminine word "Shekinah" does not exist anywhere in the Bible suggesting that someone, or a group of Israelites, specifically put a feminine ending to the word for "dwell," to denote the presence of God. What is important for us is that they made it a feminine manifestation.[374] In this way Shekinah had similar, if not identical, function as the Holy Spirit. In Leviticus it describes how Moses anointed the tabernacle (משכן) and all in it.[375] This is one instance where we can see a possible connection between Shekinah and the Holy Spirit since anointing is linked with the Spirit and the Tabernacle where the idea of Shekinah developed.

In Ben Sirach chapter 24, which explicitly deals with the personified feminine Wisdom, it says in verse 8 that God said to her, "Make your dwelling in Jacob . . . ." A couple lines down in verse 10 it says, "In the holy tabernacle I ministered before him, and so I was established in Zion." The root of Shekinah would be present here in the original Hebrew in "dwelling" and "tabernacle." We can thereby recognize how the idea of Shekinah could be cultivated from Old Testament passages like this. Consequently, the third Book of Enoch, which continued the Enoch tradition, likely drew from Ben Sirach. Both Ben Sirach and 1 Enoch were found in the Dead Sea Scrolls. This helps us understand the development of Shekinah as God's Divine Feminine presence.

SHEKINAH BECOMES ESTABLISHED AND POPULAR

Shekinah was developed in Midrashim literature, and in the Talmud she is the Spirit of God's manifested presence on earth connected to prophecy, inspiration and happiness. Later in medieval Hasidic 'Aškenaz and Spanish Kabbalah, this if further explored. Belief in Shekinah exists to this day. The word "glory" was also developed by these latter mystics with a role similar to Shekinah and the Holy Spirit despite being a masculine word. Jewish texts that the Kabbalah is derived from also personify the Torah as a Goddess.[376]

Shekinah in the Kabbalah as explained today was always part of God, and the one through whom creation was created, metaphorically making her the Mother. God has ten emanations, and in the last one, *Malkuth*, meaning "kingdom," she is present. We can here see the parallels to the Holy Spirit. For example, Jesus said, "unless one is born of water and the Spirit, he cannot enter the kingdom of God."[37] God's Kingdom is intrinsically tied to the Holy Spirit. Shekinah is another sign of the early presence of a more widespread belief in the Divine Feminine as part of the Hebrew religion. The femininity of the Holy Spirit being a prime part of Jesus' teachings was therefore not odd. Shekinah continued to be developed within Judaism, although it was and is not accepted as part of Jewish orthodox monotheistic principles and belongs to the mystical aspect of the faith.

The belief in Shekinah was the Jewish parallel development to the Christian Holy Spirit, and we can see another similarity here with Shekinah not being accepted to what was done to the Holy Spirit's femininity later in Christianity. Though the Holy Spirit retained her prominent position, she was changed. First she became neuter, then later she became male in an all-male Trinity. This silenced the messages and theology her gender carried. The parallels between Jesus and his disciples and the early Enoch texts provide more signs that Jesus and his followers likely declared Wisdom as personified since she was part of the Enoch manuscripts. Shekinah parallels the Holy Spirit and both are identified with Wisdom and all of them, Shekinah, the Holy Spirit, and Wisdom, can be understood as expressions of God's Divine Feminine aspect. I want to emphasize here though that only the Holy Spirit and Wisdom are verified in the Bible. Shekinah is not. It is a development from a masculine word outside of Scripture while the Holy Spirit and Wisdom are originally feminine and Biblical.

DIFFERENT SCHOOLS OF THOUGHT IN EARLY CHRISTIANITY

While mystical texts about the Divine Feminine in the form of Shekinah continued as an offshoot of Judaism, it was not the only path forged for this. In the first few centuries of the Christian era, a whole plethora of texts and beliefs about this subject, taking many different forms, developed from sects/schools that grew and drew from the earliest Christian sources as well as the Hebrew Scriptures. Although they developed many beliefs that deviated from Christianity and the Hebrew Scriptures, they are a vital historical aspect to study for numerous reasons. The first is their ideas about a Divine Feminine, because this view was not something they just made up.

Most, though not all, remaining traces of a divine mother were found in the Nag Hammadi library discovered in Egypt 1945. These texts are classified by modern scholars as being Gnostic, derived from the feminine Greek word *gnosis*, which means "knowledge." I mentioned Gnosticism earlier but want to reiterate here that this is a term scholars use today to describe these beliefs. It was also used early on, but not in the same way as it is done today. Epiphanius wrote in the late fourth century about "Gnostics" as one sect among many, and sadly the Nag Hammadi texts are clumped together today under the old heading negatively applied to heretical sects. Since *gnosis* means "knowledge" and was used to initially refer to a secret/initiated type of knowledge, it was also an early association to the "Nazarenes."

Early in Christianity, different ideas were referenced by the name of the one who developed and promoted them. Valentinus (ca 100-175 A.D.) was an influential theologian who started his own school and one example of such a person.[378] He believed procreation was impossible on the divine level without a female and added a spouse to the Father called "Sige."[379] The gospel of Truth and the gospel of Philip are believed to be productions of the Valentinian School. In the early days after Paul, Peter, and Jacob (James) were martyred and the Temple fell, the official Catholic Church was still forming, there were an array of Christian groups. This is also supported by how different the various texts that have been found are. Significant for us is that many of these texts developed the feminine presence. In a way, one could say these Christian authors, as well as Jewish writing about Shekinah, were early feminists. Since their ideas were derived from Biblical texts, the same claim can be made for the Bible. The major difference between those who wrote about the Divine Feminine then and the feminist movement that developed nearly two millennia later, is that the ancient one was perpetuated by men. Most of all, these devout Christian writers championed the feminine aspect more than anyone in Christianity has done since.

THE BOOK OF GIANTS

There is a manuscript called the Book of Giants, which was also found in the Dead Sea Scrolls validating its antiquity. It was preserved by a group called the Manichaeans, whose founder was a Persian man called Mani that lived in the third century in Babylon and spoke a form of Aramaic. This group believed in Jesus as the Messiah but did not think he was divine. St. Augustine was Manichaean before he converted to Orthodox Christianity. Mani was a dualist like Zoroastrians who believed in one good God and one evil.

Relevant for us is their belief in the Divine Feminine. In an excerpt from their texts, her origin was explained this way, "Now he, the glorious Father, summoned from him

139

three emanations. The first is the Great Spirit, the first Mother, who came out of the Father.[380] Another illustration of their belief in her is found in a manuscript he wrote called the Living Gospel. It goes as follows,

> the Maiden of Light, head of all wisdoms. It was praised and is praised, the holy church, by the power of the Father, by the praise of the Mother, and (by the wisdom of the son), and on the speakers and hearers of the true word.[381]

So, Manichaeans adhered to a belief in a Heavenly feminine force. St. Augustine related many things about them. For instance, they were vegetarians, did not drink wine, and believed plants and trees could feel pain when injured.[382] These things support the likelihood of John the Baptist, Jesus and his inner circle having similar ideas about a divine Mother.

THE APOSTLE THOMAS AND INDIA

Early testimonies say that the Apostle Thomas evangelized India, and Bartholomew brought the Hebrew Gospel of Matthew to India, wherefore I want to address some passages from the Apocryphal text of "the acts of Thomas." This is not one of the manuscripts from Nag Hammadi, but it is usually classified as belonging to the same theological category. Acts of Thomas is an early writing that has been preserved in both Greek and Syriac.[383] It is of great antiquity and was already known in the first and second century.[384] This script, ascribed to Thomas, reflects how the Gospel tradition brought to India was based on Hebrew texts, not Greek, because of what it says concerning the Holy Spirit.

First, in this text Thomas baptizes with oil and not water, which is in line with a belief emphasizing the Holy Spirit. For this reason it was understood by many as heretical. Yet, John the Baptist proclaimed that he baptized with the water of repentance, but Jesus with the Holy Spirit and fire.[385] Shem-Tob's Matthew said "fire of the Holy Spirit," which also makes more sense because lamps in those days were literally olive oil burning. Thus oil was symbolic of the Holy Spirit because she represents light.[386] Oil was, then and now, used for anointing and signifies the presence of the Holy Spirit. Fire, oil was symbolic of the Holy Spirit because she represents light. Therefore, baptizing with oil would be both a sign of following Jesus and the presence of the Holy Spirit.

Moreover, there is a bridal song in this manuscript sung by Thomas at a wedding. It ends like this, "and they glorified and praised, with the living spirit the Father of Truth, and the Mother of Wisdom."[387] Wisdom as a Divine Feminine aspect of God could not be more obvious. This line has been understood to refer to the Gnostic Trinity. Yet, it would be a bit odd calling Jesus "the living spirit." Maybe the "living Spirit" was not a reference to Jesus but meant to define the Father of Truth *and* the Mother of Wisdom; a duality that can also be understood as One, especially if this song was older than the rest of the text. This manuscript also claims that Jesus is "the God of all" and "the Father of truth," which signals the Trinitarian ideas.[388] However, Father, Mother and Son depict a family, but the later construction of the Trinity did not do so. It was an all-male entity in an attempt to preserve monotheism. The parts proclaiming Jesus is God could also be is a sign of later reworking of the text as it circulated.

It is specifically mentioned in this text that Thomas spoke in Hebrew. The only one who understood him in India was a flute girl who happened to be a Hebrew. Later the Apostle is anointing a king and his brother with the seal of the Holy Spirit through oil. While he does, he proclaim these words,

> Come, holy name of Christ that is above every name;
> Come, power of the most high and perfect compassion;
> Come, highest gift;
> Come, compassionate mother;
> Come, fellowship of the male;
> Come, you that reveals the hidden mysteries;
> Come, mother of the seven houses, that your rest may be in the eighth house;
> Come, elder messenger of the five members—understanding, thought, prudence, consideration, reasoning,
> Communicate with these young men!
> Come, Holy Spirit, and purify their reins and their heart
> And give them the added seal in the name of the Father and Son and Holy Spirit.[389]

The attributes of the Holy Spirit in line eight and nine in this poem reminds us of Wisdom. The word "understanding" is virtually synonymous with Wisdom in the Wisdom texts, and the other meanings rings true of her as well. A fresh reminder is for example Proverbs, who list Wisdom's many characteristics and at one point quotes Wisdom herself saying "I, wisdom, dwell in prudence, and I find knowledge and discretion."[390] The Holy Spirit and Wisdom are repeatedly the ones who enter into people and cause them to do all that is right and good, which positively cements them as one and the same. She is again the one who reveals, "hidden mysteries." Additionally, this text definitely correlates with the Gospel of the Hebrews. The seal invokes first Christ, then the Father, and the rest is about the Mother, who is identified as the Holy Spirit.

The very last line in the above song, "And give them the added seal *in the name of the Father and Son and Holy Spirit*" (my italics) is identical to the second final verse in the canonical Gospel of Matthew where it says "Go therefore and make disciples of all nations, baptizing them *in the name of the Father and of the Son and of the Holy Spirit*" (my italics).[391] As I mentioned earlier, this has often been understood as a later interpolation or a sign of Matthew's late authorship because of what is seen as a Trinitarian formula, which is otherwise not an idea expressed in the New Testament. It was also noticed by scholar F.C. Conybeare nearly a century ago that when Eusebius of Caesarea quoted this last part of Matthew, sixteen times the Trinitarian formula and the baptismal command were always missing.[392] This then would suggest it was not an original part of the Gospel. There can be explanations such as Eusebius simply having skipped that part, plus the wording of the baptismal formula necessarily representing the later Trinitarian doctrine. It could just be a command to baptize in the name of these *three*: God *and* Jesus *and* the Holy Spirit. If it did not include the later notions of same substance but different personas, it does not have to characterize a later authorship. Thomas could have brought this formula with him when he travelled to India to evangelize. In other words, the presence of this phrase in both Matthew's Gospel and Acts of Thomas could instead be a sign of its antiquity.

This baptismal expression, where the Father, the Spirit, and the Son are all joined, is likewise found in other early sources. One of those supporting that it was done in all three names is called "the Didache."[393] This text is remarked on by Eusebius as part of the works that some accepted as canonical and others did not. The text itself was a modern discovery found 1873 in its complete form in a convent in

Istanbul.[394] Written in Greek, it is "widely understood as citing either Matthew's Gospel or some combination of the Matthean or Lucan traditions."[395] This in itself may mean it has strong relations to the Gospel of the Hebrews. Because of this, the date of composition is believed by some to be later than the standard dates for Matthew and Luke, i.e. later than around 80 A.D. Estimates range between mid-first century to late second century. It is mostly placed at the turn of the first century A.D.,[396] which relies heavily on the belief that it draws from especially Matthew's Gospel. Since all the Synoptic Gospels are dated rather late, around 70-80 A.D., academics place other, possibly interrelated, texts after that. This may be inaccurate, and many scholars dispute the Didache or gospel of Thomas' reliance on any canonical Gospel, believing it is written independently of them.[397] Whether you believe that or not, this text is a potentially quite significant source.

> The Baptismal formula in the Didache is as follows,
> (And) concerning baptism, baptize thus: Having said all these things beforehand, immerse in the name of the Father and of the Son and of the holy Spirit in flowing water– if, on_the_other_hand, you should not have flowing water, immerse in other water [that is available]; (and) if you are not able in cold, [immerse] in warm [water]; (and) if you should not have either, pour out water onto the head three times in the name of [the] Father and [the] Son and [the] holy Spirit.[398]

Here then we conceivably have this possibly extraordinarily early source for the phrase to be used in baptism, which include all three: Yahweh, the Holy Spirit and Jesus.

Another script that some scholars believe originated in the first century, while others deem it later, is called "Recognitions." Reportedly authored by Clement, who knew Peter and was one of the earliest to succeed him as

Bishop of Rome, it tells of one occasion when Jacob (James) the brother of Jesus and first Bishop of Jerusalem defended Jesus to be the Christ at the Temple. While doing so he said that,

> . . . unless a man be baptized in water, in the name of the threefold blessedness, as the true Prophet taught, he can neither receive remission of sins nor enter into the kingdom of heaven; and he declared that this is the prescription of the unbegotten God.[399]

Again, expressing these three names does not automatically make it Trinitarian. What it does imply though is that this wording helped defend the case for the later Trinitarian creeds. Acts of Thomas testifies that anointing followers with oil instead of water while using this formula was another form of valid baptism.

If what is referred to as the "Trinitarian formula" in Matthew as well as Acts of Thomas was indeed added later, it could reveal an internal strife between baptizing with oil versus water. As the early church formed, it was perhaps not too long after Jesus' passing that disciples more officially articulated how baptism should be done the way it is specified in the Didache.[400] But again, debates about the baptismal formula did not necessitate a Trinitarian belief. The emphasis on baptism to be in *three* names can simply be just that: include all three when you baptize. If, as many academics suggest, the baptismal formula was inserted in Matthew later, it might be somewhat far-fetched that it would end up affixed to Acts of Thomas to justify baptism with oil.

It is important here to remember that the focus on the "Trinitarian formula" can detract from what is needed to be "saved" which is the internal change, not the various rituals. Jesus followed the baptismal formula up with in Matthew 28:20, "teaching them to observe all that I have commanded you . . . " because without it, baptism has no effect. Baptism symbolized the washing away of sins after repentance, just as anointing with oil represented the Holy Spirit's presence. However, these things were not magical tools that changed someone, but physical enactments of what had or was taking place inside spiritually. We all know people who have been baptized and anointed but are not righteous or Bible believing Christians. What matters for this outer ritual to have significance is the internal change. Speaking about the need for a spiritual birth, Jesus said, "unless one is one is born anew, he cannot see the kingdom of God."[401] Jesus did of course not minimize or negate baptism, but he emphasized the teachings that will lead you to an inward change, not the rituals accompanying this. Because Jesus' teachings are true, they will lead to God if you follow them and receive the Holy Spirit. This is therefore the most important element.

The New Testament itself plus a variety of early historical texts are full of tales about the disciples' travels in order to evangelize. All these texts allow us to see there was a specific tradition that linked; Thomas, Bartholomew, Matthew, India and the Gospel of the Hebrews. It preserved the Hebrew form of the Holy Spirit as not only a feminine word, but as a divine Mother.

VARIOUS EXTRA BIBLICAL, CHRISTIAN TEXTS ALL FEATURING A HEAVENLY MOTHER

Acts of Thomas was not an isolated incident in having a concept of a divine Mother, but it was a trend that was quite extensive. In many early Christian texts, there was a re-occurring theme of a celestial Mother accompanying the divine Father. It can be misleading to call them all Gnostic texts today, because they did not all come from the same place or source. Some were deemed heretical by different church fathers, yet others were not condemned by early church fathers and were popular such as Shepherd of Hermas.

The Divine Feminine was prominently featured in Christianity's initial stages even if those texts were not canonized Biblical texts. Even if various Christian sects developed ideas that deviated from the Gospels and included stories about Jesus later that cannot be considered historical, many of their ideas were established from legitimate sources. They can be traced back to the Hebrew Scriptures, and they drastically raise the chances of Jesus having the Holy Spirit as a Divine Feminine aspect of God being part of his teachings. The fact that this is such a strong feature in these Christian historical texts tells us these ideas did not develop out of thin air.

A Christian text suggested to be from around 140-180 A.D. called the "Gospel of Truth" elaborates on the Word and its totality.[402] It says that it is, "purifying them, bringing them back into the Father, into the Mother, Jesus of the infinite sweetness."[403] The Father's bosom is the Holy Spirit and Jesus is what was hidden, now revealed.[404]

There is one early manuscript found at Nag Hammadi called the "The Secret book of James," which claimed to have been written in Hebrew. Therein Jesus is quoted saying, "Become better than I; be like the son of the holy spirit!"[405] We are used to the phrase "Son of God" where God of course is the "Father," but here we have a roundabout way of calling the Holy Spirit "Mother" since the text claimed to have been written in Hebrew where the Holy Spirit is feminine. For this reason the phrase "son of the Holy Spirit" makes it a necessary grammatical conclusion that the Holy Spirit is a "Mother." It was also likely the intent.

The "Apocryphon of John," whose main compositions existed before 185 A.D.,[406] has some complicated stories regarding creation, God, and numerous heavenly beings that have clearly wandered off from the historical Jesus' teachings. Still, there are traces of important information. It opens up describing a Pharisee approaching John, the son of Zebedee, at the Temple asking him where Jesus, his master, had gone. John told him he went back from where he came, and then the Pharisee said that "this Nazarene" deceived them.[407] Following this interaction John goes to the desert full of grief and questions. The heavens open up, and Jesus comes to give him instructions about the past, present, and future. John quotes Jesus saying he is the Father, Mother, and Son; thereby connecting the Divine Feminine Power to the faith. Following a long grandiose description of God, John says that, "the Monad [is a] monarchy with nothing above it."[408] It then says about God that "he is more than a god, since there is nothing above him."[409] By doing so the author is acknowledging other "gods" but distinguishing them from "the God." Then it describes this,

> And [his thought performed] a deed and she came forth, [namely] she who had [appeared] before him in [the shine of] his light. This is the first [power which was] before all of them (and) [which came] forth from his mind, She [is the forethought of the All] – her light [shines like his] light – the [perfect] power which is [the] image of the invisible, virginal Spirit who is perfect.[410]

This inevitably reminds us of the Wisdom texts, which describes her as God's first creation or emanation, and a reflection, or radiance, of His light and an image of his goodness.[411] It continues saying, "she became the womb of everything for it is she who is prior to them all."[412] It then lists several titles beginning with the "Mother-Father" and among them also "the first man" and "the holy Spirit" and "thrice male.[413] We can certainly see how it was written later and in Greek caused confusion by the change of language along with the emerging Trinitarian ideas. The feminine aspect of God is preserved and thoroughly presented yet simultaneously the Holy Spirit can be seen as male, revealing later influences from Greek and Latin. She is here called "Barbelo," and though she here is a mix of several identities, the point is the text tells of an original heavenly feminine Power.[414] The Mother-Father concept occurs numerous times in this text, as does, Mother-Father-Son. The text is full of complex explanations focused on the origins of the divine entities. In it all, the divine Mother plays a prominent role.

Christ is described as the "word" and the "light" following Johannine tradition.[415] This is introduced later than the feminine aspect signifying that she came first. The Holy Spirit is also called "the mother of the living"[416] and Sophia (the Greek word for Wisdom) is likewise called, "Life, which is the mother of the living, by the foreknowledge of the sovereignty of heaven."[417] Though the Holy Spirit and Wisdom are here sometimes described as the same deity, and other times not, this is one instance suggesting they are. Sophia is also called "Sophia of the Epinoia."[418] Eve was considered the "counter-image" of Adam and she was created in the likeness of "Epinoia"[419] So, Eve was reportedly formed in the image of a female deity, Wisdom, not Father God.[420]

The Apocryphon of John digresses from Scripture in several major ways regarding a number of issues in its vivid expansions on creation. Eloim (Elohim) and Yave (Yahweh) do not represent God as in Hebrew Scripture but are two sons of Eve (or Epinoia, the text is dubious).[421] Another example is that it interprets Epinoia to be the Tree of

Knowledge of Good and Evil becoming part of Adam as his rib and who caused them to eat of its fruit.[422] It takes quite some effort to keep up with the many elaborate accounts and intricate details which at times are hard to make sense of. Despite this there are core ideas taken from the Wisdom books. For instance, we can find the first created feminine emanation of God and the duality of male-female Power in the heavenly realm. Likewise present are concepts such as the Holy Spirit as Mother, a heavenly marriage of a divine male and female and parallels between the Holy Spirit and Wisdom.

There is another text that deals exclusively with Sophia. It is a letter from a teacher to his pupils. It is believed a Christian took the letter, copied and changed in places, and renamed it "the Sophia of Jesus Christ."[423] It was possibly composed as early as the latter part of the first century A.D. in Egypt, which makes it important to look at.[424] Here Sophia is the female name of the Son of God. She is "First Begettress Sophia, Mother of the Universe," who some call "Love."[425] She was the counterpart of Jesus though, not God. Particularly interesting to note in this manuscript is that it only mentions Philip, Matthew, Thomas, Bartholomew as Apostles, who, with their connections to India and the Hebrew Gospel, are the same Apostles having ties to the Divine Feminine. It also talks about Mary Magdalene and Mary, the mother of Jesus. These two women played the most significant roles in Jesus' life according to the canonical Gospels.

Another manuscript in this genre is called "The Teachings of Silvanus." It is dated to the late third century but includes traditions that could go back as far as the first century. Found in Nag Hammadi in Coptic, it is believed by scholars to have been originally written in Greek.[426] It elaborates on Wisdom and even though it states that Christ is the Wisdom of God, it also describes her the way she is depicted in the Wisdom books. At one point it says,

> My child, return to your first father, God, and Wisdom, your mother, from whom you came into being from the beginning. Return, that you might fight against all of your enemies, the power of the adversary.[427]

Wisdom is personified as our heavenly Mother, while making the fusion between her and the Holy Spirit all the more obvious. It was not a far out fringe belief but was seen as legit because of what the Hebrew Scriptures teach about Wisdom.

I earlier quoted from "Recognitions," another manuscript assigned to Clement of Rome is called "Clementine homilies," which has a disputed age of origin but is possibly an early source. It consists primarily of the teachings of Peter, after Jesus has passed, but touches on the Divine Feminine too. When discussing the creation story and the "beginning" Peter said, "and the Spirit of God was borne above the waters. Which Spirit, at the bidding of God, as it were His hand, makes all things, dividing light from darkness."[428] The Spirit is described as a separate being that is "borne" and follows God's orders. We can here see a link between God's hand and the Spirit too, which was discussed earlier. Shortly thereafter, speaking of water, Peter says,

> ". . . water makes all things, and water receives the production of its movement from spirit, and the spirit has its beginning from the God of all. And thus you ought to have reasoned, in order that by reason you might attain to God, that, knowing your origin, and being born again by the first-born water, you may be constituted heir of the parents who have begotten you to incorruption."[429]

The Spirit has "its beginnings from the God of all" and when you are baptized and born-again he speaks of "parents," i.e. the divine Mother and Father, who have now spiritually begotten you.

Later Peter is making instructions about the Golden Rule and what it entails to love your neighbor as yourself. He said, "this perfect love towards every man is the male part of philanthropy, but the female part of it is compassion . . . ."[430] He proceeds to list things, which constitute showing "compassion on him who is in misfortune" such as feeding the hungry and clothing the naked.[431] Again, we see the duality of the feminine and masculine displayed. Expounding on the doctrine of philanthropy Peter said it was possible through the fear of God. Then he said, when one does deeds of love,

> ". . . the bride LOVE is, as it were, brought to the bridegroom FEAR. And thus this bride, bringing forth philanthropic thoughts, makes her possessor immortal, as an accurate image of God, which cannot be subjected in its nature to corruption."[432]

Once more we see the feminine and the masculine as complementary forces. The bride is the Spirit, and here the bridegroom symbolizes the believers who become transformed by her.

Particularly noteworthy for us is what was written about the pre-Christian Jewish Ossaeans and their later leader called Elxai. Judging by the name "Ossaeans" alone, it is possible that they were related to the Essenes, perhaps an offshoot sect. Elxai was a follower of Jesus, who lived around a century after Jesus' death, and he believed the Holy Ghost was feminine in line with the Hebrew language. When Epiphanius wrote about him in the 4th century the language switch from Hebrew to Greek had already taken place. Thus, the Holy Spirit had been neutered whereby the specific mention of the Holy Spirit's femininity is important. His name meant hidden (xai) Power (El). The Ossaeans observed the Sabbath, kept the whole Law, practiced circumcision and rejected both sacrifice and the eating of meat. Elxai and his followers believed that Christ was a man, invisible to the eye, with very specific huge proportions. Opposite him was the Holy Spirit, with the same dimensions, except in the form of a female.[433] By all indications Elxai's name, "hidden power," is a reference to the Holy Spirit. Elxai was additionally associated with Nazoraeans and Ebionites.

Jesus shared a number of specific customs and beliefs with Jewish groups who were around just before and after he lived such as the Essenes. For instance, the authors of the Dead Sea Scrolls were both apocalyptic and adhered to Wisdom teachings. The beatitudes is an example of Jesus as a Wisdom-teacher[434] and some previously unknown Wisdom texts were found in Qumran that according to scholars demonstrate a particular similarity to these. Here is a short excerpt from one:

> Blessed are those who seek her with pure hands, and do not pursue her with a treacherous heart. Blessed is the man who has attained Wisdom, and walks in the Law of the Most High. He directs his heart towards her ways, and restrains himself by her corrections, and always takes delight in her chastisements.[435]

This shows a strong resemblance to the beatitudes while it contains the familiar Biblical Hebrew way of describing Wisdom; a personified feminine force who is tied to the Law.[436]

Other sects with particular parallels were the just mentioned Ossaeans, the Nasaraeans, the Nazoraeans and the Ebionites. Since we know that the Nazarenes and the Ebionites both adhered to the Gospel of the Hebrews, and

Elxai from the Ossaeans understood the Holy Spirit as a feminine divine power, Jesus speaking about the Holy Spirit as his Mother would not be strange. All of this gives us a window into the theological significance the feminine Holy Spirit had in ancient Israelites. She was understood as a personal force that was God's active Power on earth and her femininity was not a grammatical side note.

The entire New Testament itself testifies to the prominent role the Holy Spirit takes for Jesus compared to the Hebrew Scriptures. Christians are so used to it that most barely reflect on how the emphasis on the Holy Spirit is not an obvious continuum of most of the Old Testament and how it differs from Orthodox Judaism. You see her if you search deeper and know the Hebrew language and once you understand that she is Lady Wisdom who is openly present. But, since nearly everyone neglects the personified Wisdom she remains "hidden." Still, all this tells us that Jesus calling the Holy Spirit "my Mother" is highly likely to have taken place. Hopefully new discoveries await us that will lend more knowledge about Jesus' belief in the Holy Spirit as our Mother.

The last illustration I want to give in this section is from a book called the "Shepherd of Hermas." When introducing it in her book scholar Carolyn Osick wrote, "no other noncanonical writing was as popular before the fourth century as the *Shepherd of Hermas*."[437] It contains numerous teachings on how to live the right way versus the wrong, has apocalyptic elements and warns of what will happen to those who do not follow God's Law. It is believed to have been written in Greek, in Italy, within a timeframe stretching from the late first century to the first part of the second century.[438] Clement of Alexandria, Origen in Egypt, Irenaeus in Gaul, Hippolytus, Jerome, Augustine, Eusebius were among those who had a positive view on. Additionally, it was attached to Codex Sinaiticus.[439] Some believe it was written in stages by different people; others by one single author albeit using material from several sources.[440] There is a general agreement that the first section (1-4), which is the one mostly relevant for us, is the oldest.[441]

The content in Shepherd of Hermas is a series of visions received by a former slave called Hermas. It opens up with an incident and apparition of the woman he was sold to many years earlier. Just shortly after he has a vision of an "older woman in a shining robe."[442] This elder Lady comes back to him repeatedly. At one point Hermas had a revelation in a dream where a young man came to him and asked if he knew who this elder lady was. Hermas said, "The sybil" (a female prophetess) and the man said, "Wrong."[443] This is the conversation that proceeded,

> "Then who is she?" I asked. "The church," he said. I said to him: "Then why is she elderly?" "Because," he said, "she was created before everything. That is why she is elderly, and for her the world was established."[444]

The word "church" in Greek is *ekklesia* and literally refers to the "assembly" of believers. The concept of the believers being "created before everything" is not found elsewhere but Lady Wisdom, on the other hand, was created first according to the wisdom books.[445] In Ephesians Paul speaks of the church as the Bride of Christ[446] and he says this among other things,

> To me, though I am the very least of all the saints, this grace was given, to preach to the Gentiles the unsearchable riches of Christ, and to make all men see what is the plan of the mystery hidden for ages in God who created all things; that through the church the manifold wisdom of God might now be made known to the principalities and powers in the heavenly places.[447]

The church represents the Wisdom of God because Wisdom is present in believers. As shown several times, Wisdom was said to take her place in Jacob, Israel was her dwelling.[448] Believers see and understand hidden mysteries, and Wisdom is therefore revealed through the church. While expounding on the church as the body of Christ, Paul wrote in Ephesians 5:29-32,

> For no man ever hates his own flesh, but nourishes and cherishes it, as Christ does the church, because we are members of his body. "For this reason a man shall leave his father and mother and be joined to his wife, and the two shall become one flesh." This mystery is a profound one, and I am saying that it refers to Christ and the church . . .

Christ as the bridegroom and the Church as the bride is a symbolism present in the early Christian church. Her appearance as a bride and the church is likewise present not only in the New Testament but other early texts too. Yet, in Shepherd of Hermas the church is more than the body of Christ: she is fused with the Divine Feminine aspect. What is quite profound here is that not only is Wisdom personified, but he saw her in the figure of a woman. This Lady further appeared in different ages, which reflected certain elements in Hermas that was explained to him.[449] She appeared as a bride that came forth from the bridal chamber commending him for trusting in God completely and not being double minded, a topic heavily emphasized in this text.[450] Wisdom/Holy Spirit, representing the Church, seen in visions as a heavenly woman reveals her feminine gender and personhood in a crystal clear way in the text.

The Lady tells Hermas a parable about a tower. She herself is the tower (the Church), which was built on water and "founded by the word of the almighty and glorious name, and is sustained by the unseen power of the master."[451] There were six young men building the tower who were holy angels of God, created first, and all creation was turned over to them "to increase, build up, and govern."[452] However, later she also showed him seven women around the tower. These were the ones sustaining it. Each one was the daughter of the previous one, and the first one was called "Faith." The others in subsequent order are "Restraint." Simplicity," "Innocence," "Reverence," "Knowledge," and lastly "Love."[453] It says of these that, "When you do all the works of their mother, you can live."[454] The use of "mother" here is yet another occasion for the spiritual use of this term within the early Christian faith.

Now in the third part of this book, Similitudes, the tower is addressed again, and the Archangel Michael appears. However, since it was possibly written by someone else, or derived from another source, I want to address this section separately. Note that while there were six men there are seven women. The foundation of the tower was, "the word of the almighty and glorious name, and is sustained by the unseen power of the master." We can read this to mean that Jesus is the "Word" and God the "almighty and glorious name" and "the master." But, in light of the complete absence of Logos-theology here, it likely only refers to God. The Mother "Faith" being the founding Mother of the others could therefore be understood to correspond to the Father, which would make the other six young women correlate in number to the six young men.[455] Observe too how both the young men (angels) and young women (virtues) were essential in the tower's existence. It is telling us that the church needs a female-male balance.

After the visitations Hermas has from this Lady, the part of this manuscript believed to be the oldest ends. He then begins to be guided by a shepherd. At one point the shepherd tells him, "The son is the Holy Spirit. The slave is the Son of God."[456] The shepherd explains that the world is a vineyard where the Son labors hard to purify people's sins, showing them the paths of life and giving people the Law that God had given him. The slave/servant (same word in Greek) concept is present in the New Testament, used by Jesus as a metaphor for being free from sin or in bondage to it, and similarly professed by Paul.[457] The Son as The Holy Spirit is not something present anywhere in the New Testament. We can shortly see how this is a figure of speech meaning he has the Holy Spirit. The shepherd proceeded to explain,

> The preexistent Holy Spirit, which created all that was created, God made to dwell in the chosen flesh. This flesh, in which the Holy Spirit dwelt, served the spirit well, living in a manner distinguished and pure, in no way defiling the spirit. Because it conducted itself well and with purity, cooperating with the spirit and working with it in every respect, acting stoutly and bravely, God chose it as partner for the Holy Spirit. For the behavior of this flesh pleased God because it was not defiled while it bore the Holy Spirit on earth. So he took the son and the noble angels as counselors, to the effect that this flesh, which had served the spirit without blame, should have some dwelling place, and not seem to have lost the reward for its service. For all flesh in which the Holy Spirit has dwelt, which is found to be undefiled and spotless, will receive its reward.[458]

When deconstructed, the passage means that the Holy Spirit took her place in Jesus, not that Jesus actually is the Holy Spirit. Plus, any flesh that the Holy Spirit dwells in must be pure, and will receive its reward, meaning Jesus is not the only flesh that the Holy Spirit is dwelling in. Furthermore, it is the Holy Spirit that is pre-existing and through whom creation was created.

The last chapters of this manuscript have a very different tone and style, suggesting a different authorship.[459] Keep in mind it has just been specifically explained by the Shepherd that the elder Lady, called the church, is the Holy Spirit. Despite this, the Shepherd later says to Hermas, "I want to show you whatever the Holy Spirit showed you, who spoke with you in the form of the church, because that spirit is the Son of God."[460] We can perhaps try to apply the former explanation here that Jesus had the Holy Spirit but it gets muddier further on. Later it is stated that "The Son of God was born before all his creation, so as to be counselor to the Father about creation."[461] There are now apparent changes between the earliest and the later parts. The focus is at first all on the Lady, who is the church and bride, while the Son of God is not even mentioned. Then she is identified with the Holy Spirit and pre-existent. However, she can be called the Son of God because she dwelt in Jesus. Towards the end, it is the Son of God who is born before all creation instead of her, and she is not even present in such an important passage. This sequence mirrors the development that happened within the church itself with regards to the Holy Spirit/Wisdom and Jesus, which later led to and culminated in the concept of the male Trinity.

The important part is that the Holy Spirit was understood early on as feminine and personified. In the Shepherd of Hermas, she was revealed in the form of a woman in vivid and profound visions. She gave Hermas long detailed teachings about how to have complete faith in God. This combined with the popularity and recognition of this text is in itself telling of the early acknowledgment of the Holy Spirit as an unmistakable Divine Feminine power. As we continue to the next segment I want to add that these early texts featuring the Heavenly feminine are a few examples among many more. I will discuss one more because of its particular relevance to this topic which entails enough to warrant its own heading.

To sum up this segment, the Holy Spirit and Wisdom were personified and featured as no less than a divine Mother in numerous early writings. Some are today deemed heretical and referred to as Gnostic texts and other manuscripts are just extra Biblical texts. Whether we see them as invalid or valid, the writers saw themselves as Christians. For this reason it seems highly likely that Jesus declaring, in the Gospel of the Hebrews, the Holy Spirit as his Mother strongly appears to have sent vast ripple effects in the faith. While all Christians believed in the Holy Spirit we can see a later divergence on this matter between those who retained the femininity of the Spirit and those who did not. It was the latter group that later came to require that priests and bishops should be unmarried and later morphed the Spirit into the male Trinity. In this sense, the understanding as well as the misunderstanding, of the Holy Spirit's gender had concrete consequences.

THE GOSPEL OF PHILIP

The Apostle Philip was part of the group described in "the Sophia of Jesus Christ" along with Matthew, Thomas, and Bartholomew. We can see traces of his connections to them elsewhere too. Acts of Thomas starts off with the disciples being together in Jerusalem dividing the regions of the world to go out and evangelize. When they are named, Philip, Bartholomew, Thomas and Matthew are counted up one after another in that order just like in the canonical Gospels.[462] Philip is said to later live in a house in Caesarea and perhaps it was even he who brought the Gospel of the

Hebrews to the library there where Jerome much later said it still resided.[463]

There is also a gospel of Philip estimated to have been written in the second half of the third century A.D. It may have Syriac (Aramaic) origins because of how the writer expounds on the language and what words mean in Syriac throughout the text and other "Eastern sacramental practice and catecheses, and its ascetic ethics."[464] The author discusses many subjects pertinent to the Divine Feminine and it seems he had several collections of writings handed down to him that he mixed in with his own commentaries. This gospel was not written by the Apostle himself, but probably named so because Philip is the only Apostle mentioned by name in it. The writer refers to the Apostles in third person and to himself as someone who was anointed by them.[465] Note the word "anointed," because it will be the first topic of discussion as we see what we can learn from this manuscript and its relation to the Divine Feminine. In fact, the oldest surviving Christian inscription from the 2nd century found in Rome is linked by scholars to the Gospel of Philip, because it mentions "the bridal chamber," which is often present in this text.

DUAL BAPTISM - WATER & ANOINTING WITH OIL

In light of the earlier mentioned scenario of baptism being done with oil instead of water in the Acts of Thomas, the gospel of Philip proclaims, "it is from the olive tree that we get the chrism, and from the chrism, the resurrection."[466] It goes on to say,

> The chrism is superior to baptism, for it is from the word "chrism" that we have been called "Christians," certainly not because of the word "baptism." And it is because of the chrism that "the Christ" has his name.

> For the father anointed the son, and the son anointed
> the apostles, and the apostles anointed us. He who
> has been anointed possesses everything. He possesses
> the resurrection, the light, the cross, the holy spirit.[467]

"Chrism" is the Greek word for "anointing" and correlates
to the Hebrew term "messiah." which is the adjectival form
of the word meaning "anointed one." Here then, we see a
clear comparison of the two rites of baptism, and anointing
with oil, "the chrism," is far more valued and gives you
access to the Holy Spirit. Peter said in Acts 2:38 "Repent, and
be baptized every one of you in the name of Jesus Christ for
the forgiveness of your sins; and you shall receive the gift of
the Holy Spirit." The meaning of baptism was a three part
event; repentance, forgiveness, and receiving the Holy Spirit.

Being baptized with the Holy Spirit was not used as a
figure of speech though but was done ritually like the one in
water. In Acts 19:2-7 when Paul was talking to some
disciples in Ephesus it says,

> And he said to them, "Did you receive the Holy Spirit
> when you believed?" And they said, "No, we have
> never even heard that there is a Holy Spirit." And he
> said, "Into what then were you baptized?" They said,
> into John's baptism." And Paul said, "John baptized
> with the baptism of repentance, telling the people to
> believe in the one who was to come after him, that is,
> Jesus." On hearing this, they were baptized in the
> name of the Lord Jesus. And when Paul had laid his
> hands upon them, the Holy Spirit came on them; and
> they spoke with tongues and prophesied. There were
> about twelve of them in all.

This shows us that even though they had been baptized in
water for repentance, they were baptized again in the name
of Jesus. It does not reveal if this meant the people were

immersed in water again or if this baptism solely meant the laying on of hands to receive the Holy Spirit, but it strongly suggests the latter.

The fact that the Holy Spirit's presence was of utmost importance with regards to Baptism for Jesus and his followers is also made quite clear in Acts 8:14-17. It is said,

> Now when the apostles at Jerusalem heard that Sama'ria had received the word of God, they sent to them Peter and John, who came down and prayed for them that they might receive the Holy Spirit; for it had not yet fallen on any of them, but they had only been baptized in the name of the Lord Jesus. Then they laid their hands on them and they received the Holy Spirit.

As we can see illustrated here, when someone got baptized in water in the name of Jesus, it did not necessarily encompass the Holy Spirit. It was the baptism to receive the Holy Spirit that truly transformed and unified believers. Paul put it this way, "For by one Spirit we were all baptized into one body–Jews or Greeks, slaves or free–and all were made to drink of one Spirit."[468] It was the Holy Spirit who was needed to fill every believer. To receive her was an equal opportunity, because it was not based on your position in the world but on an internal belief in God and surrendering your own will and desires to seek those of the Father. This is what enables one to receive the Holy Spirit.

The gospel of Philip has much more to say about baptism. At one point it says,

> Through the holy spirit we are indeed begotten again, but we are begotten through Christ in the two. We are anointed through the spirit. When we were begotten we were united. None can see himself either in water or in a mirror without light. Nor again can you (sg.) see in light without water or mirror. For this reason it

is fitting to baptize in the two, in the light and the water. Now the light is the chrism.[469]

Here it openly declares there to be two baptisms; one in water and one in oil (chrism), and they are both necessary. Being cleansed of sins and receiving the Holy Spirit is how baptism "united" believers. Oil was not the only thing representing the Holy Spirit, but light too. As earlier mentioned, they were intrinsically intertwined since lamps burned with olive oil. This symbolism is suggested during Jesus' baptism when it says that the heavens "opened" and the dove descended on him.[470] The heavens opening can be understood as clouds parting letting the sun come shining through.

This new form of baptism was modeled after what happened to Jesus when John baptized him, and the Holy Spirit landed on him.[471] Baptism done in all three names: God, Jesus and the Holy Spirit. Each one represented a component of the baptism.[472] God was represented by water referring to repentance, as in changing your ways and turning back to God. Jesus stood for forgiveness of sins signified by a new clean heart and realized in his physical death and resurrection. The Holy Spirit was able to enter the believer after repentance, and she was received in anointing with oil or the laying on of hands. Through her you would have a new spiritual insight and understanding and be connected to God as well as other believers.

FAREWELL COMMANDS BY JESUS

Though the baptismal formula is only present in Matthew the core contents of Jesus' last instructions are paralleled in the other Gospels. His last words in Mark before he ascended were,

"Go into all the world and preach the gospel to the whole creation. He who believes and is baptized will be saved; but he who does not believe will be condemned. And these signs will accompany those who believe: in my name they will cast out demons; they will speak in new tongues; they will pick up serpents, and if they drink any deadly thing, it will not hurt them; they will lay their hands on the sick, and they will recover."[473]

The command to evangelize is there, and the last part concerns gifts of the Holy Spirit.[474]

The same goes for Luke. Jesus' last charge is presented in the context of the Messiah having suffered, died and being raised again. It says this was done so,

that repentance and forgiveness of sins should be preached in his name to all nations, beginning from Jerusalem. You are witnesses of these things. And "behold, I send the promise of my Father upon you; but stay in the city, until you are clothed with power from on high."[475]

The Gospel of Luke concurs that the final directives of Jesus was to proselytize, and we have a slight variation regarding the reference to the Holy Spirit who is here called "power from on high." "The Power" usually refers to God, but this phrase in Luke can be understood to mean the Spirit, especially when compared to Acts where it says, "you shall receive power when the Holy Spirit has come upon you."[476] The Holy Spirit was the instrument for God's Power.[477]

The final Gospel of John ends a little differently being focused on Jesus' interaction with Peter. The farewell commands come just prior to that in the second to last chapter,

> Jesus said to them again, "Peace be with you. As the Father has sent me, even so I send you." And when he had said this, he breathed on them, and said to them, "Receive the Holy Spirit. If you forgive the sins of any, they are forgiven; if you retain the sins of any, they are retained."[478]

We again see the emphasis on the disciples to be missionaries once Jesus is gone. He gives them the Holy Spirit through breathing on them, exhibiting the meaning of the Hebrew word for Spirit, *ruah*, which is "breath" or "wind." This passage yet again reveals how Jesus had the Holy Spirit in addition to one way of how he shared it. The prime importance of the Holy Spirit is again exhibited. We have now seen three actions accompanying the transmission of Spirit: Jesus breathing on the disciples, anointing with olive oil, and laying on of hands.

The first chapter in Acts more or less starts where the Gospels end and states that right before Jesus had been "taken up" he gave "commandment through the Holy Spirit."[479] He urged the disciples to stay in Jerusalem saying, "you heard from me, for John baptized with water, but before many days you shall be baptized with the Holy Spirit."[480] It then says they came together and asked him when the kingdom would be restored to Jerusalem. Jesus' response to this, before being lifted up in a cloud, was,

> It is not for you to know times or seasons which the Father has fixed by his own authority. But you shall receive power when the Holy Spirit has come upon you; and you shall be my witnesses in Jerusalem and in all Judea and Sama'ria and to the end of the earth.[481]

Jesus' final words were about receiving the Holy Spirit, which is how the Power of God is transmitted. He also commanded the disciples to first stay in Jerusalem for the particular reason of being baptized with the Holy Spirit. Then they should go out and evangelize to not only Israel, but to all nations, which is what they did. In other words, all the Gospels plus Acts of the Apostles declare that Jesus' last words were about sending out the Apostles to teach this form of baptism, which included forgiveness of sins and obtaining the Holy Spirit.

It is somewhat obscure when the Holy Spirit was given to the Apostles. In John it says Jesus breathed it upon them; while Acts, who most believe have the same author as Luke, related Pentecost as the event that brought about the Holy Spirit.[482] At the same time, it is difficult to perceive the disciples not having been anointed with the Spirit earlier when they were busy baptizing other people.[483]

When the Holy Spirit came as a mighty wind at Pentecost enabling the Apostles to speak in other tongues, the multitude, with "devout men" gathered in Jerusalem, they too experienced a miracle.[484] They heard others speak in their own language.[485] This has been understood by scholars to be a symbolic reversal of the tower of Babylon where language was confused to hinder people from committing more evil. Believers were now united by the Spirit of God and understood each other. Simultaneously the Holy Spirit was, and had been throughout the Hebrew history, already present in certain people.

In the Gospels, her presence is particularly described before Jesus' official ministry in Luke. This is the Gospel that pays the most attention to women, and it may not be an accident that it likewise speaks more about the Holy Spirit. John the Baptist was filled with the Holy Spirit, and she was instrumental in Jesus' conception.[486] Mary, Elisabeth, Zechariah and Simeon were all said to be filled with the Holy Spirit prior to Pentecost or any baptism by Jesus.[487] Jesus also claimed that the Father would give the Holy Spirit to those who asked.[488] The Holy Spirit could of course enter or leave people, just like Satan.[489] One thing is for sure, the Holy Spirit is a principal player of the faith that Jesus inherited, believed in, manifested and passed on to his Apostles and disciples.

In all the Canonical Gospels, and the Gospel of the Hebrews, baptism in water and baptism in the Holy Spirit were of utmost importance. If anything, baptism in the Holy Spirit was even more important while baptism in water was a pre-requisite and preparation. It is the Holy Spirit that enables a person to understand and "see."

THE BRIDE AND THE BRIDEGROOM

"The bride and bridegroom" was a concept John the Baptist used, present in Jesus' teachings, and also had a prime role in Philip's gospel. The bride represents the Holy Spirit and is therefore vitally important with regards to the Divine Feminine to examine and we already looked at this a bit in chapter 2.

Acts (8:14-17) demonstrates baptism in water needs to be followed by receiving the Holy Spirit. This concept is echoed in a paragraph from the gospel of Philip declaring that it is of essence that the first baptism in water requires the one in oil to make it complete. It says,

> If one go down into the water and come up without having received anything and says, "I am a Christian," he has borrowed the name at interest. But if he receive the holy spirit, he has the name as a gift. He who has received a gift does not have to give it back, but of him who has borrowed it at interest, payment is demanded. This is the way [it happens to one] when he experiences a mystery.[490]

This shows that the understanding here of baptism was, at least for the most part, receiving the Holy Spirit simultaneously to the baptism in water, but that it was the baptism in the Holy Spirit that was the one of prime significance. As discussed earlier regarding the baptismal formula in Matthew, if baptism lacks an inner change, which is the result of receiving the Holy Spirit, then it has no value. It was also a mystery, which is something that needs to be revealed to be understood. A revealer was needed which was part of the meanings in the title "Nazarene."

On another occasion the gospel of Philip says, "The lord [did] everything in a mystery, a baptism and a chrism and a eucharist and a redemption and a bridal chamber."[491] This mirrors the many components described in the New Testament for baptism; water, oil/Holy Spirit, Jesus, and forgiveness of sins. The "eucharist" is specifically explained to mean "Jesus" in the gospel of Philip.[492] The last one, the bridal chamber, is a word that occurs repeatedly in this gospel and it is of prime significance as to why the words bride and bridegroom are used to begin with. The following passage helps signal why:

> There were three buildings specifically for sacrifice in Jerusalem. The one facing west was called "the holy." Another facing south was called "the holy of the holy." The third facing east was called "the holy of the holies," the place where only the high priest enters. Baptism is "the holy" building. Redemption is "the holy of the holy." "The holy of the holies" is the bridal chamber. Baptism includes the resurrection [and the] redemption; the redemption (takes place) in the bridal chamber.[493]

The Holy of the Holies **is the bridal chamber,** because it was the place where the Ark of the Covenant was situated, and **God was literally present**. It is the bridal chamber because it is where the masculine and the feminine unite. A veil separated it from the rest of the Holy places.[494] Hebrews chapter nine describes that only the high priest could enter this place once a year on the Day of Atonement to sprinkle sacrificed blood as a compensation for the sins of himself and the people of Israel. The Holy Spirit had until then let them know that "the way into the sanctuary" was not opened as long as the outer tent stood.[495]

But, Christ, appearing as the high priest in the order of Melchizedek, entered the Holy of Holies once and for all and secured eternal redemption by his sacrificial blood. It says, "the blood of Christ, who through the eternal Spirit offered himself without blemish to God, purify your conscience from dead works to serve the living God."[496] Jesus was the mediator and his blood was the blood of the new covenant because in ancient Israelite belief forgiveness of sins included the shedding of blood. This was part of the purification rituals. The sacrificial role of Jesus is a tenet in Christian belief. However, what is often overlooked is the Holy Spirit's part in this. It was the Holy Spirit who revealed *"the way into the sanctuary"* (my italics) to the followers of Jesus, and it was *"through the eternal Spirit"* (my italics) that Jesus offered himself.[497] The Holy Spirit is a key character in this mystery of mysteries.

Going back to the passage in the gospel of Philip about the Holy of Holies it says that the bridal chamber is located in that which is superior. Following this the text is too broken off to make sense of what it says, including the bridal chamber's relationship to why the veil in the Temple was torn in two immediately after Jesus drew his last breath.[498] Again, the bridal chamber is just what the name itself stands for: it is the place where the feminine and the masculine forces unite. It says, "Bridegrooms and brides belong to the bridal chamber."[499] Right after proclaiming the chrism to be superior to baptism in water, the author declares,

> it is from the word "chrism" that we have been called "Christians," certainly not because of the word "baptism." And it is because the chrism that "the Christ" has his name. For the father anointed the son, and the son anointed the apostles, and the apostles anointed us. He who has been anointed possesses everything. He possesses the resurrection, the light, the cross, the holy spirit. The father gave him this in the bridal chamber; he merely accepted (the gift). The father was in the son and the son in the father. This is [the] kingdom of heaven.[500]

The anointed Jesus and his followers have accepted the gift, which is a form of marriage of the heavenly and earthly realm. It is not only in the bridal chamber where the mystery of God and the Holy Spirit reside but where Jesus gained his crown of life and enabled his disciples to follow suit.

At the end of this manuscript the author repeats what he likely said in the instance where the text was earlier broken off concerning the Holy of holies. It says that the bridal chamber was hidden and "It is holy in the holy" and "The veil at first concealed how God controlled the creation" but when it was rent, and the insides revealed, the godhead had to flee to the holies of the holies.[501] The veil was rent from both top to bottom meaning "Those above opened to us the things below, in order that we may go in to the secret of the truth."[502] It continues, "Therefore the perfect things have opened to us, together with the hidden things of truth. The holies of the holies were revealed, and the bridal chamber invited us in."[503] In other words, when Jesus died, truth was revealed and access to God became available in a new way. This mirrors how the Holy Spirit was given to the Apostles and the core of the mystery of marriage and God's presence behind the veil is the mystery of Creation itself. Creation is the mixing of male and female and this applies on both levels: human and divine.

Following this, it essentially says that as long as evil is concealed it has power but once it is revealed, brought to the light, it loses it. This can be applicable on numerous levels, two of them being confession of sins and repentance that are necessary components to leave evil behind which the water of baptism represents. The text speaks of how everyone who enters the bridal chamber will kindle its light and this type of marriage, unlike the earthly, is perfected in the day and light. This kindling of light, i.e. fire, reminds us of when John the Baptist said that Jesus would baptize with the Holy Spirit and fire.[504] Shem-Tob's has it as "fire of the Holy Spirit" which is probably more accurate. Anyone who becomes a son of the bridal chamber will receive this light/fire. When you receive it the truth is revealed to you and this day and light never sets. Once this human leaves from here he/she steps right into eternity where suffering holds no power over this soul.

The gospel ends with these words "This is the way it is: it is revealed to him alone, not hidden in the darkness and the night, but hidden in a perfect day and a holy light."[505] The truth sets you free, the lie is evil. Hidden in a holy light again suggests that the key to receiving this is the Holy Spirit. The Holy Spirit is the truth, light and the Revealer. What is hidden will be revealed to believers. The Nazarene is someone whom the truth has been revealed to and in turn reveals it to others. The chain of command is: God to the Holy Spirit to Jesus the Nazarene, to the followers who became Nazarenes. When you receive the light, eternal life is gained. In other words, the gospel of Philip explains the Way to everlasting life and the very key to that is internally receiving the Holy Spirit.

Because the Holy Spirit is the bride, believers are sons and daughters of the Bridal chamber. This in turn makes the Holy Spirit the Mother of believers. We can see this in the gospel of Philip as well. One line goes as follows, "When we were Hebrews we were orphans and had only our mother, but when we became Christians we had both father and mother."[506] This is odd in light of God's role as the Father, in particular for Jesus to say the least. In order to appreciate it one must understand the context. It is the Holy Spirit that is called "our Mother," and when Christ came, he restored a broken unity. Somewhat later it says,

> Through the holy spirit we are indeed begotten again, but we are begotten through Christ in the two. We are anointed through the spirit. When we were begotten we were united.[507]

The line of thinking reveals an emphasis on the divine duality of male and female, here represented by Christ and the Holy Spirit and it is yet another example of how the Holy Spirit was understood as a Mother. Baptism in Jesus' name and being anointed by the Spirit gave new spiritual life, which also brought you to the Father.

In another instance a disciple asks Jesus for something from this world and he answered, "Ask your mother, and she will give you of the things which are another's."[508] The answer is peculiar, and the context a bit hard to understand, but it is likely not referring to the disciple's earthly mother but a heavenly mother. If so, then this is yet another quote where Jesus calls the Holy Spirit "Mother." This along with the Holy Spirit being called "Mother" elsewhere in the text suggests that one of the sources or inspirations for this text was the Gospel of the Hebrews.

If the Holy Spirit was understood as "Mother" and God "Father" but together they are One, a separation of the two would be inconceivable and impossible. Jesus encouraged us to strive to mirror heaven on earth so his instructions about marriage may have been a strong admonition to adhere to God's intent with it as it also reflected our Heavenly origin.[509]

The last thing I want quote here from the gospel of Philip links the Holy Spirit to life. This is important.

> By perfecting the water of baptism, Jesus emptied it of death. Thus we do go down into the water, but we do not go down into death in order that we may not be poured out into the spirit of the world. When that spirit blows, it brings winter. When the holy spirit breathes, the summer comes."[510]

Winter is when flowers and greens die while in the summer they are alive and bloom. The symbolism here is evident; the Holy Spirit represents life. She is the breath of God, described to give life when she breathes.[511] The name of first female human, Eve, represents this as it was given to her "because she was the mother of all living."[512] On the opposite you have the blows of winter, which kill. Breath in itself, of course, represents our ability to breathe, which means our hearts are beating and we are alive. The Holy Spirit parallels this by giving us spiritual eternal life with God.

CHAPTER 5

THE EFFECTS OF THE DIVINE FEMININE IN THE EARLY CHURCH & WHY SHE DISAPPEARED

I commend to you our sister Phoebe, a deaconess of the church at Cen'chre-ae, that you may receive her in the Lord as befits the saints, and help her in whatever she may require from you, for she has been a helper of many and of myself as well.

Paul in Romans 16:1-2

OFFICIAL ROLES FOR WOMEN IN THE FIRST CHURCH

Jesus is not cited discussing the role of women in official settings in the canonical Gospels. This could perhaps be because it was not relevant for him in the same way that it came to be later, because of the new church that emerged after Jesus' departure. However, we do know that Jesus had many female disciples, and one of his premises for teaching was that his teachings should be passed on.[513] Jesus himself was consistently referred to as a teacher.

In the story where Jesus visits the house of Martha, he is teaching. Her sister, Mary, sits at Jesus' feet attentively listening to him. Martha becomes frustrated and wonders if Jesus does not care that her sister is letting her do all the housework. She asks Jesus to tell Mary to help. Jesus responds, "Martha, Martha, you are anxious and troubled about many things; one thing is needful, Mary has chosen the good portion, which shall not be taken away from her."[514] This is a significant sentence. Jesus does not demean the importance of service or doing housework, but he declares listening to his teachings is the priority. For Jesus to tell a woman being a disciple was more valuable than fulfilling her role of typical female chores was not a side note. When he said, "one thing is needful," Jesus pointed to always keeping God first. Everything else in life is secondary; or rather, it would fall into place once you have your priorities straight. Jesus also sternly pointed out Mary had chosen the better part, and it would "not be taken away from her." Jesus praised Mary for making the right choice.

This passage simultaneously gives a deep insight into female discipleship, which translates into women's role in the church. Though Jesus' twelve Apostles were all male, and they were the only ones sent out to travel to evangelize, Jesus did not declare only men should be disciples. Instead, he had numerous female followers. The above story of Mary and Martha, where Jesus stated discipleship was an important role for women, suggests in a roundabout way that women should pass the teachings on. Women would inevitably do so anyway because by raising children their influence was/is more direct and greater than anyone else's. It is undoubtedly the most powerful time and setting of all.

Jesus made a distinction about tradition and the Law, stating that the Law superseded traditions.[515] When we read this we have to understand that only men had official roles in the Temple and the Synagogue. Rabbis were teachers and interpreters of Scripture. The priesthood was given to Aaron, the brother of Moses, and his sons in the tribe of Levi, and they performed sacred rituals in the Temple.[516] Early on sacrifice was offered on outside altars and did not necessitate an ordination, which continued for some time after Moses as well. Women were allowed in synagogues, but men and women sat separately. Likewise women went to the Temple, and one of the main courts was specifically named and designed for them."[517] So, the men were the religious leader and women only participatory.

With the absence of any direct Mosaic commandment barring women to teach or speak, the sentiments reflected in some of Paul's letters must then be derived from either tradition, or possibly not part of the original Gospels but inserted later.[518] If it was tradition, it is believed by some to be derived from Genesis 3:16 where Eve's punishment after the fall was to be ruled by her husband. As discussed earlier, this is incompatible with the redemption Jesus brought from the fall. The justification for the barring of women teaching or speaking in Paul's letters not being original to the Gospel texts is based on how prominently several women are featured in Paul's letters, indicating that women were busy evangelizing, and thus teaching. Paul worked along many female disciples whom he praised. Some had the position of deaconesses, and one was possibly even referred to as an Apostle.[519] Paul had no opposition to these women working within the church.

There were no female priests or rabbis in ancient Israel, as recorded in the Old Testament, because the priesthood was male and hereditary. However, women functioned as prophetesses proclaiming the Words of Yahweh. There were several ancient prophetesses and the Hebrew Scriptures record Miriam, Deborah, Hulda, Noadiah, and Isaiah's wife as such.[520] In the New Testament, Anna was a prophetess and spoke of Jesus in the Temple when his parents took him there for the purification ritual.[521] Also in the New Testament, the Apostle Philip had four daughters who were prophetesses. Acts 21:8-9 claims,

> On the morrow we departed and came to Caesare'a; and we entered the house of Philip the evangelist,

who was one of the seven, and stayed with him. And he had four unmarried daughters, who prophesied.

When Jesus' own Apostle had daughters who did this it was most certainly an approved part of the faith. At Pentecost the Apostle Peter quotes a prophecy in Acts 2:17-18 by the prophet Joel (2:28-29) about the Day of the LORD. God proclaims that in the last days ,

> I will pour out my Spirit upon all flesh, and your sons and your daughters shall prophesy . . . and on my menservants and my maidservants in those days I will pour out my Spirit; and they shall prophesy.

The outpouring of the Spirit would be equally distributed among men and women meaning that Peter understood that women should prophesy.

Essentially, the Biblical support for prophetesses is solid and had been in place for hundreds of years by the time Jesus was born. Their prominence continued in the early Christian church. Prophets and prophetesses were vessels of the word of God and did whatever God commanded them to do. An illustration of this is when Jeremiah, whom God consecrated to be a prophet while in the womb, tried to tell God he was too young, but God would not have it. It says,

> But the LORD said to me, "Do not say, 'I am only a youth'; for to all to whom I send you you shall go, and whatever I command you you shall speak." . . . Then the LORD put forth his hand and touched my mouth; and the LORD said to me, "Behold, I have put my words in your mouth."[523]

Because prophetic words also came to women, this indirectly tells us that if anyone makes rules opposing women to teach, and even speak, in the church, this could muzzle God's word. Consider this, if a church did not allow a woman to prophesy on its premises, would that be a true Christian church?

Before we leave this section I want to mention that there was an early traditions that elevated female prophetesses named "Sibyl." Different Sibyls are known from the beginning of the mid-first millennium B.C. and onwards. The Sibylline tradition was wide spread and included pagan Sibyls too. Though no one in the Bible is referred to as a Sybil there was an ancient Jewish belief in Sibyls that continued within Christianity. The Jewish version of her origins is that she was a daughter or daughter-in-law of Noah.[524] An example of a Christian Sybil is the German Christian mystic Hildegard of Bingen, who lived in the middle Ages being born in Germany 1098. She was also called Sibyl of the Rhine. Relevant to mention here is that Hildegard claimed to have personal spiritual experiences with the personified Wisdom.[525]

There are ancient Jewish and Christian texts called "The Sibylline Oracles" which were written starting in the mid-2nd century B.C. until the 7th century A.D.,[526] believed to be directed to Jew and Gentile alike. Introducing the Sibylline Oracles scholar Barnstone wrote that,

> "Her" words glorify the history of the Jews, denounce animal sacrifice, sexual immorality, and worship of idols, and proclaim the truth of monotheism and the absolute sovereignty of its self-sprung, invisible God.[527]

In addition to this the Sybil oracles were apocalyptic.[528] The fact that this was a renowned tradition that originated far back and continued into Christian times testifies to a strong tradition of Jewish and Christian prophetesses which in turn places them into a position of authority.

THE FIRST FEMALE DISCIPLES - DEACONESSES

Deaconesses were present in the early church at time of the Apostle Paul. The Christian communities originally allowed female deacons, which was later prohibited by the emerging political Catholic Church. This official role for women flourished more in the east than in the west. In one of the canons written at the first council of Nicaea in year 325, it said regarding women that "they have no imposition of hands," meaning they were not officially ordained and were counted among the laity.[529] However, in the Council of Chalcedon 451 additional canons were written, and deaconesses are mentioned. These canons said women were to have been "ordained" by "imposition of hands" at the Nicene council, "But this did not imply any sacred commission such as deacons receive, nor any properly ministerial function," making the issue of women's roles somewhat unclear.[530] Women existed in an official way early on in the Church as apparent in the New Testament Scriptures. Later they had an unofficial role, which lasted a little longer in the east than in the west. By the Middle Ages, no genuine roles for women existed in the Church.[531] Roles for women resurfaced in Protestant Churches in the 19th century but are still not allowed in Catholicism.

Interestingly, the idea of outlawing priests and bishops from marrying came about at the same time as the first moves to prohibit deaconesses. These developments were parallel. The council of Elvira in Spain that took place circa 300-310 decreed that bishops and other clergy should not marry.[532] Various councils and voices promoted a celibate clergy even though Paul warned against prohibiting marriage in 1 Timothy 4:3. It was not until the start of the second millennium such practices were more firmly established, and priest were not allowed to marry in the

Catholic Church. When the Charlemagne Empire declined during the tenth century, there was social instability and moral failings regarding celibacy. In efforts to inhibit scandals and keep church property from being lost to the descendants of the priests, Pope Benedict VIII (1012-1024) made regulation to protect them.[533] Shortly thereafter Pope Gregory VII (1073-1075) finally made sure celibacy was consistently observed by the priesthood. It should be noted too at the council of Trent (1545-1563), it was acknowledged laws pertaining to celibacy were not divine laws but church laws.[534]

The validity of deaconesses came to be questioned even though the New Testament endorsed them having an official role in the first church. Romans 16:1 Paul says, "I commend to you our sister Phoebe, a deaconess of the church at Cen'chre-ae . . . ."[535] In 1 Timothy 3:11 Paul discusses rules of behavior for deacons and then says "The women likewise must be serious, no slanderers, but temperate, faithful in all things."

The likelihood the primitive Christian Church gave women an authorized role as deaconesses and this is what Paul talked about is substantiated by numerous early documents. For instance, St. Basil (died 379) wrote letters to deaconesses.[536] Epiphanius was another person who wrote about them.[537] Women are mentioned in Pliny the Younger's letter to Emperor Trajan, which is an extraordinary early Roman account of Christians. In it Pliny writes about torturing "two maidservants, who were called deaconesses" to learn about the truth of what Christians did and believed.[538] These are some of the rather strong evidences for the presence of deaconesses in the earliest church.

Another source supporting deaconesses can be found in a Syriac document called "the Didascalia." This title comes from the Greek word to "teach." It is uncertain how old this text is, but it was quoted by Epiphanius (4th century) wherefore it was at least written earlier than that.[539] The Didascalia manuscript followed the same genre as the Didache but was more elaborate in its instructions of the new church. It is written as if the twelve Apostles wrote it firsthand and mainly spells out the role of the bishops in the church. However, it discusses several other issues as well. Most importantly for us, at one point it explains how the role of the hierarchy in the church resembles the hierarchy in heaven. It says,

> For the Levite and the High Priest is the Bishop. He is a servant of the Word of God and a Mediator, but to you a Teacher and your Father after God, who has begotten you by means of water. He is your Head and Governor, and he is a powerful king to you. He governs in the place of the Almighty, but let him be honoured by you as God, because the Bishop sits for you in the place of Almighty God; but the Deacon stands in the place of Christ; and ye should love him, but let the Deaconesses be honoured by you in the likeness of the Holy Ghost. Moreover, let the Elders be to you in the likeness of the Apostles, but Orphans and Widows be considered by you in the likeness of an Altar.[540]

This testifies to a time before the all-male Trinitarian concept was present. Thus, it has a much closer relationship to Jewish roots of the faith, which suggests it was written early on in Christianity.[541]

The fact that the text states Deaconesses represent the Holy Spirit is profound. It is not out of the realm of possibility that this text, or ideas in it, originated in the lifetime of the Apostles. In organizing the first Church the Apostles established these positions as described in the New Testament.[542] The Didascalia underscores the vital role the gender of the Holy Spirit played in the early church, which was eventually lost. The femininity of the Holy Spirit and her place in the Heavenly hierarchy was well-defined. Jesus was not originally on par with Yahweh, but paired with the Holy Spirit and placed under Him. There were initially no "priests" because in Jewish customs they offered sacrifices, which had ended. Instead the Church had bishops who were over the deacons and deaconesses. Presbyter (elder) was the official role later turned into priest. Part of the women's role as deaconesses included to anoint newly baptized women, as well as to teach and educate them in order that "the unbreakable seal of baptism be with purity and holiness."[543] According to the Didascalia, women had a significant role serving within the church.[544] It further states that,

> Therefore we affirm that the service of a woman, a Deaconess, is necessary and obligatory, because even our Lord and Saviour was served by the hand of women deaconesses, who were Mary the Magdalene, and Mary (Cod. S. daughter) of James, the mother of Joses, and the mother of Zebedee's children, with other women. This service of Deaconesses is necessary also to thee for many things, for in the houses of the heathen, where there are believing women, a Deaconess is required, that she may go in and visit those who are sick, and serve them with whatever they need, and anoint (S. wash) those who are healed from sicknesses.[545]

The role of the Deaconess was to primarily serve women. The role models for this were Jesus' female disciples, and on top of this list was Mary Magdalene. When the femininity of the Holy Spirit disappeared, it went hand in hand with women's roles disappearing in the initial structure of the Christian church.[546]

Earlier in the Didascalia, a discussion among the Apostles is quoted and recorded by a man called Baltous.

This segment is titled "The Teaching of the Twelve Holy Apostles."[547] In addition to the twelve men were two women: Mary and Martha. Here women are yet again featured as prominent disciples. They are both cited as follows,

> Martha said, about Mary, I saw her laughing between her teeth joyfully. Mary said, I did not surely laugh, but I remembered the words of our Lord, and I rejoiced, for ye know that He said to us before, when He was teaching, He that is weak shall be saved by means of the strong.[548]

These two tiny inclusions of Martha and Mary mirror the tension between them in the Gospel of Luke where Martha was upset with Mary because she was doing all the serving when Jesus visited them.[549]

Right before these quotes, the text suggested the role of women as Deaconesses was instituted by one of the Disciples. The text states, "Andrew said, It would be very good, my brethren, that we should appoint women as Deaconesses."[550] Cephas (the Syriac name for "rock," in Greek "Petros," English "Peter") said there should be three widows appointed, whereby two should continually pray for those in temptation, but also for revelations and signs. In other words, the prophetic role of women was validated and continued. The other woman should be with the sick, and serve as a liaison to the Elders regarding what was needed for them.[551] Peter also pointed out women's heads should be covered when they take communion.[552]

In other words, according to this manuscript the Apostles themselves spelled out specific spiritual roles for women that would be an official part of the church.

Later in the Didascalia, it says it was not necessary or required that women should teach. It states,

> Therefore it is not required nor necessary that women should be teachers, especially about the name of

Christ, and about salvation by His passion, for women were not appointed to teach, especially not a widow, but that they should make prayer and supplication to the Lord God. For even Jesus the Christ, our Teacher, sent us the Twelve to make disciples of the people and the nations. There were with us female disciples, Mary Magdalene and another Mary, and He did not send [them] to make disciples with us of the people. For if it were required that women should teach, our Teacher would have commanded them to make disciples with us.[553]

This is in line with what Paul wrote in 1 Timothy 2:12, "I permit no woman to teach or to have authority over men; she is to keep silent." which is the main reason used still today for prohibiting women to teach or preach by the Catholic Church and other denominations. However, it is important to know that there is no ban spelled out backed up by an actual law. Paul specifically states, "I permit no woman to teach" so, not the Law and not Jesus. Forbidding women to teach was *debated* specifically because Jesus's Apostles were all male, yet at the same time there were female disciples. Jesus' great commission was for the Apostles to make more disciples who in turn would also pass on Christ's teachings. This does not include everyone being an official teacher, but it would inevitably include women passing on teachings. Though there were no female rabbis, Jesus never declared women unfit to teach. Maybe it was a given thus not mentioned. There would certainly have been practical and safety reasons for why women were not sent out to evangelize in the world by Jesus. At the same time, if Jesus specifically instructed and supported a ban on female disciples to teach it is difficult to conceive that it would not be used by Paul as a reference in the New Testament letters when he wrote about this. So, this was based on tradition, not the Law. Jesus defended the Law and said that tradition did not supersede it wherefore this question is worth exploring.[554]

Worthy to note about the Didascalia is that it quotes Matthew's Gospel more than any other (much like the Didache) with a great deal from Proverbs, using the title "Wisdom" when referring to this book.[555] This is another trace of the prime role the Divine Feminine as Wisdom played in the early church.

Speaking of Matthew, in the Apocryphal work "Acts and Martyrdom of St. Matthew the Apostle," Matthew appoints a king to the office of presbyter, his wife a "presbyteress," the king's son a deacon, and the son's wife a "deaconess."[556] They were also given new names as they converted to Christianity. The queen's new name was "Sophia," meaning "Wisdom," and the son's wife, "Synesis," meaning "Understanding."[557] This could be yet another hint of women once having had an official role in the early church modeled after the personified Divine Feminine force of Wisdom. For men to support and write about women having such roles were surely not grounded in personal opinions similar to modern notions of "equality." Instead it was rooted in the Holy Scripture about the Divine Feminine force personified as Wisdom and the Holy Spirit. Lastly, of all the Apostles, this manuscript is about Matthew. The reason is likely due to the legacy Matthew had for writing the first Gospel where Jesus addressed the Holy Spirit as his Mother. This had ripple effects, yet another positive sign that Matthew and consequently Jesus adhered to a belief in the Holy Spirit/Wisdom as a Divine Feminine Power.

Paul's references to Deaconesses are verified by early extra Biblical accounts that support this title as part of the initial structures of the church instituted by the Apostles themselves. Deaconesses represented the Holy Spirit, because both were feminine. The Holy Spirit's femininity had direct consequences for women's role as the church formed. The above-cited manuscripts corroborate New Testament declarations of prominent women in the early church.

THE CONSEQUENCES OF NEUTERING THE SPIRIT

How and why the femininity of the Holy Spirit changed from feminine, to neuter, and then finally masculine, can be attributed to a few factors. The main reason though was the consequence of Hebrew losing to Greek and Latin, as the primary language of believers. Theology then gradually followed the linguistic change. Simultaneously, the prominent role of Wisdom decreased. Changes in the early church were gradual in the first few decades and continued over the next centuries, branching out into differing beliefs and practices.

The Holy Spirit and Wisdom understood, as a heavenly Mother, was rather widespread and popular judging by the many historical texts testifying to it. An illustration of a continuing but changing tradition of the Holy Spirit as a feminine divine aspect can be found in a text called "Odes to Solomon." It was written in Syriac, which is a form of Aramaic, and therefore preserved the Spirit female. These odes were a continuation of the tradition of Solomon's Wisdom texts but incorporated new Christian elements. It was estimated to be written around year 100.[558] The first few lines of Ode 24 go as follows, "The dove fluttered over the head of our Lord Messiah, because he was her Head. And she sang over him, and her voice was heard."[559] Later in the same ode it continues, "And the Lord destroyed the thoughts, of all those who had not the truth with them. For they were lacking in wisdom, they who exalted themselves in their mind."[560] As we can see, it is a Wisdom text. The dove, representing the Holy Spirit, is feminine in line with the language. At the same time, the new Christology is emerging, evident in how the writer wants to make sure that even though the Spirit landed on Christ, Christ was ranked higher saying; "he was her Head."

Though the Heavenly female was prominent in many texts in the first few centuries, changes, which can at least partly be attributed to the language change from Hebrew to Greek, came and conquered. The femininity of the Holy Spirit eventually disappeared completely, and the original interpretation of the Wisdom texts took a backseat to the new understanding that Jesus was the Wisdom of God.[561] By the fourth century, major developments in Christianity took place. Constantine was the first Roman Emperor favorable to Christianity. The Edict of Milan year 313 gave protection and legal status to the long suffering, persecuted Christians. The Nicene Creed was penned down around this time, and with it the Holy Spirit went from neuter to masculine. She was now part of an all-male Trinitarian doctrine. With this, our divine Mother's open presence vanished.

THE LASTING LEGACY OF MARY AND ITS RELEVANCE TO THE DISAPPEARING FEMININITY OF THE SPIRIT

After the Christian church changed the Holy Spirit's femininity to be a masculine part of the Trinity and Lady Wisdom was fused with Jesus, the divine Mother was in some essence replaced by the role of Mother Mary. After the Protestant Reformation Mary's important role in the church prevailed only in Catholicism. Though the new Protestants focus was *Sola Scriptura*, meaning relying on Scripture alone, they were ignorant to the true feminine gender of God's Spirit in Scripture. Consequently, the all-male Trinity was blindly reinforced to numerous new denominations.

Manuscripts devoted to Mother Mary such as the Protoevangelium of James (Jacob) also known as the Infancy Gospel of James, developed early. This one tells the story of Mary's birth. Its vast popularity is evident by the fact that some hundred and thirty Greek manuscripts have been found. Most of them originate after the tenth century, and the earliest is from the third.[562] In addition it exists in many translations such as early Syriac, Armenian, Slavonic, and Ethiopic to name a few.[563] It is also probably the inspiration behind the 19th century institution of the feast day for the Immaculate Conception celebrated December 8, which refers to when Mary was conceived.

Some traditions existed in the early centuries that were devoted to Mary. For instance, a group in early Christianity located in the eastern parts of the Roman Empire called the Kollyridians offered sacrificed bread to Mother Mary. They were condemned by Epiphanius who suggested that "such women be muzzled by Jeremias."[564] This was a reference to the prophet Jeremiah and his offense at women baking cakes to the Queen of Heaven.[565] Here then, an early parallel can be drawn between goddess worship and Mariology. Perhaps this was in fact not a new tradition invented for Mary, but the ancient one that lingered in which Mary now replaced "the Queen of Heaven."

The widespread Marian devotion for the last two thousand years demonstrates a strong foundation for the devotion of a heavenly Mother. It did not disappear, but was just expressed through Mother Mary instead of the Divine Feminine. Jesus' mother continues to this day to fill this void in many Catholic believers.

CHAPTER 6

RESTORING THE BALANCE

"Hear, O Israel: The LORD our God is one LORD."

Moses in Deuteronomy 6:4

GOD IS NOT ALONE: MONOTHEISM

The Holy Spirit being feminine must include a little time spent on the concept of monotheism, which does not preclude the inherent duality of God being both masculine and feminine. The all-male Trinitarian concept was born as an attempt to preserve monotheism. However, monotheism, as depicted in the Bible, needs to be examined closer. To begin, Jesus used Scripture that spoke about "gods" to defend being the Son of God and therefore "divine" or "a god."[566] The Bible itself speaks of the "divine council" consisting of "gods,"[567] as well as Yahweh being "above all gods."[568] Scholars explained such passages as remnants from the Canaanite mother-religion. Regardless of their origins or other religious influence, these statements are preserved in Scripture and endorsed by Jesus. This inevitably presents a dilemma to the conventional idea of monotheism. If God having a wife or Divine Feminine counterpart, who could technically be called Goddess, were perceived as heretical, it would be intellectually dishonest to not address Jesus supporting the idea of other gods in Holy Scripture.

Let us take a look at one of the foundational passages for Biblical monotheism. Moses met Yahweh on Mount Sinai and exclaimed, "Hear, O Israel: The LORD our God is one LORD."[569] Traditionally this has been understood to mean that God is alone, as in there are no other gods. Some scholars though have recognized that this is not a declaration of monotheism but henotheism, which is the belief and worship in one supreme God but yet acknowledging the existence of other gods. Either way, this Scripture is what set the Israelites apart from the surrounding cultures. They believed in many gods, whereas the Hebrew national Deity was not only the God of the entire cosmos but no other divinities existed at all. If "one" meant "alone," as the traditional reading goes, this verse could interpreted in a couple of ways. Either Moses met only Yahweh on Mount Sinai, or Yahweh told him that there were no other gods in the heavenly realm. The first does not necessarily exclude others, while the latter does. But, everything hinges on what exactly Moses said.

Observe that the passage does not say Elohim (God) is one, but rather Yahweh (LORD) is one. Usually, the personal name of someone is for obvious reasons not in the plural. There cannot be two Yahweh, unlike the word Elohim, which can designate "gods." If Moses aimed to convey that there was only one God, it would have been worded, "there is one God - Yahweh is God." But, the sentence in Deuteronomy is literally the opposite, "Yahweh our God - Yahweh (is) one."[570] In order to figure out what this means, we have to look more at the word for "one," in Hebrew אחד and in transliteration 'ehad.

Though 'ehad has been mostly understood to mean "alone," the Hebrew word usually used for "alone" is another word, בד transliterated as bad. This hints at another meaning for the word "one" rather than "alone." The word *'ehad* is not only the cardinal number "one" but can also mean "first." The intention of the passage may not have been that Yahweh was alone, but a proclamation that He was the First: the Creator of everything and everyone. Though Melchizedek blessed Abraham by El Elyon, "God Most High, maker of heaven and earth" we must remember that when Moses led the Israelites out of Egypt, he had to first learn about the Hebrew God.[571] He did not know His name, and it was emphasized repeatedly that Yahweh was the God of his forefathers. Yahweh was Moses' rightful God since he was ethnically a Hebrew.[572] Having lived in Egypt all his life, Moses seemingly needed to learn that his forefathers' God, El-Shadday, now known as Yahweh, was not only his rightful ancestral God, but the Creator of everything and everyone. If Yahweh told Moses that He was the "first," the emphasis could have been that, as the Creator of all, Yahweh was the *only one* to worship. What follows this famous line in Deuteronomy 6:4 is the command, that "you shall love the LORD your God with all your heart, and with all your soul, and with all your might."[573] The motive for the proclamation that Yahweh is "one" was to decree a complete and exclusive worship of only Him. This Scripture does not automatically mean any other deities do not exist; only that others are secondary, created *by* God and *not* to be venerated. Yahweh wants full loyalty and His people's whole heart. As the Creator of all Life, He has the right to ask this. However you look at all this, the Bible points to an original singularity, which is Yahweh.

The sense of Deuteronomy 6:4 referring to Yahweh being the first, without denying the existence of other "gods," is also encoded in the first commandment given to Moses. It says, "You shall have no other gods before me."[574] "Before" can also be translated as "besides," and both statements announce that you must put Yahweh first.[575] This is why it was controversial for the Jews that Jesus would be seated at the right hand of God in heaven. But, as God's Son, this is the place that Jesus announced to be his, and it was Scriptural. Any authority Jesus had was given to him by Yahweh. But, to preserve monotheism, with this perceived theological dilemma, the church fathers arrived at idea of the all-male Trinity.

When Satan asked Jesus to fall down and worship him in exchange for all the kingdoms of the world, Jesus responded, "Begone, Satan! for it is written, 'You shall worship the Lord your God and him only shall you serve.'"[576] Jesus' answer testifies to Yahweh being the only One to worship. The Devil himself is not human, but a being from the spiritual realm. In this spiritual realm sense he can be understood as "a god." Not a good god, and not the Creator of the universe, nevertheless a form of deity above frail flesh.[577]

The meaning of the Hebrew word "god," in transliteration *El*, is not only a reference to God, as in Yahweh. It can mean a supernatural being, a minor god/deity, or someone divine with limited powers as well. Though we often look at other religions as heretical, due to believing in many gods, Christianity supports the belief in angels and a devil with his own demons. The Hebrew meaning of "angel" is "messenger," which serve as a go-between God and humans. An angel and a minor god are both categorized as supernatural and have a limited power and knowledge. The difference is angels are described as all good, servants and messengers of God. Demons are all evil, deceivers, tempters, attackers, and serve Satan. Ancient pagan gods, on the other hand, were more like humans, having both good and bad traits. Nevertheless, angels and demons in the New Testament fall in a spiritual category between God and humans. This spiritual hierarchy is identified in the Bible. For this reason, these spiritual beings could theoretically be called minor "gods."

This inevitably leads to the question: where does God's Divine Feminine aspect fit in? There are different ways to answer this question. Ben Sirach states that "From eternity, in the beginning, he created me, and for eternity I shall not cease to exist."[578] The Wisdom books furthermore say she was "created"[579] and is "a breath of the power of God"[580] and "came forth from the mouth of the Most High . . . ."[581] This begs the question, if she is the breath of God, can He live without her? Additionally, Genesis does not testify to a creation of God's Spirit; instead she is already present in the beginning.[582] In Book of Proverbs, Wisdom says, "the LORD created me at the beginning of his work, the first of his acts of old. Ages ago I was set up, at the first, before the beginning of the earth."[583] The word translated as "work" is *derek* which can also mean "road," "path" or "way." It can additionally refer to "journey." Moreover, the word, here in Proverbs, for "created" can mean "acquired" too. In Hebrew it is the root קנה in transliteration *qnh*. It can also mean "take" and is for instance the word used to describe how Boaz took Ruth to be his wife.[584] The word can mean "bought," too which is how some translate that part in Ruth. But, if we think of adding the meaning "buy" or "acquire" to this word in Proverbs, it would not make sense. God would not "buy" Wisdom and thus "own" her. She came from Him, and there is no one from which He would buy her. This is why the word *qnh*, is mostly translated as "created," or "possess" instead of "owned" in Proverbs. In other words, *qnh* can indicate taking someone in marriage while have nothing to do with monetary means or values. For these reasons, Proverbs can suggest that Wisdom is God's feminine aspect, who can also be seen as Yahweh's counterpart, and together they are One. If this Scripture read, "the LORD acquired me at the beginning of His *journey*" it could signal the start of time. The journey of creation is one that began with God and His feminine Holy Spirit and inherently consists of the two of them.

The Hebrew word for "beginning " in Proverbs 8:22 is *rosh*. It is the same word used in Genesis 1:1 "In the beginning . . . ." Proverbs is in this sense alluding to her origin with Him either before or right at creation. Ben Sirach 24:3 put it this way, "I came forth from the mouth of the Most High, and covered the earth like a mist" hinting at Genesis 1:2 where it says, "the Spirit of God was moving over the face of the waters." All this could be indications that she came forth from Yahweh either the instance time came into being, or she was always present because she was a part of Him reflected in the story about Adam and Eve. If she existed prior to time, it naturally becomes irrelevant for Scripture to discuss her origin.

Another way to see this is that Yahweh was the original singularity, the first, and she came into being in His first division, much like the first cell division when a new baby is created. First it is one cell, then two. When discussing these ideas with a friend he said, "The same entity, divided in two to create balance."[585] By seeing it from this unique perspective, it is also possible that God became a distinguishable He only after She was created, in the same way some view the creation story of Adam and Eve. Eve was fashioned from what was taken out from Adam's side, and only at the creation of her, did he become solely male.[586]

Moses' declaration that Yahweh is One, as in undivided and whole, could have undertones of the creation story. The same word for "one" in Deuteronomy 6:4, *'ehad*, is the same used to describe marriage in Genesis 2:24, when it says Adam and Eve are again by marriage "one flesh." Claiming Yahweh is "one" could theoretically be a roundabout way of saying, He is married to Wisdom/His Holy Spirit. She can be understood as part of God in a

Divine Marriage and God's other half. God is on the throne in heaven. She is the one present on earth, who enters into believers exemplified in Biblical texts. It could also be that God (Yahweh) was the "First," but it was simultaneously a pun on "one." As stated earlier, the Two being One could also signal an indirect reason for God's objection to divorce and His wish for humanity to strive to implement this value of oneness on earth.[587]

All this leads us to the question that if God's Feminine Spirit is a Goddess in her own right, does she have a mind apart from God and is she God's equal? How does a monotheistic belief work with her presence? How is she different from what the Trinity proclaims about Jesus? The major differences between Jesus and her are that the Holy Spirit/Wisdom is not a human. Scripture places her in the beginning. One way to look at this is using the metaphor of a brain, since we are created in God's physical image. It has two parts, the left and the right. The right side is creative and diagonally controls the muscles on the left, while the left-brain is logical and in charge of the muscles on the right. These two parts make a whole, and we all need both.

As far as equality with God for Wisdom/Holy Spirit, the answer is both yes and no. Let us begin by exploring the no answer. They are not equal, because Wisdom is portrayed in the Bible as God's first possession or creation.[588] But, while she is second compared to Him from our human perspective, she is first for Him. Jesus also said, in John 16:13, the Spirit of Truth, (synonym for the Holy Spirit) did not speak on her own accord.[589] The second answer regarding equality would be yes, if we look at the Creation story. There is no reference to God's Spirit being created in Genesis. She can be understood as always having been present within Him, and at the creation of time she came forth. If so, it becomes meaningless to discuss equality. She and He are part of the same original entity. She was present when God created everything, and regardless of this question, she was the co-creator of humans and as such: our Mother.

She is part of Him, and we feel and know God through her. We can think of it in the way of a good marriage. The partners are of one accord, and there are no secrets or sin, because sin and secrets separates. Neither is this a master and slave marriage, because she is not a servant of God, she is part of God. Wisdom of Solomon says, "She glorifies her noble birth by living with God, and the LORD of all loves her. For she is an initiate in the knowledge of God, and an associate in his works."[590] This depicts her as having a mind of her own, albeit in complete harmony/unity with God.

Another aspect of this is looking at the significance of God's sentiment when He said that it was not good for Adam to be alone. In the Garden of Eden, God planted trees to give food for Adam, while the animals were created to help his loneliness.[591] However, they were not sufficient for this role and Eve entered the story. In the first creation story, God declared that everything He had created was very good, which included man and woman who were to "Be fruitful and multiply" together.[592] Jesus also said that God is all good.[593] This may be a roundabout way of declaring that God is not alone.[594] He is not alone in particular because, yes, He has all of His Creation, but He also has His matching other feminine half. Ben Sirach put it this way, "All things are twofold, one opposite the other, and he has made nothing incomplete."[595] Life is very lonely if it is not shared, and the meaning of "One" in Deuteronomy 6:4 may not mean God is alone, but just the opposite.

With regards to classical monotheism, believing that God has a feminine counterpart is undoubtedly controversial, especially if we consider her having a mind of her own. Yet, that is how Jesus talked about the Holy Spirit. This is why she was deemed to have her own persona in the

Nicene Creed. With this in mind, why should any of the feminine aspects regarding the Holy Spirit present a problem for Christians who have already accepted the Trinity concept claiming that Jesus, Yahweh and the Holy Spirit all have different personas but are part of one God? Given the belief in the virgin birth, i.e. divine origin where God is Jesus' Father, plus Jesus' own claims of divinity, the Trinity could be understood differently and instead constitute a Holy family.

True monotheism does not need to be disregarded either, if it is understood as believing in one single origin of everything, where either He and She are One from the get go, or He existed first and she was is His first creation. Created from Him she came forth and they are in this way One. What is a more difficult question is if there is one Spirit or two since God is a Spirit.[596] The Holy Spirit is the Spirit of God and this must, as I see it, be answered that there is but One Spirit. The only way to try and grasp this is through the lenses of Biblical Marriage: they are One in a heavenly Marriage, which is the blueprint of Adam and Eve's first earthly marriage. The Bible testifies to God being male and the Holy Spirit female, and their Oneness is best understood this way.

Regardless of how this concept can be grasped, it is long overdue for Christians to stop overlooking the Divine Feminine present in the Bible from beginning to end. If we avoid acknowledging the Divine Feminine, it is we who are sexist, not God, and certainly not the authors of the Bible relaying God's word. Even without the presence of the feminine Holy Spirit we have to face the reality that the Bible does not present a case for monotheism in the sense that God is the only existing supernatural being. Other heavenly beings are described who can just as well be called minor gods. It is a question of semantics. Most of all, Jesus called himself "a god" or "divine" and defended it as Scriptural.[597]

This constitutes henotheism, which is the worship of one God, without denying the existence of other gods. Yet, this is not an entirely accurate label either, because it does not specify the distinctions that the Bible shows, such as no other gods are to be worshipped. Yahweh is the supreme Creator, and no one has any power apart from Him. He is the Creator, and if other "gods" exist, they were all created by Yahweh and subject to His rule.

Right from the first three chapters in Genesis we are forced to confront the question of monotheism because of the presence of evil while God is good. God is portrayed as love in Scripture, but love cannot exist without free will because you must be able to choose it.[598] Otherwise, humans would be marionettes. In this way, the devil is a necessarily existing consequence of free will. Because there is no limit on love, the inevitable consequence is that there is no counter limit on evil. In the beginning, at the start of creation, the presence of the male Yahweh and the female Holy Spirit can present a divine Marriage—an act of love—just the same way as when a man and women come together and their union creates a child. In this way all of Creation itself comes from love represented by the union of male and female as One.

The lack of a sharp division between pure monotheism and a variant of henotheism in the beliefs of both the ancient Israelites and Christianity is undoubtedly present in the Bible. Even so, the ancient Israelites set themselves apart by worshipping only Yahweh. The first commandment to have no other gods besides Yahweh did not only refer to other gods, or inanimate objects. It could mean anything that may come before Him, such as another human, desire for power, fame, possessions or a political party.[599] Putting anything before Him constitutes a form of idol worship.

All this to say that the Bible's description of monotheism is simply this: to worship/serve only Yahweh, because He is the Creator and Source of all. In Isaiah 45:5, Yahweh declares there is no God except only Him, but Chronicles and Psalms say Yahweh is above, and to be feared, over all other gods.[600] So, there is mixed Biblical verses regarding strict monotheism or a modified henotheism, where some passages do not deny the existence of other divine beings. This is why Jesus did not blaspheme by calling himself "a god" or "divine" when defending his title "Son of God." The Holy Spirit though, is not simply another deity, but represents something more profound. As the expression goes for marriage: She is His other half.

CHAPTER 7

THE CONCLUSION

Jesus answered him, "Very truly, I tell you, no one can see the
kingdom of God without being born from above."

John 3:3[601]

BRINGING IT ALL TOGETHER

The idea of a spiritual feminine force understood as
one with Yahweh in a heavenly marriage is found in the
Hebrew Scriptures. She comes in the form of Wisdom and
the Spirit of God (the Holy Spirit) who are one and the same
heavenly Power. She is described as an emanation of God as
well as the first creation by Yahweh. The concept of a Divine
Feminine was not a heresy, but Scriptural and part of
accepted theology both in the Old Testament and early
Christianity. We can see her openly in places like the book of
Proverbs, accepted by all Christians and Jews. We can detect
her throughout Scripture in the language of Jesus and his
ancestors, who spoke and wrote in Hebrew/Aramaic. She is
present in the first book of Genesis 1:1, where it describes in
the beginning "the Spirit of God was moving over the face of
the waters" all the way through Scripture to one of the very
last verses in the Book of Revelation where "The Spirit and
the Bride say 'Come.'"[602]

There is abundant evidence that the very first Gospel was written in Hebrew and possibly many more texts were written in Hebrew by Apostles and later disciples as well. Most of all, in testimonies for the Gospel of the Hebrews, claimed to be written by the Apostle Matthew, Jesus himself called the Holy Spirit, "my Mother." The Gospel of the Hebrews may very well belong to one of the oldest most accurate textual witnesses of all for what Jesus did and said. Jesus calling the Holy Spirit his "Mother" would explain the vast amounts of extra Biblical texts developing the Divine Feminine in the first few hundred years of the Church. While most of these texts are today popularly labeled as "Gnostic," and often described as part of a movement whose origins remain unclear,[603] the Divine Feminine idea was present even before the time of Jesus and accentuated by the dawn of Christianity. The "Gnostic" name given to those texts, derived from the focus seeking "knowledge" can be quite misleading. Attaching this name to all of them in retrospect can be quite misleading though. When Epiphanius wrote his "Panarion" in the late 4th century the Gnostics were merely one sect among many Christians. By grouping these texts as Gnostic, it makes it seem like they are wholly separate from anything the historical Jesus taught, which is incorrect. The very first followers of Jesus were called "Nazarenes." Later Nazarenes kept the Hebrew Gospel where Jesus called the Holy Spirit his "Mother," and it would be disingenuous to call them "Gnostic," because by doing so distances them from the first church.

Jesus' own brother, Jacob, was the first bishop of Jerusalem and he took on Jesus' role as the leader after he had passed. After Rome destroyed Jerusalem and the Temple fell, the bishops of the Church were no longer part of Jesus' family or Apostles. They were not even Jews. In essence, the Church was now run by Gentile converts, which facilitated the disappearance of several Hebrew customs and beliefs. Some Jewish followers never went along with the gentile those changes and held on to their original Hebrew Gospel, along with certain practices like the belief in the Holy Spirit as feminine.

It does not appear one single overarching unified group adhered to beliefs in the Divine Feminine. Historical testimonies show up in several places, and some who were "people of the Book," yet not Christians, adhered to beliefs in the Divine Feminine too. This tells us that the idea of the Divine Feminine did not originate with Jesus, which the Hebrew Scriptures themselves testify. The personified Wisdom and the feminine Holy Spirit reveal the ancient Hebrew tradition and were the foundation for this early Christian belief

The Gospel accounts tell us how much Jesus respected women, which enhances the likelihood of him understanding the significance of the Holy Spirit as a Divine Feminine aspect. Not only did Jesus consistently defend, heal, and interact positively with women, but the disciple closest to him could have been Mary Magdalene. The extra Biblical accounts of her strong relation to Jesus are quite early. The Gospels describe her as the first person Jesus revealed himself to as resurrected. In the light of how there are no indications of any female authors of Scripture, it is unlikely that a man would falsify the accounts detailing Jesus' devotion to Mary Magdalene and her status as an important disciple.

In ancient Israel and early Christianity, the femininity of the Holy Spirit was a well-known fact. Numerous texts reveal the Holy Spirit and Wisdom were understood as one and the same heavenly divine aspect of God. Most of all, the New Testament itself is the ultimate proof that Jesus' ideas about the Holy Spirit represented a specific strand within Judaism. The role of the Holy Spirit was developed, from the Hebrew Scriptures, to where she was an individual being with a more defined role for Jesus and his followers. Her role in Jesus' life is even a key factor as to why the all-male Trinity developed. Jesus' words about the Holy Spirit described her as a distinct entity wherefore the idea of a Trinity developed instead of a duality (Jesus and God). Additionally, the Nicene Creed set in motion ideas that changed Jesus from *being one* with the Father, to Jesus and the Father being the *same being*.

The only reason we cannot fully recognize her today is because the Holy Spirit is grammatically neuter in the Greek language and all the earliest New Testament texts we have yet found are written in Greek. This is why the translations today do not reveal how the Spirit is feminine via feminine pronouns. Latin subsequently became another major language of the Church, particularly after Jerome translated the Bible into Latin in the 4th century, commissioned by Pope Damasus, referred to as the Vulgate. It was this version that was the primary Bible translation used for centuries to come, all the way until the Reformation. Sadly, the Holy Spirit in Latin is grammatically masculine. This further facilitated her being combined as one aspect in the all-masculine Trinity. Her true identity came to be deeply buried by later Christian creeds of the emerging official, political church. Parallel to the disappearance of the feminine Holy Spirit were women's official roles in the church, their presence as wives to bishops and presbyters along with some early Hebrew elements of Christianity that were discarded one after another.

The languages that dominated and thus "conquered" in Christianity during the early centuries following Jesus' death, as stated, were Greek and Latin. It is ironic because both the Greek and Roman Empires were so severely oppressive towards the Israelite nation. They tortured and killed the Hebrews and tried repeatedly to have them to denounce their faith. In a roundabout way, ultimately the enemy succeeded in one aspect. It finally repressed the femininity of the Holy Spirit of God. Otherwise, Christian theology would definitely have been more closely related to what Jesus himself taught about the Spirit of God. If the role of Hebrew, as the sacred language, had continued to be emphasized, it would have presented a major obstacle to the male Trinitarian concept.

More urgently, though Biblical scholars are well familiar with the Holy Spirit's feminine gender in Hebrew Scriptures, she is virtually unknown among ordinary believers that the Spirit is a "she." Likewise, the stunning evidence from possibly the earliest Gospel that quotes Jesus calling the Holy Spirit "my Mother" is essentially information that is unheard of among regular Christians. While the femininity of the Holy Spirit eventually got lost in Christianity, Mother Mary's popularity grew. Elevating her was undoubtedly, at least partly, an unconscious compensation for the newly neutered Holy Spirit.

While the Trinity concept masculinized the Holy Spirit, it was also a game changer in separating Christianity once and for all from the Hebrew religion that Jesus lived and taught. Subsequent believers made changes that were not in line with the fundamental beliefs of Jesus and his forefathers. The Holy Spirit's femininity creates a problem for the doctrine of the all-male Trinity, and should be cause for Christians everywhere to reevaluate our own history before blindly following the traditions of men as Jesus warned.

WOMEN'S ROLE IN THE CHURCH TODAY

Most Christians agree on the profound significance of the Holy Spirit, but the fact that her gender has been lost in translation is not generally known. If churches worldwide would be true to what the Hebrew Scriptures, and the Aramaic/Hebrew speaking Jesus taught about the femininity of the Holy Spirit, it would revolutionize Christianity. Today many focus on things like the "right" for women to do everything men can and see this trend as representing equality. However, this is both false and superficial. We have equal worth *in spite* of being different which often means we do different work, have different roles, and so forth. For example, some people are angry that Catholicism does not allow female priests, but rarely consider that Jesus was not an earthly priest. He was a teacher of the Law. The Jewish priesthood was hereditary for males within the tribe of Levi, as part of the Mosaic covenant. Jesus was not a Levite but from the Davidic line of Judah, which is why he could be considered to be the king of Israel. The priesthood and kingship were separate.

The theology of Jesus as a spiritual priest formed soon after his death and resurrection. The letter of the Hebrews states that God declared Jesus to be a high priest forever in the order of Melchizedek.[604] This ancient Canaanite priest blessed Abraham, in the name of God the Most High, as they shared bread and wine (parallel drawn between Melchizedek and the Last Supper). The meaning of the name Melchizedek is "king of righteousness." Being the king of Salem (Jerusalem), he was also the "king of peace."[605] At the Last Supper Jesus asked the breaking of the bread and drinking of wine be done in his memory. The bread represented his body and wine his blood, shed to ratify the new covenant for forgiveness of sins prophesied by Jeremiah.[606]

The main function for the Levitical priests was to perform the sacrifice and declare blessings. The priest offered sacrifice at the Day of Atonement, and Jesus' sacrifice of himself gave him a priestly function in that sense. For the Christians, Jesus' one time sacrificial death substituted all future sacrifice. The new Christian priesthood mimicked Jesus' actions at the Last Supper and in this way continued to perform the "sacrifice" of the body/bread and blood/wine. They also took on the role of preaching/teaching, wherefore the ancient role of priests and later rabbis were combined. For these reasons Jesus came to represent both. Yet, Jesus' priestly title was fulfilled just before, and when, he died. He did not live and function as a priest in Israel.

The story of Mary and Martha where Jesus commended Mary for choosing the good part that would not be taken from her, can be understood as giving women, not just the right to learn, but indirectly the authority to teach.[607] In light of Jesus defending the Law as trumping traditions of men there is an argument to be made in support of women teaching.[608] Especially if we can sort out the difference between teaching and the ancient priestly function of performing the sacrifice. The early church had female deaconesses representing the Holy Spirit contrasting the male deacons who mirrored Christ. The early document called Didascalia testified for women's role to be baptizing, anointing, prophesying, and most of all, teaching. The Didascalia mentions that Jesus himself was served by female deacons and lists a series of female disciples, Mary Magdalene being the first one. This is another early seal of approval for an official role for women in the church, which included ministering to men too. If women could have an official position within the church that represent the work of the Holy Spirit, there ought to be no conflict in keeping the priesthood male. The role of a deaconess could fulfill this. It would then simply be a division of labor, where women's voices and work would be fully present and *complement* the work of men.

The many testimonies to an early Hebrew Gospel, where Jesus calls the Holy Spirit his "Mother," are

significant. This is not out of character given Jesus'
validation of women, his belief in a personified feminine
Wisdom, and his strong emphasis on the Holy Spirit as an
individual force. His passion for the Holy Spirit was no
small matter, as shown when he said, "And every one who
speaks a word against the Son of man will be forgiven; but
he who blasphemes against the Holy Spirit will not be
forgiven."[609] Jesus, whose message so heavily emphasized
forgiveness, drew a line in the sand when it came to who
you could blaspheme. It stopped right at the Holy Spirit.[610]
The significance of the female and male duality in ancient
Israel has been neglected in favor of an all-male Trinity, but
this is not an accurate picture of how things were neither
before Jesus was born, nor after his death and resurrection.

OUR MOTHER

Here is a re-cap of the main features about the Holy
Spirit, our Mother, and some interrelated matters. The new
covenant prophesied by Jeremiah announced the Spirit
speaking directly to our hearts. She *is* the Law and the
spiritual life-giver. The Holy Spirit represents life, which
Paul expressed this way in 2 Corinthians 3:4-6,

> Such is the confidence that we have through Christ
> toward God. Not that we are competent of ourselves
> to claim anything as coming from us; our competence
> is from God, who has made us competent to be
> ministers of a new covenant, not in a written code but
> in the Spirit; for the written code kills, but the Spirit
> gives life.

Paul does not proclaim doing away with the Law, such as
declaring what is evil is no longer evil. While speaking about
Yahweh being the God for Gentiles too he said, "Do we then

overthrow the law by this faith? By no means! On the contrary, we uphold the law."[611] It is a reference to death as a consequence of breaking it, and the new covenant promises of a return to life via a living relationship with God through the Holy Spirit. He also provides assurance of forgiveness for sins when we repent. Paul put it like this, "So you also must consider yourselves dead to sin and alive to God in Christ Jesus."[612]

The life force that was blown into the nostrils of Adam and Eve was called *nephesh* and gave physical life to our bodies. One of the several meanings of this word is "soul." The Holy Spirit, in Hebrew *hokmah ruah*, entering the prophets, the disciples and other believers, parallels *nephesh* by being the spiritual life force. She gives life to our faith and reveals the truth.[613] Jesus explained to the Pharisee Nicodemus what being born again meant, and stated,

> "Truly, truly, I say to you, unless one is born of water and the Spirit, he cannot enter the kingdom of God. That which is born of the flesh is flesh, and that which is born of the Spirit is spirit."[614]

Receiving the Holy Spirit gives you an insight that is not worldly and leads to everlasting life. Being an encompassing life giver is also reflected in Eve, the first woman, whose name literally means "mother of all living."[615] Proverbs 3:18 says that Wisdom is a "tree of life to those who lay hold of her" and in Genesis, it is eating from the Tree of Life that lets you live forever.[616] In Revelation the Tree of Life is situated in the middle of the main street by the river, bearing fruit each month with its leaves for the healing of the nations.

In addition, the culmination in heaven is described as a marriage. Jerusalem symbolizes God's people and represents the Bride of Christ mirroring how Israel was God's wife. One of the very last lines in Revelation is,

The Spirit and the Bride say, "Come." And let him who hears say, "Come." And let him who is thirsty come, let him who desires take the water of life without price.[617]

We can read this as either: the Spirit and the Bride are two, or they are one and the same. If they are two, the Spirit is the Holy Spirit of God making her our Mother.

Jesus said, "if any one thirst, let him come to me and drink. He who believes in me, as the scripture has said, 'Out of his heart shall flow rivers of living water.'"[618] The Hebrew word for "heart" is a symbolic reference to someone's intent, but the word itself can also mean "belly" or "womb." This suggests that either the correct translation is "heart," referring to the purification of the inside of a person such as thoughts and feelings, or the original Hebrew may have been "out of the ("her") womb shall flow rivers of living water" indicating salvation from God's Wisdom. The purpose of the sentence is ultimately the same, but the second makes the presence of our divine Mother apparent. If the latter is true, it again intertwines the Divine Feminine with being "born again," plus we can see how inspiration and intuition, often physically felt in the heart and belly, are tied to the divine Mother.[619]

The female being the vessel for new life parallels the role of the Holy Spirit, who envelops you in your spiritual birth and leads you to eternal life. If she was the one next to Yahweh in the creation of mankind the picture of her as our divine Mother is complete. Through her, also represented as the Tree of Life, we gain not only eternal life, but bliss. "Life" in the Bible is in essence a synonym for "good." When God had finished creating He looked at it all and called it "very good."[620] The consequences of Eve and Adam tasting the forbidden fruit caused an imbalance between the two sexes, as well as the relationship between humans, the rest of creation, and the earth itself. Jesus, the Messiah, came to teach and lead us to the Way back to life, and the prophesied Messianic age is a restoration of the original harmony and balance between man/masculine values and woman/feminine values.

When Jesus taught us to pray to "our Father" and say "Thy kingdom come. Thy will be done, On earth as it is in heaven" he let us know that life on earth is about our journey in learning how to live here as close as we can to how it is in Heaven.[621] Our Mother has been sent to live in us in order to gently lead us to know the truth and eternal life.

Because the Holy Spirit is feminine, a sole emphasis on the masculine Yahweh does not give an accurate picture of what the Bible declares. As mentioned in the beginning of this book, some promote gender-neutral language to be used when God is addressed in Scripture, to "fix" what they see as sexism. The irony is that altering these sacred texts because of modern political correctness would distort what the Bible says and even more hinder the presence of the Divine Feminine.[622] The neuter form does not even exist in Biblical Hebrew, and changing what the texts say constitutes censorship, which is strictly forbidden in the Bible.[623] It is because of the meticulous transmission of Scripture by countless faithful scribes that the Bible is so brutally honest. It does not always give an idyllic picture of people or events in history. Neither does it answer things in the way we think it should. Jesus himself was certainly not a people pleaser. But, it is in the midst of this honesty that God can be found. The faithful copying of the texts was done because for millennia the texts have been, and continue to be, believed to be inspired by God. The Law was given by God directly to Moses, whom He spoke to face to face. The prophets had visions and prophetic words from God and spoke on His behalf. Numerous others throughout Scripture had direct interactions with God. Jesus taught what he learned from

Yahweh, and for all these reasons we can find God by reading and studying the Bible. This is why transmitting the words and genders accurately are essential.

Jesus is the prophesied "tested stone," who is the cornerstone of the Christian faith.[624] However, the concept of the male Trinity has served as a stumbling block, effectively concealing the true identity of the Holy Spirit. The reason the Jews accused Jesus of blasphemy was because of his claimed divinity and having a seat in Heaven at the right hand of God. His comments later developed into making Jesus to be God Himself. The whole reason the idea about a Trinity, instead of a Duality (Yahweh and Jesus), emerged was because the Holy Spirit's individual identity was so pronounced. She was understood as more than just part of God. Jesus' teachings about her testify to a belief within ancient Israel where a distinct heavenly feminine force played a major theological role. She is God's counterpart complementing Him. His abode is Heaven and hers is earth.

With the Holy Spirit's true gender lost in translation, the Divine Feminine is consistently hidden. Since the Holy Spirit has a prime-role in the New Testament, from beginning to end, it makes it all the more problematic that the Spirit's femininity is not known. She was instrumental in the conception of Jesus, and she is present in, and leads us to, the Heavenly Jerusalem. Jesus let the disciples know that it was she who would go with them when he sent them out into the world to evangelize.[625] She guides the Church, and as such she is the Bride. The merging of the Holy Spirit and Wisdom as one and the same feminine force crystallized her identity and role, which is seen in the New Testament. It is most likely Jesus' specific teachings about the Holy Spirit as a "Mother" that led to so many early texts, now referred to as "Gnostic," where she plays such a prominent part.

Jesus did not invent notions about a heavenly Mother. She was derived from all of the Hebrew Scriptures.

Acknowledging the Holy Spirit and Wisdom to be the same force and that it is she who is next to Yahweh in the Creation story would give God's "better half" back her rightful identity in Christianity. Yahweh does not appreciate anyone changing His words; thus Yahweh would not approve of any man changing her identity so that she would be referred to as a "he," when He so clearly identified her as a "she." If Jesus is sitting on the right hand of the Father, surely the left is reserved for someone else very special. She is the one seated next to Yahweh. She belongs by his side, just like He belongs next to her.

OUR FATHER

It is not just Jesus' emphasis on the Holy Spirit's role that testifies to the duality, but the fact that Jesus called Yahweh "Father." There is something usually overlooked in Jesus' use of this term. While calling the Creator, "Father," is a prevalent epithet for God in the New Testament, it is, in comparison, rare in the Hebrew Scriptures.[626] God is more so referred to variants of the phrase, "the LORD God of your fathers" pointing to how Yahweh/El was their ancestral God."[627] On a few occasions God is described specifically as the Father with reference to a specific person with messianic references. One of those is Psalm 89 that has a long vision given to the faithful about Yahweh's covenant with His anointed David and the Davidic line. God said He would never break it, saying "Like the moon it shall be established for ever; it shall stand firm while the skies endure."[628] God also said that David will cry to Him, "Thou art my Father, my God, and the Rock of my salvation."[629] So, in the small number of instances that an individual is described to have God as "Father," they are all references to Solomon or King David.[630] Jesus calling God "Father" is in this sense fulfilling yet another Messianic prophecy. Jesus is revealing himself as

Yahweh's Messiah of the Davidic line in an everlasting covenant by calling God his "Father."

At the same time, the whole notion of addressing Yahweh as "Father," by implication of its definition, requires the existence of a Mother. In other words, Jesus so frequently using of the term "Father" can indirectly support a belief in a heavenly Mother. The fact that the Gospel of the Hebrews confirms her identity is no small matter. When Jesus taught his disciples to address God as "our Father," he indicated that his followers would be able, like him, to have a close relationship with God and become sons of God.[631] This ties into what was discussed earlier; that becoming a child of God was not a matter of being born, but being born anew, spiritually.[632] The Greek word used for "anew" in John 3:3 can also mean "again" or "from above," where "above" refers to heaven. Peter explains that being born again is not referring to a human seed but the word of God, which cannot be destroyed[633] In the letter of John, it is explained this way,

> Every one who believes that Jesus is the Christ is a child of God, and every one who loves the parent loves the child. By this we know that we love the children of God, when we love God and obey his commandments. For this is the love of God, that we keep his commandments. And his commandments are not burdensome. For whatever is born of God overcomes the world; and this is the victory that overcomes the world, our faith. Who is it that overcomes the world but he who believes that Jesus is the Son of God?[634]

This Scripture reveals the relationship that being a child of God entails. It means believing that Jesus is God's anointed, and loving God means following His commandments.

214

The missing piece is that Jesus as the Messiah (the anointed) had the Holy Spirit. It was Jesus' emphasis on having her in order to get to know God that he passed on to the Apostles and countless disciples. Being born from above was explained by Jesus. In John's Gospel we read,

> Jesus answered, "Truly, truly, I say to you, unless one is born of water and the Spirit, he cannot enter the kingdom of God. That which is born of the flesh is flesh, and that which is born of the Spirit is spirit. Do not marvel that I said to you, 'You must be born anew.'"[635]

When Jesus spoke of water he referred to the waters of baptism. This too parallels birth in the sense of how a baby bathes in amniotic fluid before being born. A woman's water "breaks" before the baby is born forth paralleling the receiving of the Holy Spirit after being baptized. Matthew describes Jesus' baptism this way,

> And when Jesus was baptized, he went up immediately from the water, and behold, the heavens were opened and he saw the Spirit of God descending like a dove, and alighting on him . . .[636]

Jesus' own baptism was followed immediately by the baptism of the Holy Spirit, in the form of a dove, coming down on him. The life Jesus guides us to is one where we too can have the Holy Spirit as *our Mother*.

LIFE IS A DANCE

The focus on equality between women and men today is misleading because it is equal *worth* that matters, not being able to do the same things. We are neither physically nor mentally identical, not on the outside nor the inside. There

215

are many physical features and traits we share of course, and many things we can do equally well. But, there are also many traits we do not share, and many things we cannot do equally well, or even at all. The most important thing that is lost in the equality debate is what women have traditionally done for millennia, such as raising children and preparing food, which should be valued instead of the focus only being on women proving they can do what men do, and believing that when they have done that they will gain equal worth.

Women today try to "do it all." Yet, it is still not recognized that women have *always* worked very hard and done more than raising children. It is a physical impossibility to raise a young child and be at work, outside of the home, full time. If you are physically absent, someone else must raise your child the majority of the time the child is awake since you cannot be at two places at once. The one thing that children demand more than anything is our time. Seeking women's equality today has translated into lessening her role as a mother instead of appreciating it more. It expresses to our culture that being a mother who raises her own children is not significant. When we diminish something as profound as motherhood and *strive* to create a world where we place children in the earliest, most important, years of their lives in the care of paid workers, we declare that making money is worth more than raising children. Making sure that children interfere as little with our lives as possible, so women can be recognized in what is often referred to as a "man's world" is hardly progress. It is a woman's role that should be treasured instead of downplayed and devalued. We do not want to diminish the danger an imbalance of worldly power by only men can present to women, but attempts to correct this have, in vital aspects, gone awry and have led to the degradation of our society as a whole.

When Jesus selected 12 male Apostles, many men have thought, and continue to think, that it was because he did not find women worthy. But, the Gospels themselves tell us differently. Jesus defended female discipleship. Yet, there were practical reasons, along with physical dangers, for women to do what the male Apostles did, and women are often in the exact same predicament today. Jesus was protective of women, and this is a trait that is not only incredibly good, but something that most women crave from men in a primal way.

The Bible urges men to treat women with honor and respect. It also teaches us that women and men *complement* each other, not that women are the same as men. Humans are divided in two genders: male and female, which mirror God in the form of the male Yahweh and the female Holy Spirit. This is what the Creation story in Genesis is ultimately about.

It is a fact that the Holy Spirit in Hebrew and Aramaic is feminine. It is also a fact that Jesus, who spoke Aramaic and Hebrew, made specific illustrations about the Holy Spirit that made it certain the feminine gender of the Spirit is theologically significant. It is not just a grammatical matter. Nicodemus, a Pharisee, came to Jesus secretly at night because of how dangerous it had become to be associated with him. This is the conversation that transpired:

> This man came to Jesus by night and said to him, "Rabbi, we know that you are a teacher come from God; for no one can do these signs that you do, unless God is with him." Jesus answered him, "Truly, truly, I say to you, unless one is born anew, he cannot see the kingdom of God." Nicode'mus said to him, "How can a man be born when he is old? Can he enter a second time into his mother's womb and be born?" Jesus answered, "Truly, truly, I say to you, unless one is born of water and the Spirit, he cannot enter the

kingdom of God. That which is born of the flesh is flesh, and that which is born of the Spirit is spirit. Do not marvel that I said to you, 'You must be born anew.' The wind blows where it wills, and you hear the sound of it, but you do not know whence it comes or whither it goes; so it is with every one who is born of the Spirit."[637]

Jesus made a clear distinction between being born in the flesh by a woman and being born again by the feminine Spirit. It is precisely because the Spirit is feminine that Jesus uses this imagery. The message is that it is the latter birth of the Spirit that makes you a child of God. When you have the Holy Spirit you know God; you feel Him and you hear His voice.

Peter, the Apostle, put it this way, "You have been born anew, not of perishable seed but of imperishable, through the living and abiding God . . . ."[638] Here, we see how the Word of God is the seed, signifying God being male. The seed fertilizes the Holy Spirit, and you are born again. The word for "again" can also mean "from above" referring to heaven as just stated earlier. This all describes the process of becoming a child of God, which is an exact parallel to how children are born on earth. Via the mixing of male and female, we are conceived. Yet, we grow and are finally birthed by the female. The feminine is the chosen vessel by God where we are both earthly and spiritually born. To downplay, or deny, the importance of the Spirit being feminine is just plain wrong. If we are born again via the Holy Spirit, she is our Mother.

Wisdom of Solomon 7:24-30 says,

For Wisdom is more mobile than any motion; because of her pureness she pervades and penetrates all things. For she is a breath of the power of God, and a pure emanation of the glory of the Almighty;

therefore nothing defiled gains entrance into her. For she is a reflection of eternal light, a spotless mirror of the working of God, and an image of his goodness. Though she is but one, she can do all things, and while remaining in herself, she renews all things; in every generation she passes into holy souls and makes them friends of God and prophets; for God loves nothing so much as the man who lives with wisdom. For she is more beautiful than the sun, and excels every constellation of the stars. Compared with the light she is found to be superior, for it is succeeded by the night, but against wisdom evil does not prevail.

Wisdom conquers sin, and as the battle between good and evil is raging on more than ever throughout the globe, we need to turn to her. Wisdom has always included intuition, which is a typically feminine attribute; even known as "women's intuition." No wonder this is the case since the Holy Spirit is feminine It means listening to another voice inside that is not your own, i.e. not feelings, but the voice of God. The door (Jesus) that opens for this to be possible is faith; believing in and surrendering to Yahweh and His will, not our own. This divine Source is what gave Jesus authority. It is inside of us where Yahweh's new covenant is written. He said, "I will put my law within them, and I will write it upon their hearts; and I will be their God, and they shall be my people."[639] The Law (Torah), yet another synonym for the Holy Spirit, leads us to do the will of God, which is for our own good.

The role of the feminine on an individual basis as well as on a worldly plain is in a constant relation to the masculine, the way the Star of David depicts it. The feminine triangle pointing downwards (earth) and the masculine upward (heaven) triangle are intertwined, together forming the pattern of a star. The triangle pointing downwards represents the feminine pubic triangle, passive (peaceful) and receptive. The triangle pointing upwards is the active male aggressor. Think of dancing: the man leads and the woman follows, but it is the tension between the two that the dance depends on. If either one is too forceful or too weak, it does not work, the pattern falls apart. But, if it is just right, it flows. This is when you experience bliss.

One of the Ten Commandments is, "Honor your father and your mother . . . ."[640] This is a micro-instruction that is also applicable on the macro level. We need to honor not only our earthly parents but an equilibrium that the world hinges on. We need to respect both feminine and masculine values and traits equally, understand how both are needed, complement each other to create a balance. If we honor both Yahweh and the Holy Spirit, we will restore the balance.

The Hebrew word for "Spirit" is *ruah*, which also means "wind," as well as "breath." When addressing the Apostles Jesus, "breathed on them, and said to them, 'Receive the Holy Spirit.'"[641] The breath of God originates from within God and is given to us. This illustrates the layers of meanings the feminine Spirit has. The Tree of Life is no accidental symbol for the Holy Spirit. We rely on trees for our very existence, they breathe out oxygen for us and we carbon dioxide for them. We literally exchange breath every day. The roots of trees save the soil and keep the water clean. While half of the air we need to breathe comes from trees and plants on land, the other half comes from phytoplankton in the oceans. These are the lungs of the earth that breathe life into ours. The Holy Spirit is in the same way the lungs of God. She can enter into people, yet she is part of God. Breath in humans is a sign of life. When we physically die, we stop breathing. When the Holy Spirit enters us we are spiritually born, and we gain spiritual life. This life is eternal life with God.

We can see God and the Holy Spirit as One with two equal parts, distinct but inseparable, like a Heavenly Marriage, which brings us back to them being One. We can also perceive Yahweh as the first: the singularity that started creation and time and the instance He did, she was by His side, possibly created then or an inevitable part of Him before. However we view it, God is not alone because life, even for Yahweh, does not have much meaning if it is not shared. It is time for those of us who adhere to the Holy Scriptures to acknowledge that both the female and male aspects of God are present in the Bible. We need to deeply think about what it means. It applies especially to those of us who have more of the Wisdom books such as my own Church: Roman Catholicism. This is denomination has been the lone voice to retain an elevation of a feminine feature in Christianity, because of its high reverence for Mary. Her motherly love is what eventually led me to the discoveries of the Holy Spirit shared in this book.

We need to recognize the implications of the Holy Spirit/Wisdom being a feminine force in the Bible. Jesus said, "seek, and you will find."[642] She can be found in Scripture, and in the living Church, the body of Christ who is the Bride. She is God's presence on earth yet hidden from the physical eye, just like the wind, the other meaning of *ruah*, the Hebrew word for Spirit. You cannot see the wind, but you know it is real because of its effects. Likewise, you see and know the Holy Spirit is real because of how she affects you and others who have been touched by her. Once she takes her place inside a person, she fills him or her with divine love and a joy that is not dependent on events in this world. The Holy Spirit changes a human from within and bestows a Wisdom that comes from above.

When the disciples asked the resurrected Jesus if he would now restore the kingdom of Israel, the last thing he said to them before being lifted up was,

"It is not for you to know times or seasons which the Father has fixed by his own authority. But you shall receive power when the Holy Spirit has come upon you; and you shall be my witnesses in Jerusalem and in all Judea and Sama'ria and to the end of the earth."[643]

It is the Power of the Holy Spirit that transforms believers and consequently the world. Jesus sent out his Apostles to preach and teach, and make disciples of all nations.[644] By doing so everyone would be invited to the Kingdom before the return of the King, and it is up to each person to answer yes or no. Jesus, the Hebrew Messiah and Son of God, came to show us the Way to true salvation through our Mother to our Father. The Way of Life is the way home.

"And do not fear those who kill the body but cannot kill the soul; rather fear him who can destroy both soul and body in hell."

Jesus in Matthew 10:28

ABBREVIATIONS

Abbreviations of Biblical and Apocryphal books:

Old Testament:

Gn	Genesis
Ex	Exodus
Lv	Leviticus
Nm	Numbers
Dt	Deuteronomy
Jos	Joshua
Jgs	Judges
Ru	Ruth
1 Sm	1 Samuel
2 Sm	2 Samuel
1 Kgs	1 Kings
2 Kgs	2 Kings
1 Chr	1 Chronicles
2 Chr	2 Chronicles
Ezr	Ezra
Neh	Nehemiah
Tb	Tobit
Jdt	Judith
Est	Eshter
1 Mc	1 Maccabees
2 Mc	2 Maccabees
Jb	Job
Ps	Job
Prv	Proverbs
Eccl	Ecclesiastes
Sg	Song of Solomon
Wis	Wisdom of Solomon
Sir	Sirach
Is	Isaiah

Old Testament: (continued)

Jer	Jeremiah
Lam	Lamentations
Bar	Baruch
Ez	Ezekial
Dn	Daniel
Hos	Hosea
Jl	Joel
Am	Amos
Ob	Obadiah
Jon	Jonah
Mi	Micah
Na	Nahum
Hb	Habakkuk
Zep	Zephaniah
Hg	Haggai
Zec	Zechariah
Mal	Malachi

New Testament:

Mt	Matthew
Mk	Mark
Lk	Luke
Jn	John
Acts	Acts of the Apostles
Rom	Romans
1 Cor	1 Corinthians
2 Cor	2 Corinthians
Gal	Galations
Eph	Ephesians
Phil	Philippians
Col	Colossians
1 Thes	1 Thessalonians

New Testament: (continued)

2 Thes	2 Thessalonians
1 Tm	1 Timothy
2 Tm	2 Timothy
Ti	Titus
Phlm	Philemon
Heb	Hebrews
Jas	James
1 Pt	1 Peter
2 Pt	2 Peter
1 Jn	1 John
2 Jn	2 John
3 Jn	3 John
Jude	Jude
Rv	Revelation
1 Esd	1 Esdra (in Catholic appendix this is 3 Esdra)
2 Esd	2 Esdra (in Catholic appendix this is 4 Esdra)

Abbreviations of other Biblical Sources:

DRA	The Bouay-Rheims, American Edition
KJV	King James Authorized Version
NAS	New American Standard Bible
NRS	New Revised Standard Version

General Abbreviations:

A.D.	Anno Domini (Latin for: "in the year of our Lord")
B.C.	Before Christ
ca	circa
chap.	chapter
Ibid	In the same place (Latin: ibidem)

General Abbreviations: (continued)

i.e.   In other words (Latin: id est)
p.   page
Vol(s)   Volume(s)

Abbreviations of Ancient Sources and who they were:

Eusebius: Eccl Hist, The Fathers of the Church: Eusebius Pamphili, Ecclesiastical History, Books 1-5. Eusebius of Caesarea was a Christian Historian and Bishop, who lived ca 260-339 A.D.

Josephus: Ant, Jwr, Apn, The Works of Flavius Josephus: Antiquities of the Jews (Ant), Against Apion (Apn), The Jewish War (Jwr). Flavius Josephus was a Jewish Historian, who lived ca 37-95 A.D.

Philo: Her. The Works of Philo Judaeus, the Contemporary of Josephus: Who is Heir of Divine Things (Her). Philo of Alexandria was a Jewish, Greek speaking, Alexandrian Philosopher who lived ca 10-15 B.C.- to sometime around 45-50 A.D.

Abbreviation of Lexicon:

BDB   *A Hebrew and English Lexicon of the Old Testament*

FOOTNOTES

CHAPTER 1

1. *The Oxford Companion to the Bible*, Edited by Bruce M. Metzger and Michael D. Coogan, New York, Oxford, Oxford University Press 1993, p. 501.

2. *The New Oxford Annotated Bible with the Apocrypha*, Edited by Hebert G. May and Bruce M. Metzger, expanded edition, Revised Standard Version, New York, Oxford University Press, Copyright, 1962, 1973, p. xiii. All Bible quotes, *unless specified otherwise*, will be from this Bible.

3. Waltke, Bruce K. and Connor, M., *An introduction to Biblical Hebrew Syntax*, Eisenbrauns, Winona Lake, Indiana, 1990, p. 28

4. Ibid p. 3.

5. Ibid p.19

6. Though three of them, *waw*, *yod* and *he* were also used to indicate vowels, referred to as "matres lectiones."

7. The earliest parts of it done in the 3ᵈ century B.C. in Alexandria, Egypt for Greek-speaking Jews. This is usually abbreviated as "LXX" because it was according to history 70 scholars who did the translation.

8. Jl 2:30.

9. "Targums" (an Aramaic word meaning "translation") are Aramaic interpretations of the Hebrew Bible, done by Palestinian Jews since the Second Temple period. They went beyond translating and paraphrasing, and even added things in the interpretations, but nevertheless they are important in the history of textual transmission of the Hebrew Scriptures. See *The Oxford Companion to the Bible*, p.754-755.

10. A medieval scroll, although it is preserving a much older tradition, see *The Oxford Companion to the Bible*, p. 672.

11. Commentaries of Jewish Scriptures.

12. 4th century manuscript of the Greek Bible discovered in a Sinai monastery in the mid 1800's.

13. Translation of the Old Testament (Hebrew) and the Gospels (Greek) into Latin by a scholar named Jerome who was appointed by Pope Damasus in 382 A.D. to do this, which he did in twenty years. See *The Oxford Companion to the Bible*, p. 790.

14. 4th century manuscript of the Greek Bible residing in the Vatican.

15. The Syriac (Aramaic dialect) version of the Bible and the official text for the Church of the East. It has ambiguous origins with earliest remaining manuscript from the fifth and sixth century A.D. See *The Oxford Companion to the Bible*, p. 752-753.

16. Ibid p. 159-160.

17. See *The Oxford Companion to the Bible*, p. 102-104 for a good summary on the New Testament and p. 100-102 about the Hebrew Bible and Old Testament.

18. *Harper's Bible Commentary*, James L Mays General Editor, Harper & Row, Publishers, San Francisco, 1988, p. 32.

19. *The Oxford Companion to the Bible*, p. 758.

20. *Josephus: Apn* 1:38-42.

21. Many leaves of the Old Testament were unfortunately missing.

22. Passages Hebrews 9:14-13:23 are also missing.

23. Relevant to mention here is that it is uncertain when the Jewish canon was established. Many refer to the council of Jamnia (Jabnah) 90 A.D. as where the Jewish canon was established. However, there is no evidence for this and appears to only show a debate between Rabbis over the canonicity of Ecclesiastes and Song of Songs. It is worth noting too that the Sadducees only accepted the Torah and the Old Testament mentions books that have been lost for a long time like "the Book of the Wars of the Lord" and "the Book of Jashar" for example. See Nm 21:14, 2 Sm 1:18 & Jos 10:13.

24. *The Old Testament Pseudepigrapha*, Volume 1 & 2, Edited by James H. Charlesworth, Doubleday, 1985.

25. The Prologue of Sir.

26. Ibid p. 820-821. See also The New Oxford Annotated Bible, the Apocrypha, p.102.

27. See for example, Sir 51:27 and Mt 11:29, Sir 10:14 and Lk 1:52, Mk 4:5, 16-17 and Sir 40:15, Mt 7:16, 20 and Sir 27:6, Jas 1:19 and Sir 5:11.

28. For brief history of the Apocrypha see The New Oxford Annotated Bible in the introduction for it, p. xi-xxii.

29. The Greek word "headlong" and "swollen" are nearly identical in Greek wherefore the idea is that a scribal error occurred and "swollen" was the original meaning.

30. Mt 21:1-9, Mk 11:1-10, Lk 19:28-38, Jn 12:14-16.

31. Gods also rode donkeys. Asherah, the mother goddess in ancient Canaan rode a donkey when going to see El, the Father of the gods. See Parker, Simon B. (Editor), *Ugaritic Narrative Poetry*, SBL Writings from the Ancient World Series, Scholars Press, 1997, p. 126.

32. 2 Sm 16:2, 1 Kgs 1:38-40. For other examples see Gn 49:10-11, Jgs 5:10.

33. Zec 9:9. John's Gospel does as well (12:14-16) but has a shortened version of it. Is 62:11 is also possibly alluded to.

34. Mt 21:5.

35. See for example the contrast in Rv 19:11.

36. *A Hebrew and English Lexicon of the Old Testament* (based on the lexicon of William Gesenius as Translated by Edward Robinson), Edited by Francis Brown, with the cooperation of S.R., Driver and Charles Briggs A. Brown, Francis, Driver S.R., Briggs Charles A, Clarendon Press: Oxford, (note by Driver about the re-issue, Nov. 1951), p. 776-777. I will refer to this lexicon from here on as *BDB*.

37. Zec 9:9.

38. *Harper's Bible Commentary*, p. 974.

39. See *BDB*, p. 446. This word is from the same root as Jesus' name, meaning "deliver." In Hebrew the noun *Yeshuah* means "salvation." This word being in the niphal means to "be saved," "liberated" or "victorious" (as in battle). Since it is not the Messiah that needs to be saved "victorious" is a better fit.

40. Jn 18:36.

41. Possible exceptions to surrounding polytheistic beliefs would be Zoroastrianism, depending on how you view it, as it has one main God, and a lesser god, being the Devil playing an important role, and in this sense it is a dualistic faith, which Jesus' brand of Judaism and later Christianity can be understood as too. Egypt also had one ruler in the fourteenth century B.C. Amenhotep, who changed his name to "Akhenaton" for the sun god "Aton" thus denouncing the god "Amen." He enforced the belief in just this one sun god Aton, but when he died, his reforms were reversed. See Gordon, Cyrus H., Gary A. Rendsburg, *The Bible and the Ancient Near East*, Fourth Edition, W. W. Norton & Company, New York, London, 1997, p. 82-85.

42. *Harper's Bible Commentary*, p. 39-40.

43. For example, Marcus Borg & John Dominic Crossan, William G. Dever, Bart D. Ehrman. I do not mean that every scholarly assessment is necessarily always right, only that Biblical research is made available for the general public. Relevant to this is research by modern physicist Gerald Schroeder.

44. Paul's points about women being submissive will be addressed later in the next chapter.

45. Nm 26:52-53.

46. Ibid 27:3-4.

47. Ibis 27:5-8

48. Prv 31:1

49. Sg chap. 2.

50. Jgs 4:4, Neh 6:14, 2 Kgs 22:14

51. Ex 15:20.

52. Is 8:3. Some translations just have "wife" because he, being a prophet would not break the Law, but the Hebrew word used is the female word for prophet suggesting that his wife was a prophetess.

53. Lk 2:36, 38.

54. Acts 2:17-18 quoting Jl 2:28-29.

55. Ex 20:12, Dt 5:16.

56. Clearly, Sarah's idea of having Abraham getting an offspring from someone else, when she could not conceive, backfired. God showed her and Abraham that if He wanted her to have a child despite physically not being able to, it could and would be done, by Him alone. His promise that Sarah would bear a son came after she had already taken matters of getting a child into her own hands providing an illustration of the destructiveness of doing so.

57. Gn 16:11. See also ibid chap. 16 & 21:8-21.

58. Ibid 16:13.

59. 1 Sm, chap. 25.

60. Mt 27:19.

61. Acts 16:14

62. Ibid.

63. Ibid 16:40

64. Gn 3:20

65. *The Oxford Companion to the Bible*, p. 228-229.

66. Cady Stanton, Elisabeth, *The Women's Bible, a Classic Feminist Perspective*. Dover Publications, Inc. Mineola, New York, 2002 (originally published New York: European Pub. Co. 1895-1898), p. x.

67. Ibid p. 26.

68. Ibid p. 27.

CHAPTER 2

69. Jn 4:24.

70. Re-affirming reality since it is because of the mixing of male and female that humans exist.

71. For a few examples of the Spirit (*ruah*) used with both with Elohim and Yahweh see Jgs 3:10, 6:34, 1 Sm 16:14, 1 Kgs 18:12 for the "Spirit of Lord" (Lord = Yahweh) and Gn 1:2, Ex 31:3, 35:31, Nm 24:2 for the "Spirit of God" (God = Elohim).

72. See for example Jn 16:13. The reason the Spirit is male here is due to Greek grammar. The Greek is a translation of what Jesus said in Aramaic/Hebrew.

73. The Greek translation of the Hebrew Scriptures was done in the third century B.C.

74. In Latin, another relevant language in early Christianity, the Spirit is male.

75. Primarily the Nicene Creed in 325 A.D. and subsequent additions at the council of Constantinople 381 A.D.

76. The Hebrew word *Elohim* is a subject all on its own. It was dealt with in the *God is Not Alone: Our Mother – the Holy Spirit*, and will be part of another forthcoming book.

77. The Hebrew language does not even have neuter, only masculine and feminine reflecting the human condition.

78. Mt 6:9.

79. Jer 1:9.

80. Is 6:1, 2.

81. 1 Kgs 22:19. This is paralled in 2 Chronicles 18:18.

82. Rv 22:1, 3-4.

83. Is 63:10. This is a reminder of the inscriptions referring to "Yahweh and His Asherah."

84. All quotes that explicitly show the gender of God's Spirit and His hand are my translations from Biblia Hebraica Stuttgartensia.

85. See also Jn 20:22.

86. Ibid 11:5.

87. Most body parts in Hebrew that come in two are feminine in form. We can see this parallel between the Spirit and the hand in other places such as in Jb 26:13 where he announces about God that, "By his wind the heavens were made fair; his hand piercing the fleeing serpent." The word "wind" is the Hebrew word *ruah* meaning "Spirit."

88. See for example Dt 34:9 and Acts 8:18

89. The Holy Spirit landed on Jesus in the form of a dove at his baptism for example, yet it was God's voice *from heaven* that spoke. This is an example of that duality played out. See Mt 3:16-17, Mk 1:10-11, Lk 3:22.

90. Twice, but the second time in another grammatical conjugation.

91. Prv 8:29-30

92. Sir 24:3.

93. Gn 1:2.

94. Jn 20:22.

95. Ben-Sirach was originally written in Hebrew.

96. Sir 1:1-10.

97. Lk 1:15, Acts 1:8, 2:4, 38, 4:8, 31.

98. Wis 9:9-11.

99. Ibid 9:4.

100. Ibid 9:1-2.

101. Ibid 7:25-26.

102. BGT.

103. Anaxagoras (500-428 B.C.), Shi Shen (4ᵗ B.C.), Aristotle (384-322)

104. Sir 43:6-8.

105. "The hosts on high" is also likely translation of the "divine council" revealing the ancient idea of several divine beings in heaven.

106. Wis 7:25. Observe the word "glory" here, which is Shekinah.

107. I will elaborate more on this in the last chapter.

108. Wis 8:3-4

109. Ibid chap. 10.

110. Lk 1:67.

111. Acts 2:4.

112. Dn 4:8-9, 18.

113. Ibid 5:11.

114. From a scholarly perspective the book of Daniel has several connections to Canaanite themes, wherefore this could be liked to El and Asherah.

115. From a scholarly perspective these, and other instances of this, could be ancient traces of Asherah.

116. Dt 34:9.

117. Nm 27:18.

118. Ibid 27:22-23.

119. Heb 6:2. For Jesus see for example, Mt 19:15, Mk 8:25, 10:16, Lk 4:40, 13:13. It was connected to blessing, healing and the Holy Spirit.

120. The New Oxford Annotated Bible, Apocrypha, p.198.

121. Relating Her to Shekinah (will be discussed later) plus we can again see how she radiates God's light and is not only a reflection.

122. Parker (Editor), *Ugaritic Narrative Poetry*, p. 182.

123. Jb 38:7. These are the ones understood by most scholars to be the reason for the plural pronouns in Gen 1:26. My argument presented earlier for this still applies. The rest of the Canaanite pantheon may have been present, but not as co-creators.

124. Prv 3:19.

125. The mentioning of the stars shouting out in gladness is an immediate reminder of Ugaritic passages who refer to the heavenly host as the "assembly of the stars." Jer 10:12. See also Jer 51:15, Ps 136:5.

126. The word for "side" in Prv 8:30, is אצל which is not the same as "side" in Gn 2:21 being צלע from which Eve was taken out. But, only one letter sets them apart and could perhaps hint an analogy.

127. Comay & Brownrigg, *Who's who in the Bible*, p.50.

128. Ibid p. 152.

129. 2 Kgs 21:7.

130. *BDB*, p.52.

131. 2 Kgs 18:4.

132. Ibid 18:14.

133. Ibid 18:16.

134. Canaanite Asherah was particularly linked to pillars too. Again, this is a huge topic, and will be the subject of another book.

135. The word for "gate" here is not the word *shar* usually used for this. It is another word that also means "door" and the last word for "door" in this sentence is *mezuzot*, meaning "doorpost."

136. Prv 24:7.

137. Ibid 31:23.

138. Ibid 31:31.

139. *An Intermediate Greek-English Lexicon,* founded upon the Seventh Edition of Liddell and Scott's Greek-English Lexicon. Oxford, Clarendon Press, First edition 1889, p. 118.

140. The opening one stretches from Gn 1:1 through Gn 2:3 and then the next starts.

141. For metaphors with women see for example Is 46:3, 49:14-15, 66:12-13, Dt 32:18, Nm 11:12, Ps 131:2, Lk 13:20-21, 15:8-10. Regarding female animal or bird symbols see Ex 19:4, Dt 32:11-12, Ru 2:12, Ps 17:8, 36:7, 57:1, 91:1, 4, Is 31:5, Hos 13:8, Mt 23:37, Lk 13:34.

142. *The Fathers of the Church: Saint Ambrose. Hexameron, Paradise, and Cain and Abel,* Translated by John J. Savage, New York, Fathers of the Church, Inc.1961, p. 253 (book 6, chap. 7).

143. Gn 3:22.

144. Ibid 2:17.

145. Input by my daughter, Rebekah Widmalm-Delphonse, summer 2012 via personal communication.

146. *The Fathers of the Church: Saint Ambrose. Hexameron, Paradise, and Cain and Abel,* p. 254 (book 6, chap. 7).

147. Gn 1:27. When St. Ambrose says that the image of God is wisdom, it is an idea taken from the wisdom books to which I will later return to because Wisdom represented the Mother Goddess. Here though, he has equalized Wisdom with Jesus, spinning off of statements by Paul.

148. Ibid 1:26.

149. If this was simply a figure of speech it nullifies the influence of the ancient Canaanite texts where El is not alone in the heavenly realm which will now be discussed.

150. A "pantheon" refers to all the gods in a polytheistic religion.

151. Rahmouni, Aicha, *Divine Epithets in the Ugaritic Alphabetic Texts,* translated by J.N. Ford, Brill, Leiden, Boston, 2007, p. 8, 72, 275.

152. For my initial thesis on this see, Widmalm, Marianne, *God's "Wife,"* The Biblical Historian, Journal of the Biblical Colloquium West, Supervising Editor David Noel Freedman, Feb. 2005, Vol. 2, nr. 1, p. 30-32.

153. Gn 1:26, 27.

154. The word for "man" in Gn 1:27 is *ha-adam* and can refer to "mankind" or "the man" and if it means "mankind" collectively this point would not apply, but if it specified "the man" it would.

155. God speaking about "us" in the second creation story too may suggest that both creation stories have Canaanite origins.

156. Widmalm, *God's "Wife,"* p. 30.

157. See for example 1 Cor 11:7-9.

158. Jn 10:35. Jesus of course referred to the Hebrew Scriptures when he said this.

159. Phyllis Trible, Mary Korsak and Judith Mckinley are a few who have put forth alternative readings of Genesis 2-3.

233

160. Gn 2:4-7.

161. Ibid 2:18, 20.

162. The same is reflected in the English language as the word woman contains the word man as in "wo-man." Likewise the word female contains the word male in it, "fe-male" and she is "s-he."

163. Gn 1:27.

164. Trible, Phyllis, *God and the Rhetoric of Sexuality*, Fortress Press, Philadelphia, 1978, p. 98-99.

165. *BDB* p. 617.

166. Widmalm, *God's "Wife,"* p.32

167. Ibid.

168. NAS.

169. DRA.

170. KJV.

171. The inaccuracy of this translation has also been recognized by various scholars such as Phyllis Trible. See also Widmalm, *God's "Wife,"* p. 32.

172. See also Ex 18:4, Ps 30:10.

173. Gn 2:15.

174. Ibid 2:24.

175. Ibid 2:18.

176. Prv 8:30-31.

177. Jn 8:34.

178. Ibid 8:36.

179. Ibid 14:17, 15:26, 16:13, Eph 1:13, 1 Jn 4:6.

180. Mt 26:28. See also Mk 14:24, Lk 22:20.

181. Lk 24:47.

182. Jer 31:34.

183. Mk 1:8.

184. Gn 2:24.

185. The Greek word used for "unchastity" is *porneia* which refers to all unlawful sex and prohibits sex outside of marriage.

186. Gn 2:24.

187. Eph 5:32. A shared sentiment with "Gnostic" texts.

188. Ibid 5:23.

189. Is 54:6, Jer 3:1, 20, Ez 16:32, Hos 2:4, 19-20.

190. Gn 8:21.

191. Ibid 3:14-19.

192. The word translated as "curse" here (Gn 8:21) is not the same word used in Genesis 3:14 over the serpent and 3:17 over the ground. However, in the form it is in, in Gn 8:21, it also refers to "curse."

193. Sir 15:3.

194. Jn 6:35, 48. See also ibid 6:33, 51, Rv 2:17.

195. Jn 4:14.

196. Yet another sign that Jesus was a Wisdom teacher.

197. Sir 24:25-26.

198. Or, this could be an ancient tradition of identifying Jordan with Gihon.

199. Sir 24:25.

200. Ibid 24:28-29.

201. Ibid 24:30-34.

202. See also Is 41:18, 43:19-20.

203. Acts 9:17.

204. Ibid 9:11-12.

205. Jn 4:14.

206. Rv 22:1-2.

207. It is repeated in Jn 19:18.

208. Rv 21:25. The significance of the word "glory" in Rv 21:23, 24, 26 will be dealt with later in the book.

209. Gn 3:24.

210. Ibid 2:9. "Tree" is a masculine word in Hebrew. However, the tie between trees and Asherah is, as discussed, strong. The tree of knowledge of good and evil was also in the midst of the Garden, and being a tree can likewise be linked to the Mother Goddess/Wisdom who gives you understanding. This tree was not inherently evil, it just gave you knowledge of good and evil, making humans "like one of us" according to Yahweh (ibid 3:22).

211. Jn 4:14.

212. Since we do not have an ancient Hebrew version of Revelation we cannot know if "the street" here would be *hus* ("outside street") or *derek* ("way," "road," "path"). But my guess is that whichever word was used an analogy was made between "the street" of the New Jerusalem and "the way" to the Tree of Life.

213. Rv 21:4.

214. Ibid 7:17, 21:6.

215. See also Prv 3:18, 13:12, 15:4, 2 Esd 8:52 (for the Catholic Bible versions this is 4 Esd).

216. Ibid 22:17.

217. Ibid 22:19.

218. In this sentence "say" is in the Greek plural, "they said," referring to the Bride and the Spirit which points to them being two and separate.

219. Rv 21:9.

220. Ibid 21:2

221. See for example Is 54:6, Jer 3:1, 20, Hos 2:2.

222. Jn 5:31, 8:14.

223. For more on this, see Van de Sandt, Huub and David Flusser, *The Didache*, Royal Van Gorcum, Assen Fortress Press, Minneapolis, 2002, p. 271-286.

224. Mt 3:16, Mk 1:10, Lk 3:22, Jn 1:32.

225. Mk 1:8. See also Mt 3:11, Lk 3:16.

226. Jn 3:5.

227. Ibid 3:3.

228. Ibid 7:37-39.

229. Lk 1:15.

230. Ibid 1:67.

231. Ibid 1:35.

232. Ibid 2:25-26.

233. Ibid 2:27.

234. Ibid 2:40.

235. Ibid 1:15.

236. Ibid 2:52.

237. Mk 6:2. See also Mt 13:54.

238. *Josephus: Ant* 18:63.

239. And fire according to Mt 3:11, Lk 3:16. Fire is used in descriptions about hell, and also an expression of God's anger (Dt 4:24, 36). But it likewise reminds us about when God appeared to Moses as fire in the burning bush (Ex 3:2). Additionally, fire is reminiscent of the Exodus when God appeared as a pillar of cloud by day and pillar of fire by night to lead the way (Ex 13:21). At Pentecost there appeared divided tongues like fire that rested on each person as they were filled with the Holy Spirit. So, there are some instances where fire and the Holy Spirit intertwine.

240. Lk 3:22.

241. Ibid 4:1. See also Mt 4:1, Mk 1:12.

242. Mt 12:30-32.

243. Acts 2:2.

244. Ibid 2:16-21.

245. Ibid 6:3.

246. Ibid 6:10.

247. 1 Cor 1:24.

248. Ibid 1:30.

249. Ibid 2:7.

250. Ibid 12:8.

251. See also 1 Cor 1:30. If anything, this shows how large Wisdom's role was for Paul and the Jews. Though Paul may have shifted the focus of Wisdom to Jesus who had Wisdom, many others did not, and continued to emphasize both which will shortly be examined.

252. Eph 1:17.

253. Ibid 3:10.

254. *Philo: Her* 1:126-127.

255. Jn 16:7 (see also 14:16).

256. Ibid 15:26 (see also 14:17).

257. Ibid 14:26.

258. Ibid 16:7. Other translations of "counselor" are "advocate," "paraclete," "comforter."

259. The relevant passages concerning "the Counselor" is found in Jn chap. 14-16.

260. Full examination of this word in Is 9:6 will be done in another book about Jesus with regards to the Trinity. Suffice to say here that in at that instance it is not a noun but a participle.

261. Jn 16:13.

262. In Hebrew the word is actually the female version of the word *amen* which we examined regarding Proverbs 8:30 and the word "master-workman." So, "truth" is both feminine and synonym to "faithfulness." Take off the last letter *taw* and you have the Hebrew word for "mother." One way to see this is as if "truth" is built on "mother" with its added "t" which is also the ancient Canaanite feminine ending. Both of these words are the same in Ugaritic.

263. Mt 28:18.

264. Ibid 3:11, Mk 1:8, Lk 3:16, Jn 1:33, Acts 1:5.

265. For the most part baptism was done in the name of Jesus and the gifts of the Holy Spirit could be separate, highlighting the distinctions between the two. See Acts 2:38, 8:16, 10:48, 19:5-6, 1 Cor 6:11.

266. Jn 3:5.

267. Ibid 3:3.

268. Ibid 3:4.

269. Ibid 8:41, 1 Jn 3:9.

270. See for example Mt 13:18-40, 17:20.

271. Jn 1:12-13.

272. Ibid 1:29-34.

273. Ibid 3:22, 26.

274. Ibid 4:2.

275. Ibid 3:25-27.

276. Ibid 3:28-29.

277. Ibid 3:34.

278. Mk 2:19-20 (the fullest version). See also Mt 9:15, Lk 5:34-35.

279. Mt 25:1-13.

280. Rv 18:23, 19:7, 21:2, 9, 22:17.

281. As "daughter" see for example 2 Kgs 19:21, Is 10:32, 37:22, Lam 2:10, 13, 15, Mi, 4:8, Zep 3:14, Zec 9:9. For Israel as "Mother" see Is 50:1, Hos 2:2, 5, 4:5.

282. Rv 12:1-2.

283. Is 66:7. See the rest of the chapter and specifically verses 15-16 and 22.

284. Rv 21:2.

285. Wis 8:2-4.

286. Sir 24:9-11. See also Jer 2:2 how Jerusalem is portrayed as God's bride.

287. Again, this can explain the disagreement between Jesus' and John's disciples that later may have grown resulting in today's sect of the Mandaeans who are followers of John the Baptist and why their condemnation of the Holy Spirit occurred. They could have retained the belief in a heavenly Mother because it was derived from the Wisdom books but denied her to be identified with the Holy Spirit as a way of setting themselves apart from Christians yet retain John's belief in a divine Mother.

288. Is 62:1-5.

289. *The Complete Dead Sea Scrolls in English*, p. 446 (4Q434).

290. Wis 7:12.

291. Sir 15:1-2.

292. See for example Hos 2:2 and Is 54:6. Zion can refer specifically to Mount Zion, the Temple and Jerusalem as a whole.

293. Sir 24:5-12.

294. 2 Esd 10:7. 2 Esdras is part of an appendix to the New Testament in the Roman Catholic Vulgate Bible and is there called the 4ᵗʰ book of Esdras.

295. Lk 7:35.

296. Sir 40:1.

297. *The Nag Hammadi Library*, p. 244.

298. Ibid p. 254.

299. Gn 3:20.

300. *Ante-Nicene Fathers: The Writings of the Fathers Down to A.D, 325,* Vol 6, Edited by Alexander Roberts, D.D. and James Donaldson, LL.D., Hendrickson Publishers (original printing Christian Literature Publishing Company, 1886), 1995, p. 402.

301. Jgs 5:7.

302. Miller (Editor), *The Complete Gospels*, p. 432-433.

303. Ibid p. 432.

304. Jn 19:26-27.

305. *Coptic Texts: Volume V, Miscellaneous Texts in the Dialect of Upper Egypt,* Edited with English Translations by E.A. Wallis Budge, AMS Press, New York, 1915, p. 646.

306. Ibid.

307. *The Panarion of Epiphanius of Salamis,* Book I (Sects 1-46), p. 115.

308. Jn 8:11.

309. Ibid 4:5-30.

310. Ibid 5:38-43. See Mt 9:21-22, 15:22-28 of Jesus healing women.

311. Mt 26:7-13.

312. Mk 10:9.

313. Ibid 10:11.

314. Mt 12:39.

315. Ibid 12:42.

316. Lk 15:8-10.

317. Ibid 18:1-9.

318. Ibid 18:3. The Greek word used is literally "enemy" or "opponent" but it is in the masculine singular which is why it is also translated "man."

319. Ibid 21:1-4.

320. Defending the poor, the widows and orphans was of prime importance in the Hebrew religion. See for example Ex 22:22, Dt 10:17-18, 24:19-21, 27:19, Ps 146:9, Is 1:17, Jer 7:6, 22:3, Zec 7:10. It existed in other ancient Near Eastern laws too and prevalent in later Christian texts like *the Didache* and *the Didascalia*. Caring for them was also the mark of a king. Prv 29:14 put it this way, "If a king judges the poor with equity his throne will be established for ever." Jesus repeatedly speaking up for the poor along with women and children aligned his character with the Israelite concept of a true king.

321. Mt 12:49-50.

322. Ex 20:12.

323. Mt 10:34-39.

324. Gal 3:26-29.

325. Mt 15:26.

326. Ibid 15:27-28.

327. Ibid 15:22, 27. The Greek word *kurios* used here for "Lord" can also be translated "Master." It could refer to a slave owner, a Roman emperor, God or Jesus, depending on the context. On an additional side note, in Shem-Tob's Hebrew version of this the disciples ask Jesus why he is abandoning her when she first approached him which makes his answer, that he was sent for the lost sheep of Israel, more logical. See Howard, *Hebrew Gospel of Matthew*, p. 75.

328. Lk 23:27.

329. Ibid 23:28-29.

330. Mt 27:55, Mk 15:40-41, Lk 23:49.

331. Mt 28:1, Mk 15:40, 47, 16:1, 9, Lk 24:1-10, Jn 19:25, 20:1-18.

332. Which can symbolically point to Jesus coming to life on the first day of creation.

333. Lk 24:10-11.

334. Mk 16:14.

335. Ibid 16:9-14.

336. Mt 28:1-11.

337. The disciple known as the beloved disciple, or the disciple whom "Jesus loved," is understood as John. See Jn 21:24.

338. Jn 20:8.

339. Ibid 20:16-18.

340. Though some will claim that the passages where he discusses his true relatives (Mt 12:46-50, Mk 3:31-35, Lk 8:19-21) was a negative instance but, as stated earlier, he is in that instance merely making a theological point. It is not about degrading his mother and sister or women at large.

341. Lk 1:28.

342. Ibid 1:38.

CHAPTER 3

343. *The Fathers of the Church, Origen, Homilies on Jeremiah, Homily on 1 Kings 28*, p. 161 (homily 15:4.2).

344. Ibid p. 139-140 (homily 14:5.2-3).

345. Lk 7:35.

346. Mt 11:19.

347. *The Ante-Nicene Fathers: The Writings of the Fathers Down to A.D. 325*, Vol 9, Edited by Allan Menzies, New York, Charles Scribner's Sons (original printing Christian Literature Publishing Company, 1899), 1994, p. 329-330 (*Origen's Commentary on John*, book 2, chap. 6).

348. *The HarperCollins Encyclopedia of Catholicism,* p. 940.

349. Mt 12:50, Mk 3:35, Lk 8:21 (Lk does not include "sister").

350. *Ante-Nicene Fathers,* Vol 9, p. 330 (*Origen's Commentary on John,* book 2, chap. 6).

351. Though Origin simultaneously writes that he saw the Holy Spirit as made through the Word, just prior (ibid p. 328), Wisdom and the Holy Spirit were both referred to as "mother" and often interchangeable wherefore there is a strong case for making them one and the same force.

352. *The Fathers of the Church: Origen, Homilies on Jeremiah, Homily on 1 Kings 28,* p. 140 (homily 14:5.2) and see also footnote 38.

353. Edwards, *The Hebrew Gospel and the development of the Synoptic Tradition,* p. 28.

354. Ibid p. 285-286.

355. Ibid p. 32. It is said that more than 30,000 manuscripts were kept at this library.

CHAPTER 4

356. *The Complete Dead Sea Scrolls in English,* p. 578 (a Moses Apocryphon, 4Q376, 1Q29).

357. Ibid p. 545.

358. With fragments in Greek and Latin.

359. Barnstone, *The Other Bible,* p. 486.

360. Dn 8:17.

361. Ibid 7:13. Sections of Daniel are in Aramaic and *bar* is the Aramaic for the Hebrew word *ben* meaning "son." *Enosh* just like *adam* means "man" (can also mean "people").

362. *The Old Testament Pseudepigrapha,* Vol 1, p. 7.

363. Ibid p. 35.

364. Ibid. Footnote (h) of the translation here reveal that this last line literally ends with "its deeds." This gives us a parallel to "wisdom is justified by her deeds" (Mt 11:19). The contrast is between the ways of the world and the ways of Wisdom. This link is further enhanced when shortly prior it says about Wisdom that She "went out to dwell with the children of the people" (*The Old Testament Pseudepigrapha,* Vol 1, p. 33). Although that poem says she found no dwelling place among men, the point is that this is what she did in Jesus.

365. Ibid p. 35-36.

366. Ibid p. 29.

367. Ibid p. 29-30

368. Sir 24:5-12, *The Old Testament Pseudepigrapha,* Vol 1, p. 33.

369. *The Old Testament Pseudepigrapha,* Vol 1, p. 33.

370. Lk 7:35. See also Mt 11:19.

371. *The Old Testament Pseudepigrapha*, Vol 1, p. 35.

372. Ibid p. 226-227.

373. *BDB*, p. 1014.

374. See for example Ex 29:46 where the word "dwell" here signifies the presence of God.

375. Lv 8:10.

376. Barnstone (Editor and Introduction), *The Other Bible*, p. 26 (the *Creation of Adam* in the *Haggadah*).

377. Jn 3:5.

378. *The HarperCollins Encyclopedia of Catholicism*, p. 1294.

379. *Ante-Nicene Fathers: The Writings of the Fathers Down to AD 325,* Vol 5, Edited by Alexander   Roberts, D.D. and James Donaldson ,LL.D., Hendrickson Publishers (original printing Christian Literature Publishing Company, 1886),1994, p. 144 (*Hippolytus: The Refutation of all Heresies*, book 10, chap. 9).

380. Gardner, Iain and Lieu Samuel N. C. (Editors), *Manichaean Texts from the Roman Empire*, Cambridge University Press, 2004, p. 192.

381. Ibid p. 157.

382. Ibid p. 189.

383. Barnstone (Editor and Introduction), *The Other Bible*, p. 464,

384. *Ante-Nicene Fathers,* Vol 8, p. 357.

385. Mt 3:11, Lk 3:16.

386. Howard, George, *Hebrew Gospel of Matthew,* p. 11

387. Barnstone (Editor and Introduction), *The Other Bible*, p. 468.

388. Ibid p. 473.

389. Ibid p. 474.

390. Prv 8:12.

391. Mt 28:19.

392. Van de Sandt and Flusser, *The Didache*, p. 287. Eusebius lived ca 263-340. See for example *Eusebius: Eccl Hist*, Books 1-5, p. 145 (book 3, chap. 5) where he quotes Jesus saying "Going teach ye all nations in my name."

393. Milavec, Aaron, *The Didache*: *Text, Translation, Analysis, and Commentary,* Liturgical Press, Collegeville, Minnesota, 2003, p. 19.

394. Ibid p. xi-xii. See also *Eusebius: Eccl Hist*, Book 1-5, p. 179 (book 3, chap. 25). It was referred to as "the Teachings of the Apostles."

395. Milavec, *the Didache*, p. xiii.

396. *The HarperCollins Encyclopedia of Catholicism*, p. 416, Milavec, *The Didache*, p. xiii-xiv, Van de Sandt and Flusser, *The Didache*, p. 48-52.

397. Milavec, *The Didache*, p. xiii-xiv.

398. Ibid p. 19.

399. *Ante-Nicene Fathers*, Vol 8, p. 95 (*Recognitions of Clement*, chap. 69). I will address what follows this quote further on.

400. Milavec, *The Didache*, p. 19.

401. Jn 3:3.

402. *The Nag Hammadi Library*, p. 38.

403. Ibid p. 43.

404. Ibid.

405. Miller, *The Complete Gospels*, p. 337 (5:6). See also Cameron, *The Other Gospels*, p. 59, there called *The Apocryphon of James*.

406. *The Nag Hammadi Library*, p. 104.

407. Ibid p. 105 (mentioned when discussing this title).

408. Ibid p. 106. A "monad" is a "single unit" or "number one."

409. Ibid.

410. Ibid p. 107.

411. Prv 8:22-30, Wis 7:25-29, Sir 24:3.

412. *The Nag Hammadi Library*, p. 107.

413. Ibid.

414. Ibid.

415. Ibid p. 108-109.

416. Ibid p. 110.

417. Ibid p. 118.

418. Ibid p. 110.

419. Ibid p. 118.

420. In line with my core thesis of this book about Gn 1:26.

421. *The Nag Hammadi Library*, p. 118-119.

422. Ibid p. 117. In an interesting side note there are descriptions of a "fourth light" who are the "creatures which glorify the invisible Spirit" called "Eleleth" (ibid p.110). This undoubtedly sounds like El and Elat, reflecting another name for the combination of the Father-Mother. Eleleth also exists in *the Gospel of the Egyptians*.

423. Ibid p. 220.

424. Ibid p. 221.

425. Ibid p. 231.

426. *The Nag Hammadi Scriptures,* The Revised and Updated Translation of Sacred Gnostic Texts, Edited by Marvin Meyer, The International Edition, Harper Collins, 2007, p. 499.

427. Ibid p. 507.

428. *Ante-Nicene Fathers*, Vol 8, p. 289 (homily 11, chap. 22). We here again see the connection between Asherah, water, and the Holy Spirit.

429. Ibid p. 289 (homily 11, chap. 24).

430. Ibid p. 299 (homily 12, chap. 32).

431. Ibid.

432. Ibid (homily 12, chap. 33).

433. *The Panarion of Epiphanius of Salamis*, p. 46, 133.

434. Mt 5:1-12. See also, Mt 11:19, Lk 7:35, 11:49 which show he believed in a personified Wisdom.

435. *The Complete Dead Sea Scrolls in English*, p. 455.

436. The Dead Sea Scrolls also included the book of Ben-Sirach in Hebrew.

437. Osiek, Carolyn (Commentary) and Koester, Helmut (Editor), *Shepherd of Hermas*, Fortress Press, Minneapolis, 1999, p. 1.

438. Ibid p. 18-20.

439. Ibid p. 1, 4-7.

440. Ibid p. 9-10.

441. Ibid p. 9.

442. Ibid p. 46 (vision 1.2)

443. Ibid p. 58 (vision 2.1).

444. Ibid.

445. Prv 8:23.

446. Eph 5:23-29.

447. Ibid 3:8-10.

448. Sir 24:8.

449. Osiek (Commentary) and Koester (Editor), *Shepherd of Hermas*, p. 83-84 (vision 3.10-13).

450. See for example ibid p. 89-90 (vision 4.2).

451. Ibid p. 65 (vision 3.3).

452. Ibid (vision 3.4).

453. Ibid p. 76 (vision 3.8).

454. Ibid.

455. If the tower represented only the bride and the Church it could reflect Revelation where Jesus is the groom and the Church the bride, paralleling the Spirit and God. See Rv 22:17.

456. Osiek (Commentary) and Koester (Editor), *Shepherd of Hermas*, p. 175 (5.5).

457. Jn 8:32-34, Phil 2:6-7.

458. Osiek (Commentary) and Koester (Editor), *Shepherd of Hermas*, p. 176 (5.6)

459. Ibid p. 194 (from vision 8.1. onwards).

460. Ibid p. 211 (9.1).

461. Ibid p. 230 (vision 9.12).

462. Barnstone, *The Other Bible*, p. 465, Mt 10:3, Mk 3:18, Lk 6:14-15, Acts 1:13.

463. Acts 21:8, Edwards, *The Hebrew Gospel & the Development of the Synoptic Tradition*, p. 281.

464. *The Nag Hammadi Library*, p. 141.

465. Ibid p. 153.

466. Ibid.

467. Ibid.

468. I Cor 12:13.

469. *The Nag Hammadi Library*, p. 151.

470. Mt 3:16. See also Mk 1:10, Lk 3:21-22. With the light in this context we can also see a parallel with Shekinah and the Holy Spirit because it was intertwined with the word "glory." For example, in Lk 2:9 when the angel of God appeared for the Shepherds when Jesus was born it says "the glory of the Lord shone around them." John the Baptist also had the Holy Spirit judging by what Jesus said in Jn 5:35, "He was a burning and shining lamp, and you were willing to rejoice for a while in his light."

471. See also Acts 19:5-7, 1 Pt 3:21, Col 2:12.

472. Mt 28:19.

473. Mk 16:15-18 (there are theories about the last sections of Mark being later additions).

474. See also 1 Cor 12:4-13, 28, Heb 2:4.

475. Lk 24:47-48.

476. Acts 1:8.

477. Remember too that the meaning of El was "power" but so was Elat which is just the feminine form of El.

478. Jn 20:21-23.

479. Acts 1:2.

480. Ibid 1:4-5.

481. Ibid 1:7-8.

482. Ibid 1:5, 2:4.

483. Jn 3:22, 4:1-2.

484. Acts 2:5.

485. Ibid.

486. Lk 1:15, 35.

487. Ibid 1:35, 1:41, 1:67, 2:25-26.

488. Ibid 11:13, Jn 1:33.

489. See Mt 16:32, Mk 8:33, Lk 22:3, Jn 13:27, Mt 16:17 (this this last reference says God not the Holy Spirit, it describes her exact function).

490. *The Nag Hammadi Library*, p. 148.

491. Ibid p. 150.

492. Ibid p. 148.

493. Ibid p. 151.

494. See Ex 26:31-27:21. This veil is symbolic of what is between God and Man when we are here in this world. Paul alluded to it in 1 Cor 13:12. Also, the cherubim ordered to be on the veil symbolizes how they guard the gates of Eden and the Tree of Life.

495. Heb 9:8.

496. Ibid 9:14.

497. Ibid 9:8, 14.

498. Mt 27:51, Mk 15:38, Lk 23:45.

499. *The Nag Hammadi Library*, p. 158.

500. Ibid p. 153-154.

501. Ibid p. 159.

502. Ibid.

503. Ibid.

504. Mt 3:11, Lk 3:16.

505. *The Nag Hammadi Library*, p. 160.

506. Ibid p. 142.

507. Ibid p. 151.

508. Ibid p. 145.

509. Ibid 6:10.

510. Ibid p. 155.

511. Wis 7:25.

512. Gn 3:20.

CHAPTER 5

513. Mt 28:19.

514. Lk 10:41-42.

515. Mt 15:1-9, Mk 7:1-9.

516. See Ex chap. 28 and 29.

517. See for example *Josephus: Jwr* 6:415.

518. 1 Cor 14:34-36. See also 1 Tm 2:11-14. This last reference in Timothy is neglects to remember that God reprimanded both Adam and Eve for breaking His commandment and made sure they both received consequences for their actions. Also, nothing is mentioned in Genesis 1-2 how the woman or man should be saved. However, the idea of women not having authority over men reflects a certain—at face value order—in the Bible: Adam came first, and Yahweh before Wisdom.

519. Rom 16:1, 7 (if "Junia" is the name of a woman).

520. Ex 15:20, Jgs 4:4, 2 Kgs 22:14, 2 Chr 34:22, Neh 6:14, Is 8:3.

521. Lk 2:36-38.

522. Acts 21:9.

523. Jer 1:7, 9.

524. Etymology of the name is unknown but Hebrew suggestions have included the Sabbath and the divine title Sabaoths. For more see *The Old Testament Pseudepigrapha*, Vol 1, p. 317-324.

525. So did seventeenth century mystic Jacob Böhme, English late seventeenth century female religious leader Jane Leade and Russian poet and mystic Vladimir Solovyov, born 1853.

526. *The Old Testament Pseudepigrapha*, Vol 1, p. 322.

527. Barnstone (Editor and Introduction), *The Other Bible*, p. 501

528. Ibid.

529. Bright, William, *The Canons on the First Four General Council of Nicaea, Constantinople, Ephesus and Chalcedon with notes*, Second Edition, Oxford, at the Clarendon Press, 1892, p. 82 (canon 19).

530. Ibid p. 196 (canon 15).

531. Ibid p. 80.

532. *The HarperCollins Encyclopedia of Catholicism*, p. 463.

533. Ibid p. 290.

534. Ibid p. 290-291.

535. Some question this to mean "deaconess" too, because it can also mean "servant" or "helper." However, the Greek word *diakonos* is used in the feminine form, matching the feminine name Phoebe and it is this word which is used for this official role for men.

Worthy to mention is that in the Aramaic New Testament the word *shammash* which means "minister" is used in this verse.

536. Bright, *The Canons on the First Four General Council of Nicaea, Constantinople, Ephesus and Chalcedon with notes*, p. 80 (see this page for more references regarding early deaconesses).

537. Martimort, Aimé Georges, *Deaconesses, An Historical Study*, Translated by K.D. Whitehead, Ignatius Press, San Francisco, 1982, p. 112-115. See this book for many more references.

538. *Pliny the Younger, Complete Letters*, p. 279.

539. *The Didascalia Apostolorum in English*, p. v. This translation was done in 1903 and "includes additional material supplied by Gibson from a variety of sources" (see the first page). The translator, Margaret Gibson, travelled with her twin sister and made many significant discoveries in the Middle East, whereas sections of this text may not be part of *the Didascalia* and possibly even older.

540. Ibid p. 48.

541. It could also be from one of the groups retaining more of the original beliefs.

542. See for example Acts 14:23, 16:4, 26:16, 1 Tm 3:1-13, Ti 1:5-11, 1 Pt 5:1, 2 Jn 1:1, 3 Jn 1:1 ("Presbyter" is sometimes translated as "elder" or other titles). Other signs of its antiquity include lack of references to the Trinity, celebration of the Sabbath on Saturday (*Didascalia Apostolorum in English*, p. 99), reference to only one Gospel (ibid p. 19), the description of "two ways, one of life and one of death" by the Apostle John (ibid p. 13) and the child of God as a "son of light" (ibid p. 60), the presence of Jesus" brother Jacob (James), emphasis on Wisdom teachings (ibid p. 8-9) and more. Of course, it can be said to belong to the Ebionites or Nazarenes, but since these signs are simultaneously all elements of the early Church and the organizational parts, for instance, exactly what the first followers dealt with, this could have ancient origins.

543. *The Didascalia Apostolorum in English*, p. 79. Women were not allowed to baptize in water though, explained by the fact that Jesus was baptized by John. Had women been allowed Mary, his mother, would have baptized him (ibid, p. 75). So, it was not due to anything Jesus had said, but following the tradition of what had previously been done.

544. In the Didascalia women were serving other women which can be a reflection of how men and women sat separately in the Jewish Synagogues at that time.

545. Ibid. the "Cod. S" refer to explanations in the footnotes regarding Deacons.

546. *The Didascalia* also spends a great deal of time discussing the role of widows. Though it was mainly a passive role, including many restrictions, it does spell out a spiritual role for them.

547. *The Didascalia Apostolorum in English*, p. 17. See also p. 12 but here missing the word "Holy."

548. Ibid p. 17.

549. Lk 10:38-42.

550. *The Didascalia Apostolorum in English*, p. 17.

551. Ibid p. 16-17. The text use both the name "Peter" and "Cephas" taking turns.

552. Ibid p. 17.

553. Ibid p. 72.

554. Mt 15:3. 6. Mk 7:8-9, 13.

555. *The Didascalia Apostolorum in English*, p. 6, 8, 9, 58.

556. *Ante-Nicene Fathers,* Vol 8, p. 533.

557. Ibid.

558. *The Old Testament Pseudepigrapha*, Vol 2, p. 727.

559. Ibid p. 757.

560. Ibid.

561. Passages like 1 Cor 1:24, 30 were singled out for this purpose, while what even Jesus himself said about Wisdom was ignored. See Lk 11:49.

562. Cameron (Editor), *The Other Gospels*, p. 107.

563. Barnstone (Editor and Introduction), *The Other Bible*, p. 384.

564. Benko, *The Virgin Goddess*, p. 173.

565. See Jer 7:18, 44:17-19, 25.

CHAPTER 6

566. Jn 10:34-35.

567. Ps 82:1.

568. Ibid 135:5.

569. Dt 6:4.

570. The Hebrew can leave out the word "is" so that is not strange.

571. Gn 14:19.

572. Ex 3:6, 15, 6:2-3.

573. Dt 6:5.

574. Ex 20:3. See also Dt 5:7.

575. This in and of itself can be understood to assert that other gods exists otherwise there is no one else for Yahweh to be placed before, i.e. placed first. Scripture also repeatedly makes the point that false gods, in the form of manmade objects, are not real.

576. Mt 4:10.

577. Furthermore, if Dt 6:4 indeed meant "one" it flies against the Trinitarian concept. One, as in Yahweh being one single personality is incompatible with three persons in one substance.

578. Ibid 24:9.

579. Sir 1:9.

580. Wis 7:25.

581. Sir 24:3.

582. Gn 1:1-2.

583. Prv 8:22-23. See also Sir 24:8-9.

584. Ru 4:10.

585. My friend Jeff Abrams, Detroit, MI, summer 2012 via personal communication.

586. Trible, *God and the Rhetoric of Sexuality*, p. 98-99.

587. Mal 2:16, Mt 6:10, 19:8, Mk 10:5-6.

588. Prv 8:22-23. See also Wis 7:26.

589. As stated before, masculine pronouns are used for the "Spirit of Truth" in the New Testament due to Greek grammar.

590. Wis 8:3-4.

591. Gn 2:9, 18-20.

592. Ibid 1:28. See also ibid 1:31.

593. Mt 19:17, Mk 10:18, Lk 18:18-19.

594. See Widmalm, *God's "Wife,"* p. 32.

595. Sir 42:24.

596. Jn 4:24.

597. Jn 10:34-36.

598. 1 Jn 4:16.

599. Mt 19:21-24, Mk 10:21-25, Lk 18:22-25.

CHAPTER 7

600. 1 Chr 16:25, Ps 96:4.

601. NRS

602. Rv 22:17.

603. *The HarperCollins Encyclopedia of Catholicism*, p. 563.

604. Heb 5:6, 10, 6:20, 7:3, 11, 14-17. See also Gn 14:18, Ps 110:4.

605. Heb 7:2. Salem (*Shalom*) is the Hebrew word for "peace." The name for Jerusalem – "the city of peace" – has been linked to derive from the name of an ancient Canaanite god called Shalim, but it still does not take away the meaning of the name. The name Jerusalem goes back a couple of millennia B.C.

606. Heb 8:8, Jer 31:31-34.

607. Lk 10:38-42.

608. Mt 15:3-9.

609. Lk 12:10.

610. In addition, this is presents a dilemma for Trinitarians. Why could you blaspheme Jesus but not the Spirit if they are equal and if Jesus is God?

611. Rom 3:31. See also ibid 2:12-13, 6:15, 7:12, 22-25.

612. Ibid 6:11.

613. There are instances that suggests that the Holy Spirit sustains physical life too. For instance, in Genesis 6:3 Yahweh declares that His spirit (*ruah*) will not abide in man forever because he is flesh and numbers his days on earth to a hundred and twenty years.

614. Jn 3:5-6.

615. Gn 3:20.

616. Ibid 3:22.

617. Ibid 22:17.

618. Jn 7:37-38. The passage Jesus is quoting is not found in the Hebrew Scriptures and may refer to a passage now lost to us. The closest is perhaps Is 12:3, "With joy you will draw water from the wells of salvation" or Zechariah's predictions about the LORD's Day "On that day, living waters shall flow out of Jerusalem . . . ."

619. Jn 3:4-5.

620. Gn 1:31.

621. Mt 6:9, 10.

622. The same thing is played out in real life in parts of third wave feminist ideas where some now want to advance notions of gender fluidity or get rid of gender distinctions altogether and so forth. Much of it is pursued in the name of equality by suggesting that the gender notion itself supports oppression. Instead of promoting a society that honors women and feminine traits, these ideas deny them. It supports the ultimate form of suppression; saying we do not exist. Just because feminine and masculine traits overlap and are not always strictly belonging to either sex it does not mean gender/gender-traits are not real. For example, we both have feminine and masculine hormones but it is the amount and balance of it that separates us (along with chromosomes and a whole host of other things). If you advocate that the solution is to reject and deny what is unique to women, and our value *because of that*, you have not solved or learned anything. You have just made up new words to sidestep the issue altogether. More and more ideas in this field are simply deconstructing reality to the point where all definitions are rendered meaningless. A complete divorce from reality is encouraged by the notion that whatever you think, feel or want is the only basis needed to make it true.

623. Rv 22:18-19, Jn 10:35.

624. Is 28:16.

625. Jn 20:21-22.

626. Dt 32:6, Ps 89:26, 68:5, 103:13, Prv 3:12, Is 63:16, 64:8, Jer 3:4, 19, 31:9, Mal 1:6, 2:10, (also Is 9:6 depending on how you understand it).

627. Ex 3:15, 16, Dt 1:11, 21, 4:1, 6:3, 9:5, 12:1, 27:3, 30:20, Jos 18:3, 1 Chr 29:10, 20, 2 Chr 28:9. 29:5, 30:7, Ezr 8:28, 10:11.

628. Ps 89:37 (the whole vision is Ps 89:19-37).

629. Ibid 89:26.

630. 2 Sm 7:14, 1 Chr 17:13, 22:10, 28:6.

631. Mt 6:9. See also Mt 5:9, Ps 82:6. This is why Jesus called those who were committing evil a slave to sin whose father is the Devil. They were not born (pre-destined) for evil, but chose it. As such, they became sons of the Devil. See Jn 8:33-44.

632. Jn 3:3.

633. 1 Pt 1:23.

634. 1 Jn 5:1-6.

635. Jn 3:5-7.

636. Mt 3:17.

637. Jn 3:2-8.

638. 1 Pt 1:23.

639. Jer 31:33.

640. Ex 20:12, See also Dt 5:16.

641. Jn 29:22.

642. Mt 7:7. See also Lk 11:9.

643. Acts 1:7-8.

644. Mt 28:19, Mk 16:15.

Thank you for reading

Our Mother: The Holy Spirit

Made in United States
Troutdale, OR
08/05/2023

11835487R00151